Grave New World

GRAVE NEW WORLD

MICHAEL A. LEDEEN

New York   Oxford
OXFORD UNIVERSITY PRESS
1985

Oxford University Press

Oxford   London   New York   Toronto
Delhi   Bombay   Calcutta   Madras   Karachi
Kuala Lampur   Singapore   Hong Kong   Tokyo
Nairobi   Dar es Salaam   Cape Town
Melbourne   Auckland

and associated companies in
Beirut   Berlin   Ibadan   Mexico City   Nicosia

Published by Oxford University Press,
200 Madison Avenue, New York, New York 10016

Library of Congress Cataloging in Publication Data
Ledeen, Michael Arthur, 1941–
Grave new world.
Includes index.
1. United States—Foreign relations—1981–
2. United States—Foreign relations—1977–1981.
3. United States—Foreign relations—Soviet Union.
4. Soviet Union—Foreign relations—United States.   I. Title.
E876.L43   1985   327.73   84-20543
ISBN 0-19-503491-0

Printing (last digit): 9 8 7 6 5 4 3 2 1
Printed in the United States of America

To Barbara Ledeen,
for all the reasons

PREFACE

This book deals with the current international crisis, which has been made more perilous by the failure of the two superpowers to design and conduct intelligent and effective foreign policies. Perhaps because of my training as a historian and my affection for biography, I have always been reluctant to analyze events in terms of vast, impersonal forces or inevitable trends, and I prefer to look at human decisions, painful choices, foolishness, and accident. What I see in the contemporary world is mediocre leadership, lack of vision, and simple confusion. Some years ago it was fashionable to hail the end of "bipolarism," because smaller countries could assume a greater role in international affairs. This has certainly happened—but it is not good news. When countries like Libya and Cuba become major actors on the world stage, something has gone badly awry, and that something is a lack of leadership and control by the superpowers.

I examine the international consequences of the growing incoherence of the superpowers—increased danger—and attempt an analysis of the underlying causes of superpower unpredictability in the hope of being able to suggest some possible remedies. The diagnosis, as usual, is easier than the therapy. I believe the Soviet Union has entered into a structural crisis of great magnitude and potentially explosive intensity, and that the gravity of that crisis drives the Kremlin to take ever-greater international risks. The United States, on the other hand, must deal with a crisis of its policy elite—an elite that seems incapable of clearly defining and resolutely pursuing the national interest.

The remedy for the Soviet malady is structural change, but that would mean abandoning communism in favor of a workable system, and also the end of the privileges of the Soviet elite, the *Nomenklatura.* The remedy for the United States is the creation of a policy elite that is better informed about the world and thus prepared to fight for our vital interests. I believe we have a chance for a cure, but I believe that the Soviet disease will have to run its course, with potentially fatal consequences for the Kremlin. One of the gravest problems we have to face in the immediate future is that of ensuring that the Soviet crisis does not envelop us and our allies.

In the course of this analysis, I explore the reasons for our chronically poor foreign policy performance and point to a variety of causes—ranging from our educational system to the way we choose our leaders, from the influence of the media to the mentality of the professional foreign service officers. This all adds up to a general problem: it is rare that Americans fully appreciate the importance of this country in international affairs. The best way to escape this peculiarly American blind spot is to live abroad for several years and watch the way in which other countries react to events in the United States and to American decisions. In my own case, this education took place in Italy, a country remarkable for the intelligence of its citizens and the cynicism (they would call it realism) with which they approach foreign policy problems. The country of Machiavelli is a fine university for those who wish to see the world stripped of moralistic sentimentality, and there is a good deal of Italian realism in some of my claims.

On the other hand, neither foreigners nor most Americans, no matter how well informed and sophisticated, can fully understand how American policy is made unless they have seen it first hand. In 1981–82 I had a unique opportunity to watch this process from the vantage point of the Office of the Secretary of State, when I served as Special Adviser to Alexander M. Haig, Jr. Much of what follows inevitably reflects that intense and fascinating experience, and I want to thank General Haig here for having given me the chance to learn so much, and perhaps make a personal contribution as well.

In the end, I have come to believe that there are no simple, elegant solutions to our problems. We will have to seek higher performance in many areas, improving the education of our people, enforcing higher standards and accountability on our officials and bureaucrats, finding and training better leaders, freeing them so far as possible from the transient demands of domestic politics and from the clamor of the media, seeking wisdom from citizens of other countries in the West. That there is no philosopher's stone to transform our dullness into gold is not surprising, for there are no permanent solutions to the problems of defending and advancing our national interest. At best, we can devise a series of policies that, if successful, enable us to move from one threat to the next, leaving our children with a tradition of intelligence and skill, and models of good judgment and imagination.

October 1984   M.A.L.
Washington, D.C.

ACKNOWLEDGMENTS

It is always a pleasure to acknowledge one's indebtedness to friends and colleagues, for knowledge and understanding are best advanced by cooperation and dialogue. I have been unusually fortunate to be able to learn from some of the outstanding men and women of our time, and I wish to thank them here. I owe a particular debt of gratitude to two men: to General Alexander M. Haig, Jr., for inviting me to work with him at the Department of State, for having confidence in my abilities and respect for my ideas; and to the Honorable James Schlesinger, for taking the time to read part of this manuscript at an early stage, for pointing out many errors, for helping me think through some difficult problems, and for explaining to me several things I had not understood.

I am indebted to Walter Laqueur, who years ago gave me the opportunity to come to Washington, and who has patiently helped me learn the skills of which he is such a great master; to the Honorable David Abshire, currently American Ambassador to NATO, who directed the Center for Strategic and International Studies so well and permitted me to work there; to Edward Luttwak, friend and colleague, constant source of creative thought and stimulating wit; to the Honorable Richard Perle, whose strength of character, quality of intellect, and moral tenacity have been so inspiring; to the Honorable Henry Kissinger, who has encouraged me in so many ways; to the Honorable Robert C. McFarlane, who through friendship and the force of his example showed me the meaning of intellectual courage and discipline; to General Vernon Walters, one of the great person-ages of our time, whose tireless service and remarkable personal qualities have done so much for our country; to the Honorable Jeane Kirkpatrick, whose clarity of thought and political courage are so well blended with her personal warmth and breadth of human understanding; to Norman Podhoretz, whose amazing in-tuitive understanding of American culture goes hand in hand with his exceptional stylistic and logical rigor; to Midge Decter, who has somehow combined the talents of an extraordinary leader with those of the selfless colleague; to Martin Peretz, who offered me the dream of my life—the chance to write for the *New Republic;* to Rabbi Augusto Segre, whose life and thought represent a unique fulfillment of faith and action, and whose af-fection and wisdom guided me during a most difficult time; and to Renzo de Felice, who years ago gave me the opportunity to work with him on the study of fascism, who has constantly en-couraged my intellectual peregrinations and remained a dear friend. Thank you all.

Some of the material in this book appeared in somewhat different form in other publications. I wish to thank the follow-ing publications for permission to use that material:

Commentary magazine for "The Bulgarian Connection and the Media" (October 1983) and "The Lesson of Lebanon" (April 1984).

The Public Interest for "Learning to Say 'No' to the Press" (Fall 1983).

The material on Rumanian technological espionage, based on information from Ion Mihai Pacepa, appeared in a much shorter and somewhat different form in *L'Express,* July 3, 1984.

Finally, a particularly warm "thank you" to my editor at Oxford, Susan Rabiner, who had the honesty to tell me when she disagreed and the integrity to work with me when I wouldn't change it. It's a better book for her efforts.

CONTENTS

1

THE GRAVE NEW WORLD

We have now entered one more great East-West crisis, and it is quite different from what most of us expected. Instead of a direct confrontation between the two power blocs, we now witness striking indecision on both sides. Instead of a clearly defined conflict between two competing systems, two strategic designs, and two political cultures, we see the two superpowers groping for effective foreign policies. At the same time, we increasingly see centrifugal forces within the two traditional spheres of interest that threaten to fragment the two camps. The current crisis is thus more complex than earlier ones as each superpower struggles to maintain control over its own sphere of influence while trying to cope with the actions of the other.

In the East, first China and now Poland have shattered the once-solid hegemony of the Soviets; in the West, Iran, once the second pillar of America's Middle East strategy, has left the Western alliance structure and now plays a destabilizing role in that part of the world while a different sort of radical anti-Americanism spreads just south of the United States itself. The Soviet Union seems unable to resolve the Polish crisis, and the United States seems baffled by the Central American challenge. Both superpowers seem frustrated by the Middle East. Through the stages of this most recent East-West crisis, no coherent strategy has emerged—neither from the Kremlin nor from the White House.

The lack of coherence from the superpowers has greatly affected the behavior of other countries, for, generally, when other world leaders no longer believe they can depend on the superpowers to act predictably, they are driven to act on their own behalf. A major consequence of American and Soviet strategic confusion is to encourage others to take more initiative in devising their own strategies. As recently as the early 1970s, small countries were reluctant to take dramatic and dangerous initiatives because they were afraid of adverse reactions by the superpowers (reactions they considered highly likely). Nowadays several small countries play global roles and often compel the superpowers to alter their own policies to deal with situations created by these smaller countries. To take just two examples, both Cuba and Israel now conduct policies that in their power to alter world events seem to bespeak global status much greater than either possesses. To be sure, each derives special strength from its role as favored ally of a superpower, but each has on occasion far exceeded the limits its powerful friend tried to impose. Cuba's initial African adventures—for example, in Angola in the mid-seventies—seem to have been launched despite initial Soviet misgivings, even though their success enhanced Soviet strategic interests on that continent. Similarly, Israel's massive invasion of Lebanon in 1982 came despite months of American pleas for restraint, even though the destruction of the PLO as a military force in the Middle East and the humiliation of one of Russia's military clients—Syria—proved advantageous to the United States.

All this makes the world more disquieting, and to the extent that multiple sources of initiative are more difficult to manage than a few, the world has become more dangerous. Until recently, countries contemplating foreign adventures could calculate with some degree of confidence the role the superpowers would play in the most likely contingencies. Foreign leaders could say to themselves (and to those in their own governments urging foreign adventures), "We can't do that, because if we do, the Americans (or the Russians) will come down on us." Thus, although many people deplored the apparent American/Soviet "condominium" of the 1970s, it nonetheless acted as a restraining influence on international adventurism. This restraining influence is disappearing now, with evident destabilizing consequences. Countries now embark on their adventures, and then wait to see if the superpowers are capable of forcing them to back off.

The increase in international crises during the past decade stems directly from this perception that the superpowers are no longer as clear as they once were about what they want and are no longer as prepared to pursue their interests with the necessary means. This perception is reinforced at two levels: first, on the basis of the international behavior of the Soviet Union and the United States in recent years; second, on the basis of the *internal* incoherence of the two superpowers. The internal incoherence is in fact the cause of much international blundering and indecisiveness, both by the superpowers themselves, and by third countries trying to predict the superpowers' behavior.

In the current crisis, each side has powerful cards to play, but the potentially winning cards in the superpowers' hands tend to offset each other. The Soviets' cards are in the form of military power, relentlessly built up over the course of the postwar period. Although they have always held an advantage in conventional military strength, for nearly thirty years, the Soviets were inferior to the West in strategic (nuclear) power. This inferiority has now been overcome, and insofar as one side now has an overall edge in military power, it is the Warsaw Pact that leads the NATO countries. Quite naturally, the Soviets have attempted to translate their awesome new military capability into political advantage—the most notable example being the campaign of intimidation against the deployment of American Cruise and Pershing missiles in Germany and Italy in the winter of

1983 and the attempt thereby to split off Western Europe from its close alliance with the United States. It remains to be seen whether, over time, Soviet military power will be sufficient—and Soviet political skills adept enough—to impose the Kremlin's will on Western Europeans. The risk is certainly there, particularly at those moments when American leadership is weak; witness the great concern evinced on both sides of the Atlantic about the growing neutralism in some parts of Western Europe during the past decade.

The Western advantage lies in a more successful political, economic, and social system and in a more desirable and appealing way of life. Despite the imperfections and outright injustices of life in the West, there are few today who believe that life could be better under communism. If international affairs were simply a matter of people freely choosing their own destinies, there would be little doubt about the outcome: most would select some variety of democratic government and would associate themselves with the West. Unfortunately, the great majority of the earth's inhabitants are never allowed to participate in these decisions; most of their leaders base their choices on criteria other than the relative success of the two basic systems in providing for the desires and needs of the populace. Most leaders are concerned primarily with maintaining themselves in power and with the survival of their own regimes. The example of the West, with its elaborate controls on the abuse of personal power, does not often appeal to national leaders with unfettered authority. This attitude is not entirely selfish, many of these leaders worry about the stability and security of their countries and believe maintaining themselves in power is the best assurance of both. This is why, outside the West, the crucial questions of foreign policy are matters of strength, wealth, and the apparent direction of world events.

Even in the relatively secure advanced industrial democracies of Western Europe and Asia, there is profound concern about fundamental shifts in the balance of power. When Henry Kissinger ventured to say in 1980 that if current military and political trends continued, Europe would be unable to rely on the American nuclear umbrella in a nearby future, it raised a highly emotional debate, and with good reason. For the leaders of the Western European democracies know that a decisive shift in the balance of power would require them to make accommodations in their foreign policies and eventually tilt toward the Soviet Union.

For though there is considerable evidence suggesting that the Soviet Union has entered a period of profound internal and external difficulties and that all the important trends, with the exception of military strength, favor the West, it is military strength that has all too often proved to be the decisive factor. The combination of an increasingly strong Soviet Union beset by serious structural problems could well prove to be even more threatening to the West than a Soviet Union with great military might and a viable internal structure.

We often forget that the present state of affairs is in many ways the reverse of the situation that existed a generation ago. As late as the Cuban Missile Crisis, the United States was far and away the predominant military power in the world (at least in nuclear terms) and the Soviet Union was the bearer of an ideology that threatened to enlist the world's masses. At that time, we feared the spread of communism as a political doctrine of false appeal; today we fear the effects of Soviet military power pure and simple. We are concerned about Soviet arms, but we no longer believe that our system and our allies will be subverted by communism. On the contrary, today it is the Soviet Union that fears the spread of democratic ideas, whether in the form of dissident movements within Russia itself, in the form of the free trade union movement in Poland, or reformist communist leaders in Czechoslovakia. Thus have the superpowers switched strong suits; thus must superpower strategies change.

THE PARADIGM: COLD WAR TO PROXIES

The antagonism between our system and that of the Soviet Empire has been the essential fact of the postwar period, and most
of the world has long dreaded some sort of final confrontation
between the two systems. Yet, with the exception of certain
alarming moments—the Cuban Missile Crisis, the Berlin block-
ade, and a few hours of the Arab-Israeli War of 1973—there
has been no such confrontation. One may look at the details of
each of these near misses with alarm, but after the passage
of thirty-five years of world history, we are entitled to conclude
that a two-sided commitment to the avoidance of direct conflict
between the superpowers is a defining characteristic of the period.

　　Rarely in world history has there been such a fundamental
clash of ideals and interests as that between us and the Soviets.
Why, then, has there been no war and rarely the threat of war
between the two? In part, because nuclear deterrence has worked:
the American nuclear umbrella protected Western Europe from
Soviet aggression, and the threat of American nuclear forces undoubtedly played a major role in deterring Soviet adventures in
other theaters as well, from the Caribbean to the Middle East.
Prudence has also played a role: the Russians have rarely moved,
whether in first person (Afghanistan for example) or by proxy
(Africa, the Middle East, Central America) without considerable
confidence that the United States would not see the adventure
as so threatening as to require a direct response or, at least, without being prepared to beat an orderly retreat if confronted by
resolute opposition.

　　Thus, unless the balance of military power falls so far out
of balance that even the most restrained within the Kremlin
might be tempted to challenge us, a direct conflict between Russia and America has been and is extremely unlikely. The greatest
risk remains that the two great powers will be drawn into con-

flict by third powers and that a world war will break out by accident. But militating against such accidents was that the non-superpowers have, until recently, had a relatively clear sense of what each superpower was about and what each was prepared to do to protect and advance its vital interests. To be sure, this was not always so, and there were several spectacular misjudgments, even in basic East-West affairs. Yet, until quite recently, such errors could be caught in time because American strategic strength was such that the Soviets would never allow the escalation of any conflict towards the nuclear threshold. Once the Americans committed themselves to the defense of a vital interest, the Soviets were obliged to give way. Despite the fulminations of Fidel Castro, this was the lesson of the Cuban Missile Crisis, and the Russians appreciated it; they informed the Americans at the time that they would never again permit such a humiliation to be inflicted on them.[1]

Given this implicit stability from the late 1940s to the late 1960s, which was imposed by the presence of superior American military and economic power, the rules of the game evolved willy-nilly. By the late 1950s, it was generally believed that the Soviets would not tolerate anything that threatened to disrupt their total control over the East European Empire. They conducted challenges to American interests through subversion they could aid but disavow (generally Communist parties but also guerrilla movements and terrorist groups), by propaganda (the ideological struggle, both direct and through disinformation), and by establishing military bases in third countries (most notably in the Middle East and Cuba). The United States, for its part, created a series of military alliances (NATO, SEATO,* the Baghdad Pact); used its overwhelming economic power to finance the development of countries of strategic importance; and exported the American political model through its cultural diplomacy, economic assistance programs, and its worldwide radio networks.

* Southeast Asia Treaty Organization.

Throughout this period, the United States enjoyed clear-cut strategic superiority and was far and away the greatest economic force on the planet, approaching 60 percent of the industrial capacity of the world at the beginning of the postwar period. By all lights, the United States should have been able to dictate any terms it desired; yet, in practice, it did so rarely, in large part because the American political tradition holds two antithetical views on foreign policy. First, we should use our power to promote democratic change throughout the world; second, we should not interfere in the internal affairs of other countries. This manifestly ambivalent approach to the world—if we promote democracy, we automatically destabilize the governments of most of the countries of the world; if we do not challenge antidemocratic governments, we do not promote democratic change—led American leaders to abrupt and violent shifts in their foreign policies: alternately supporting Franco in Spain and calling on our allies to work with us to replace him (a little-known initiative launched by Dean Acheson in 1948[2]); conducting a massive propaganda offensive against the Soviet Union in the satellites, then not raising a finger when Hungary revolted; organizing the Bay of Pigs operation, then canceling the air strikes required to give the men on the ground a decent chance of success; warning of dire consequences if the Soviets crushed the *Solidarnósc* trade union movement in Poland, then doing virtually nothing when it happened.

Still, with all the confusion and the built-in tensions of our foreign policy, few around the world were in doubt about our ability to define our vital interests and our determination to defend them (this is not to say that everyone would have agreed on definitions because the nature of American vital interests overseas has been the object of a national debate since the days of George Washington). More recently, however, with the retreat from Vietnam, the failure to meet the Cuban/Russian challenge in Angola, and the catastrophic fall of the shah of Iran, it was legitimate for other nations to wonder if the United States still had the capacity to define and defend its vital interests.

The Russians underwent a similar evolution, albeit somewhat later. Stalin's foreign policy was of a piece with the rest of his regime: ponderous and heavy handed, but predictable. His successors have followed along. The brutal purges following the creation of the satellites, the *gulags*, and the use of foreign Communist parties to destabilize Western countries were all recognizable components of a Stalinist strategy (whether conducted by Stalin himself or his heirs). The decision to suppress the Hungarian revolt seems to have been taken only after an agonizing forty-eight hours during which Soviet tanks actually started to leave Hungary. But once the West's failure to intervene in behalf of Eastern European revolts against the Kremlin became part of the rules of the game, the suppression of the Czechoslovakian revolt was automatic.

It was not until the late seventies and early eighties that one could see the first significant signs of internal incoherence in the Kremlin's behavior. In the early eighties, the Russians faced three major challenges: Poland, Afghanistan, and Lebanon. The first was a direct challenge to their system; the second was a stalled initiative of their own that threatened to become a major embarrassment and possibly a humiliation; the third was, at least initially, a major setback for their Middle East policies.

It may be argued that the Russians simply hit a run of bad luck, but the pattern is impressive; in none of the three cases was the Kremlin able to mount a strategically coherent offensive. The pattern suggests a systematic failure, not just bad luck, and the impression is heightened when one watches the Soviets stumbling around in Poland after the proclamation of military rule. No systematic efforts are made to rebuild the Communist party and there is no attempt to woo the Solidarity leaders back into the system. Nor is there even the kind of ruthless deception that then–Soviet Ambassador, Yuri Andropov, used to liquidate the Hungarian Communist leaders in the sixties: he promised them safe passage if they would leave the Yugoslav Embassy in Budapest; when they accepted his "promise," he had them arrested and sent to their doom. And there is insufficient military repression to compel the country to work, whether at the shipyards in Gdansk or in the Silesian coal mines.

The consequences of Soviet indecision in Poland are manifold: the collapse of the Polish Communist party—unprecedented in previous challenges to Soviet hegemony over Eastern Europe—proclaims that communism has failed as a system for managing national problems. The rise of Solidarity drives the point home, with the additional—devastating—element of showing that the problems of the working class have not been solved within the Soviet system. The halfway use of military power (*not* the regular Polish Army, but the *Zomos*, an elite corps of ruthless toughs roughly equivalent to the Gestapo under Hitler) suggests that the Kremlin is trying to deal with the Polish crisis at the *political* level rather than as a national insurrection. This is a crucial distinction because it is not sufficient for the Kremlin merely to quell the Polish resistance; the country must somehow be made to function in a productive manner. This has not happened, and Poland today is in default in all but name on its foreign debts.[3]

The Polish crisis is more than another step in discrediting Soviet communism; it also indicates that the impressive Soviet military machine need not be as determinant as it was once thought to be (an impression reinforced by the duration and effectiveness of the Afghan rebellion). This in turn is linked to yet another Soviet problem: the subjects of the Empire cannot be presumed to be reliably loyal to the Kremlin. One of the elements in the decision to use the *Zomos* rather than the Polish Army regulars was probably that the Russians feared that some elements of the Polish Army would cross over to the side of *Solidarnósc*.

Today, indeed, there are two sources of political legitimacy in Poland: the Pope and *Solidarnósc*. Only they can guarantee a stable, functioning society. In the end, the Russians will have to choose between the total military subjugation of Poland or coming to terms with the true sources of legitimacy. Unfortunately for the Kremlin, they have found in the Pope a person (and an institution) as patient as themselves. In addition, the longer the Soviets flounder around without resolving the crisis, the more likely it becomes that they will face similar challenges to their legitimacy in other satellite countries. Can it be that *only* the Poles were able to organize a clandestine alternative to the Communist state? More likely, we will find organizations similar to *Solidarnósc* capable of generating popular support throughout the Empire, even in Russia itself.

The Russians, we may presume, understand the gravity of their situation, and one is inclined to believe the impressive evidence that they were deeply involved in the attempts to murder the Pope and *Solidarnósc* leader Lech Walesa. They may still worry that a brutal repression with Warsaw Pact forces in Poland might yet produce the economic sanctions from the West that they so greatly dread, and yet they must also fear that a negotiated settlement with Walesa and his mass movement would encourage others to follow in Solidarity's footsteps. There is no attractive solution, but failure to take coherent action jeopardizes the Russians' strategic objectives as well because, until recently, most people had come to view the Soviet Union as a country that would always move forcefully to protect and advance its interests. The Polish case undermines that conviction.

On the other hand, the Polish drama showed once again that the United States and its allies are unwilling to make the Soviets pay for their failures—indeed, we seem surprisingly willing to shoulder the bill ourselves. For months, it had been widely predicted that Soviet repression in Poland would lead to passionate Western actions against the Russians; in the actual event, the suppression of Solidarity produced only the most transient expressions of moral outrage and virtually nothing in the way of real action. Within two years, the United States—despite anti-Soviet rhetoric as intense as any ever used, including that in the days of John F. Kennedy—had fully embraced the policies of détente, complete with grain sales of historic magnitude. These were not interrupted even after the Soviet destruction of a South Korean passenger plane in early September 1983.

Paradoxically, the failure of the Soviet Union to act decisively in Poland may threaten world peace more than would an effective military repression of the Poles. Whatever action the United States might threaten in the event of full-scale repression, there will likely be no action seriously challenging Soviet hegemony over Poland—indeed, the deeds will seem pale and timid compared to the threats. But a drawn-out sputtering crisis in Poland might lead like-minded people in other Soviet satellites to challenge the Kremlin's control, and this might well produce a major crisis. Here again, the unpredictability of the behavior of the two superpowers contributes to instability and increases risk.

THE REQUIREMENTS FOR A PEACEFUL WORLD

Much has been written about how to maintain the peace. Some believe it necessary to confront the Soviet Union with stern military power wherever and whenever the Russians try to expand. Others believe the answer lies in détente, arguing that the Russians cannot be denied a superpower role in the world but that we should negotiate the limits of that role and demand corresponding obligations from them to respect others' traditional turf.

These options are never abstract but depend on real possibilities. It is quite useless to advocate a tough containment policy at a time when the Russians' military power may well be stronger than our own, just as it is fatuous to pretend to practice détente in the absence of the sort of equilibrium that détente requires. If the Russians eventually grow much stronger than the West, the choice of options will be denied us, and we shall see—brutally—the meaning of an often-cited Soviet goal, "a favorable correlation of forces." Americans, spoiled by two hundred years of strategic invulnerability and unused to approaching the resolution of international disputes through the eyes of other nations, invariably act as if policy decisions were simply a matter of exercising good will and simple ratiocination and demanding the same from the other side.

As the Russians—who are rather more realistic about such things—put it, "He who says 'A', must say 'B' "; meaning that if you want to carry out a certain policy you must be able to meet the requirements of having your way and be prepared to accept the consequences. Thus, if the United States wishes to practice a policy of containment, it must have enough military power to block Russian adventures (the requirements) and it must also accept the climate of tension that containment creates (the consequences). Similarly, if the United States is going to adopt a policy of refusing to use its military power (as in President Reagan's announced Central American policy in the spring of 1983), it will have to live with the consequences (Cubans and Nicaraguans unafraid to raise the level of violence when it serves their interests because they can discount the threat of American retaliation).

As will be seen in the next chapter, Americans almost never conduct this sort of analysis; they prefer to base policy on abstract moral principles. Further, they want to spell out in advance precisely what the American government is prepared to do and what it will not do, thus falling victim to what Walter Lippmann termed more than thirty years ago the folly of the "dangerous amateurs":

> In Washington today there is one way of identifying easily the amateur who causes our suffering diplomacy to suffer unnecessarily. He is the man who feels that he ought to announce publicly and in no uncertain terms what the govern-

ment will do and what it will never do on all issues in all
quarters of the globe.

He cannot seem to understand that the more rigidly he
binds our own government the more he reduces its influence,
the more he diminishes its power to negotiate—that the more
he sets our own policy on one unalterable course, the more
numerous the options among which our antagonists and
rivals can choose their course.[4]

This sort of amateurism is as prevalent today as it was
when Lippmann described it, and the situation is made even
more dangerous by our recent national penchant for changing
the rules every four or every two years. As Italy's outstanding
foreign minister, Emilio Colombo, put it to me during the Carter
years, Europe can live with a hawkish America or a dovish
America but constant shifts will in the end alienate European
sympathies and paralyze European imaginations. If our policies
are presented effectively, our allies will be able to join with us
in containment or participate in the fruits of détente, but they
find it unecessarily difficult to alternate a few years of détente
with a few years of harsh confrontational policy positions.

The worst of all possible American policies from our allies'
point of view is rhetorical confrontation and objective weakness;
this is what they feared at first from Reagan. After witnessing
and contributing to years of eroding American defense spending (and thus a relatively weaker allied position vis-à-vis the
Soviets), they feared that an aggressive American posture would
expose them to maximum Soviet pressure without a corresponding increase in American deterrence. This seems to have been
the Russian reading as well, for in 1983, the Kremlin mounted
an unprecedented effort to bully the Europeans into refusing to
deploy the American Cruise and Pershing missiles. Soviet spokes-
men traveled all over Europe warning of the dire consequences
deployment would produce. I was in Rome one day when Boris
Ponamarev, the man in charge of foreign Communist parties for
the Kremlin, lectured the Italians: "Wouldn't it be a shame," he

said on national television, "if we had to aim our SS-20s at the Vatican, and at all these beautiful monuments in your country. If only you would refuse to accept the American missiles, we would not have to target you with ours." A similar speech was delivered by Foreign Minister Andrei Gromyko in Madrid, urging the Spaniards to stay out of NATO.

In succeeding months, the Russians attempted to translate their new strategic superiority in Europe (most dramatically in the form of their SS-20s) into a European decision to accept this Soviet superiority without a Western response. From every available pulpit, the Russians threatened the Europeans; at the same time, they continued to give substantial clandestine support to the various peace movements.[5] If we can believe the press reports from Moscow, Andropov himself took charge of this campaign at the time of the West German elections in the spring of 1983, as if to say to his comrades, "Now I will show you how to get results from the Europeans." The outcome: a solid majority for the very forces in Germany (the Christian Democratic leader Helmut Kohl and liberal leader and Foreign Minister Hans-Dietrich Genscher) who seemed to be most solidly behind the deployment of the American missiles.

The Russian campaign showed a misunderstanding of the West, and also indicated a possibly fatal preoccupation within the Kremlin. The Soviet Union may eventually achieve the Finlandization, or de facto capitulation of Western Europe, but unless Soviet military superiority becomes great indeed, West Europeans are unlikely to yield their freedom of action to brazen threat. If it is ever to be, Finlandization must be brought about slowly; the process will have to permit those European leaders who submit to Soviet wishes to pose as honorable peacemakers rather than timid appeasers. There are both military and political requirements for the success of the strategy, with the military advantage being translated into political gain through implicit threat, not by public bullying. Andropov's threats to the Germans during the final phases of the 1983 electoral campaign were counterproductive. Had he spoken more softly of peace and allowed his SS-20s to be his implicit big stick, Andropov might have done better.

Andropov's actual course of action suggests that he believed he needed to demonstrate foreign policy mastery for his own purposes, quite aside from any assessment of the true state of affairs in Western Europe. Like any new ruler, Andropov was eager to demonstrate that a change for the better had taken place and that he could achieve results favorable to his side. Furthermore, Andropov was the first Soviet dictator to know in painstaking detail the internal situation of the Empire; his sixteen years at the top of the KGB gave him a unique appreciation of the structural problems of the system and of the discontent of the populace. Like few before him, Andropov knew that the Polish problem was quite different from the challenges the Kremlin had faced earlier in Hungary and Czechoslovakia; he knew that *Solidarnósc* was a mass movement, not simply a group of dissidents. Moreover, he knew that although the Russian dissidents had been silenced (he had done it himself), the "system" was widely hated and despised and that the safest way to stem possible internal problems was to demonstrate that the Soviet Union was the dominant international power. The urgency with which Andropov sought a foreign success suggests that he feared an internal crisis unless Soviet power could be demonstrated on a world scale. Hence, Andropov's ill-judged campaign against the West demonstrated both concern over the internal stability of the Empire and a lack of understanding of the political dynamics of the West.

The Soviet Union in the mid-eighties thus showed signs of erratic behavior and strategic confusion. This was rather surprising from a country that had acquired a reputation for viewing the world as a chessboard and for decisive action. Moreover, the Soviet Empire began to show signs of structural breakdown within, thus further eroding its image in the world at large. To be sure, Soviet military power was great, indeed, but history is replete with examples of mighty armies that were rendered impotent by political failure.

The American policy confusion was of a different sort, but it had the same effect: without convincing evidence that the superpowers were prepared, determined, and able to use their power effectively, the other nations of the world increasingly pursued their own more limited objectives outside the parameters that had once been defined by the Big Two.

THE FUTURE

There is a widespread perception that it is the confrontation between the United States and the Soviet Union that threatens the peace and stability of the world and that, conversely, if "peace," or "peaceful coexistence" between the superpowers could only be firmly established, the risk of war would be greatly reduced. A major corollary to this view holds that if only the two great powers would agree to end the arms race, it would then be possible to devote a far greater share of the earth's wealth to the betterment of the human condition instead of spending so much of it on weaponry and soldiering.

This utopian vision is as false as it is apparently reassuring, yet it underlies a good deal of "educated" thinking about world affairs. The realities are quite different—and generally ignored: peace between the two superpowers is impossible unless one or both abandon their revolutionary view of their role in history. And the conflict between the United States and the Soviet Union has been a godsend for the smaller countries, for it has permitted them to pursue foreign policy objectives under the safe umbrellas offered by the superpowers. Without the controlling influence of the Big Two, we would likely have witnessed many more conflicts—or, at a minimum, longer lasting wars. In 1956, the United States saved Egypt from Israel, France, and Great Britain. Similarly, two decades later, the superpowers ended the

Yom Kippur War at a time when Israel was about to destroy the Egyptian army and could have dictated terms to Syria.

As Kissinger has told us, his actions in 1973 in the Middle East were designed to prevent the Israelis from inflicting a devastating humiliation on Sadat and on Syria. But both superpowers had played the game, even mobilizing their own forces at a certain point to intimidate the belligerents into accepting peace.

In 1975, the United States unilaterally withdrew from the game. First, in Vietnam when a Senate resolution assured both sides to the January 1973 Paris Treaty that no further U.S. funds would be supplied to South Vietnam, thus guaranteeing the collapse of our former ally and the victory of North Vietnam. Then in Angola, when another Senate resolution prevented the administration from providing any covert assistance to *any* forces in Angola, thus guaranteeing the victory of the Communist-supplied forces in that country as well and willy-nilly sanctioning the use of Soviet proxies—the Cubans in this case. The leaders of the American Congress took this latter action as a welcome moral limitation on American foreign policy; for the rest of the world, it meant opening the door to Cuban forces all over Africa. In the next few years, the Cubans extended Soviet influence to the Horn of Africa (Ethiopia), to South Yemen, and elsewhere (Cubans reportedly serve as terrorist instructors in training camps from Libya to South Yemen).[6]

One should have expected these Soviet advances—and the palpable demonstration of America's unwillingness to contest them—to produce other opportunities elsewhere. And to some extent, this did take place: the Soviet-sponsored Libyan dictator, Muammar al-Qaddafi—who had expelled the Americans from Wheeler Air Force Base in Libya in 1970 without any serious reaction from Washington—attempted to expand his domains in Africa; the Soviet-supplied Vietnamese expanded into Cambodia and Laos; and the Soviet-supported Cubans and Sandinistas in Nicaragua lent their support to the insurrection in El

Salvador. The Soviets, understanding the strategic logic of the American breakdown, decided to grab whatever additional advantages they might obtain before the pendulum of American public opinion swung back.

Yet, just as Andropov's bullying in the German elections of 1983 produced a backlash, so the successes of Soviet proxies in the middle and late seventies rallied countries from Southeast Asia to Africa. ASEAN,* blessed with some of the most brilliant leaders in the world (particularly the Singaporeans), lent support to anti-Vietnamese forces in Laos and Cambodia; the King of Morocco, along with Anwar al-Sadat in Egypt, supported countries willing to stand up to Qaddafi, and the United States itself showed a limited capacity for anti-Libyan activity. And in Central America, countries from Honduras to Costa Rica openly challenged both the internal and external policies of the Sandinistas, and Guatemala obtained Israeli help for its own counterinsurgency program. Even though the United States had not fully reentered the strategic game, others were, at least, taking up part of the slack.

This activity demonstrated yet another dimension of the Soviet crisis: the failure of communism to maintain its appeal. Whereas a generation ago, a majority of the intellectuals in Western Europe were either Communists or sympathetic to the Communist world view, today Communist political culture has virtually ceased to exist. To be sure, there are still agents of influence whose anti-Western activities create a tolerance for Communist totalitarianism and for Soviet foreign policy objectives, but there is no longer a prestigious Communist intelligentsia in the Western world—with rare exceptions, communism is no longer attractive to would-be Third World leaders. To be sure, the Soviet leaders themselves still believe in communism, especially in its vision of their own ultimate triumph. But they are the keepers of a flickering flame.

* Association of Southeast Asian Nations.

The disrepute of Soviet communism as an ideology corresponds to the decrepitude of the Soviet elite and to the patent bankruptcy of the Soviet Empire. Those of us who oppose communism would normally welcome these signs of decay, but in reality, they constitute a mixture of blessing and curse.

Had communism decayed—and the parallel structural crisis of the Soviet Union taken place—at a time when the West was strong and resolute, one could look forward with optimism to a more peaceful future. For under those circumstances, the West could contain the centrifugal forces generated by the decay of the Soviet Empire and guarantee that the West itself would not be fundamentally damaged by the final disintegration of the Empire. Alas, the structural crisis of the Soviet Empire came at a time when the West was relatively weak—indeed, at its weakest point vis-à-vis the Russians since the October Revolution—and, thus, most vulnerable. This tempted the Soviets to push for quick foreign victories to forestall internal fragmentation.

The combination of fear, opportunity, and illusion is a dangerous one, and it may well be the dominant mindset in the Kremlin. Fearful of the internal problems besetting the Empire; tempted by the apparent weakness and confusion in the West (and concerned that the American rearmament program will continue, and, at a minimum, impose higher costs and substantial delays in achieving a decisively positive "correlation of forces"); and erroneously convinced that their strategic superiority will quickly permit them to dictate at least some terms to the West—the Russians may be tempted to move dramatically in the near future. The response of the West remains to be seen, depending as it does on specific circumstance, luck, leadership, and character. But the fundamental point for the world at large is that Western resolve—specifically American resolve—cannot be predicted with certainty. Consequently, although the character of Soviet adventurism is clear, Soviet behavior becomes more erratic and, at the same time, Western—especially American—power and will are also much in doubt. Thus, for different reasons, both sides of the East-West dialectic have become increasingly unpredictable.

How did the two superpowers lose control over their own destinies and encourage developments so clearly contrary to their own interests? I believe that the answers are quite different in the two cases and that the limited chances available to regain control depend on quite different actions in Washington and Moscow. It is to the specifics of the confusion in the two world centers that we must now turn.

2

THE CHARACTERISTICS
OF AMERICAN POLICY

At this crucial moment, the United States has been deprived of the essential ingredients of good foreign policy. These can be simply stated:

We must be able to identify our friends and enemies, both current and potential, in accordance with our (sometimes temporary) national interests and in keeping with our enduring national values.

We are inevitably compelled to challenge antidemocratic regimes in the long term, but this does not mean that we cannot make temporary accommodations, whether with Communist regimes or with regimes of the Right.

We must resolutely combat the ideological visions of antidemocratic societies, whether fascist or Communist. There are two reasons for this: first, because a triumph of such an ideology in America would spell the end of American democracy; second, because the spread of totalitarianism internationally would threaten the democratic revolution, which is the vital core of our own vision of the world.

We must champion the forces of the democratic revolution. When they emerge in the Soviet bloc (Solidarity for example), they threaten the structure of the Soviet Empire itself. Yet, we must work to convince the Russians that they must make some sort of accommodation with the forces of democracy. If they do not, then world peace will some day be threatened by an explosion from within the Empire. When such forces emerge within authoritarian regimes (for example, the National Front in Iran), we must similarly encourage the regime to make space for them. However, we must be under no illusions in either case: both regimes will regard our attitude as threatening, both will fear it, both will attempt to subdue the democratic forces. We must, of course, also avoid the temptation to believe that there will always be some middle ground between the two unattractive extremes; sometimes there will be no "magic middle," and we may be forced to choose among some nasty options. This, too, is part of foreign policy; one does not always have the luxury of having at least one good choice or of choosing the occasion for crisis.

It goes without saying that we must have sufficient power and will to make our causes and those of our allies successful when challenged. As James Schlesinger has put it, "the premise of the political Left that the United States had been too powerful for her own and the world's good was . . . put to the test. The outcome is hardly surprising: as the strength of the United States ebbed, so did her influence."[1]

In other words, we require understanding and seriousness: understanding of the world and seriousness in the pursuit of our vital interests. For many years now, our leaders have lacked these characteristics, and our policies along with our national policy debates have been both confused and fickle. We have tended to adopt moralistic abstractions instead of realistic appraisals of the world, and we have rarely suited our diplomatic, economic, and military means to our national objectives. Finally, we have often ignored some of the elementary facts about international reality.

That there has been a lot of confusion regarding the basic facts of international life is demonstrated by the great number of challenges to the notion—most recently enunciated by U.N. Ambassador Jeane Kirkpatrick—that there is a significant difference between totalitarian and authoritarian regimes. Many critics attacked Ambassador Kirkpatrick on the grounds that this well-established, scholarly formulation was an excuse for supporting repressive dictatorships friendly to the United States and a pretext for relentlessly attacking the Soviet Union. Such criticisms miss the point and are, moreover, misguided on scholarly grounds.

The distinction between authoritarian and totalitarian regimes is quite real and is important, as was seen during the transition to democracy in Spain following the death of Franco. Despite the common description of Franco's regime as Fascist, it was actually a classic Latin-style military dictatorship, and once the dictator died, the system itself was subject to change. It was, therefore, possible to dismantle the Francoist system within a few years and to replace it with a constitutional monarchy based on full democracy. A similar transition took place in Portugal following the death of Salazar, the country's long-time dictator, and the beginning of such a change occurred in Argentina after the fall of the military junta. This could never have taken place in a totalitarian country, where the mechanism of repression is not based on the charisma of the leader but on a system of belief imposed by systematic terror. In all cases to date, the totalitarian system has outlived any given dictator. In totalitarian countries, like the Soviet Union and China, there may be great purges or shifts in the leadership cast, but rarely if ever is there any fundamental change in the method of rule—for the perpetuation of the repression does not depend on the will of a single individual or group of individuals.

Intelligent foreign policy must take this distinction into account rather than acting—as the moralists would have us act—on the basis of a blind opposition to all tyrannies or, worse still, selective opposition based on a misguided preference for tyrannies of a given political stripe. The crucial point is that it is possible to meliorate the evils of friendly authoritarian regimes, whereas no comparable possibility exists with regard to totalitarian ones. We need to leave open the option of choosing the lesser of two evils: it is better to work with a friendly tyranny than to face an unfriendly one, both because of our own security and because of our ability to influence friendly governments. We can effect change in the behavior of friendly regimes provided that we assure them that following our lead will not result in their downfall. If we challenge them frontally or excoriate them publicly (thus giving tacit support to those within their own countries who wish to remove the government itself), they may well rear up and not only refuse to evolve in a more democratic direction, but also shift their foreign policies in directions hostile to our interests. The United States, then, has to be able to reassure disagreeable, yet friendly, governments about their own security while urging them to move steadily in the direction of greater democracy. This is not simply a political decision on our part: repressive regimes are all potentially explosive and, thus, threaten international peace (a problem that is particularly acute with regard to the Soviet Empire). Our demand for the success of the democratic revolution is accordingly both idealistic and realistic.

If we expect other countries to join with us and even to take risks in our behalf, we have to show them—at a minimum—that we understand what they are up against. Without consistent opposition to the expansionism of the Soviet Empire, we cannot offer our friends credible assurances. When friendly foreign leaders hear the president of the United States say—as President Carter did in the first year of his presidency—that the United States has lost its "inordinate fear of communism," they interpret such words as a sign that our resolve to resist Soviet

imperialism has weakened, and that our support for strongly
anti-Communist countries will be diluted. Under those circumstances, they automatically move toward greater accommodation
with the Soviet Union. But the abandonment of anticommunism
is not only a tactical mistake; it is also a betrayal of our own
values, for the democratic revolution cannot succeed if communism expands and flourishes.

The public at large seems to understand these matters far
better than our confused leadership, for the leaders are often
attempting to enhance their political status with those who decide these matters, especially the elite media. This phenomenon
will require extended treatment later, for it is one of the basic
sources of confusion in the American (indeed, the Western) political system. Let it suffice for the moment to say that fashionably correct positions on many issues are defined by a group of
journalists who are themselves ignorant of the dynamics of international affairs and who are themselves explicitly engaged in
political activity with strong professional investments in certain
outcomes. These people tend to be far more liberal than the
public. To cite one startling example: in 1972, some 81 percent
of leading journalists supported the presidential candidacy of
George McGovern, a man who carried only one of our fifty
states.[2] Yet, these people hold disproportionate influence over
which political positions will be granted respect. Before they can
address the serious problems facing us, our leaders are going to
have to overcome the influence of these reputation makers. Unfortunately, the structure of our political system is such that we
are unlikely to get such leadership now or in the near future.

AMERICA'S REAL ROLE IN THE WORLD:
THE UBIQUITOUS MEDDLER

American foreign policy is pulled in two opposite directions by
the two great passions of our international activity: the first is

to have good relations with "good" countries alone; the second is scrupulously to refrain from meddling in the internal affairs of other countries. Of the first desire, a good deal will shortly be said; it is the second that must occupy us here.

Traditionally, there have been two grounds on which American avoidance of others' political affairs has been argued: the first is the simple, pragmatic desire to avoid "entangling alliances" and overclose relationships with countries that might corrupt us or drag us into danger. So far, so good: allies should be selected with care, in keeping with real needs. But there is a second sort of rationale for refraining from an active foreign policy, one that suggests that American influence, in and of itself, is dangerous to the rest of the world. This has recently become a favorite refrain of those—Americans and foreigners alike—who view American materialism and capitalism as threatening to other cultures. Although not new, either in the United States or overseas, this theme gathered real momentum in the sixties and seventies when America's role in Vietnam was held to be proof positive that, in the words of a celebrated cartoon character, "we have met the enemy and he is us."

Those two impulses to American passiveness thus rest on opposite conceptions of the character of the United States. One version wishes to protect America from the evils of the outside world; the second seeks to defend the world against presumed American evils. Although they lead to quite different conclusions—the first demands that the United States be strong enough to defend itself against evil from without, whereas the second would have us enfeeble the country so that we are unable to exert influence abroad—both ignore the exigencies of the real world, for the United States cannot avoid playing a major role in the internal affairs of most countries in the world. American political, cultural, and economic affairs have a direct and immediate effect on the rest of the planet, with our allies in the first instance. Anyone who reads the European or Japanese or Latin American press will discover this in a matter of hours; in-

deed, citizens in those countries often follow American developments with greater attention than do Americans themselves, for
unlike us, our overseas friends must be prepared to make quick
changes in their behavior on the basis of American shifts.

One proof of this American influence—again, witting or
unwitting—lies in the constant complaints we hear from the
rest of the world about our policies, whatever they may be. If
we have—as under Carter—rising inflation and a weakening
dollar, the Europeans express panic at our willingness to flirt
with the possible collapse of our currency (as German Chancellor Helmut Schmidt never tired of repeating, along with
French President Giscard-d'Estaing); if we have instead big defi-
cits and high interest rates—as under Reagan—the Europeans
hate *that* as well (as Chancellor Schmidt never tired of repeating, along with President François Mitterrand). What the Europeans were really complaining about was not so much the American policy itself as the relentless influence of American policy
over their own social and economic programs.

Although economics provides perhaps the clearest example
of America's automatic impact on other countries' internal decisions, the same applies to culture, politics, and military questions. In 1983, America's arms-control policies were a central
question in the West German elections, and a month earlier
American culture was the object of heated debate in Paris at an
international gathering of "intellectuals" under the aegis of the
French Socialist government. American fads and fashions sweep
through the Western world, often with a multiplier effect—the
stylish Leftism that started in Berkeley in the sixties became a
tidal wave when it hit Europe, and it lasted years longer in
places like Italy and Greece than it had in the United States—
and the international effects of American language has produced
words of near-universal use, from jeans to hot dog.

So much for the notion that we can avoid influencing other
nations in a powerful and direct way, even if we wished to do

so. Our only choice is *how* to influence others. But the notion that it is somehow wrong to do so leads us to refrain from moving forcefully and coherently when it would be in our interest and, instead, standing by as we cause change throughout the world willy-nilly.

The leaders of other countries understand full well the intimate relationship between American behavior and their own imperatives, and they strive constantly to understand what makes us tick in a desperate—but usually fruitless—effort to save themselves from surprises coming from Washington. Moreover, they shamelessly attempt to use us as a swing factor in their own political battles.

There is not a country in Western Europe where this does not take place, even though no leader would acknowledge it publicly; it can be demonstrated easily enough by simply tracking the caravan of politicians that passes through the diplomatic entrance to the Department of State in any given period. Why are they all there? Many of them come for nuts-and-bolts diplomatic purposes, but many also come to be photographed with the secretary of state (even better, with the president, *whoever* he is and *whatever* the level of ostensible disagreement with American policies). Those photographs and the usually elaborate and overstated press accounts of the high-level contacts with American officials are worth a great deal back home, for they indicate that the leader is being listened to in Washington, that he or she counts at the center of power in the United States.

Often, the smaller and more insecure the country, the more elaborate the caravan to Washington. Italy, for example, sends a spectacular number of bodies through the diplomatic entrance each year. And because the Italian government is generally a multiparty coalition, each party sends its own leaders to show in Italy that each is recognized by the Americans as a personage worthy of respect—hence, worth voting for. Italian political leaders live in dread that the Americans will somehow give

greater credit to some competing politician and refuse to believe—although it is quite true—that the Americans receive them
all simply as a matter of common courtesy, not because the
United States is making active political decisions about Italian
electoral life.

Yet everything that happens to Italian politicians in Washington—and much that does not but is simply invented for the
"press event" by the politicians and their assistants—has a direct effect back home, and the same can be said for every other
allied country. Our allies would certainly design a strategy for
influencing the internal politics of other countries if they were in
our position; this is why they feel free to use us in their own internal affairs. Yet, we go by the book, by the rules of good manners, without apparent thought to our own interests. Consider,
for example, the German situation in the winter of 1982–83.
The Schmidt government had fallen and Helmut Kohl—a good
ally—was chancellor. Elections were scheduled within a few
months and the future of NATO might hinge on the outcome,
for if the Vogel/Brandt-led SPD won the elections, Germany
would take a giant step toward neutralism.

At this moment, the White House was asked to receive the
SPD* leader, Hans-Jurgen Vogel. On the question strictly of
good manners, to be sure, the American government would have
had trouble refusing the German Socialists' request. Reagan had
received Kohl in 1981 when he was the leader of the opposition
to the Schmidt government. How, then, could Vogel be denied?
Such may have been good sportsmanship, all right, but it was
bad foreign policy. Kohl, who had been denied a meeting with
Carter, had been received by Reagan to demonstrate American
support for the CDU/CSU,† and not simply because he was a
leading German politician. The central issue for Washington
should have been the impact of receiving Vogel on the outcome
of the upcoming March elections: the United States had a clear

* Social Democratic party of Germany.

† Christian Democratic party; Social Union party.

stake in a Kohl victory, therefore, nothing should have been done to improve Vogel's chances.

Finally, there was an additional dimension to the Vogel question: its possible effect on international socialism. Without attracting much public attention, the Reagan administration had spent two years quietly exchanging information about foreign policy problems of mutual interest (including Central America, southern Africa, and the East-West military balance) with moderate, democratic leaders of the Socialist International, which demonstrated, with a degree of success that surprised many people, that the Reagan administration could engage western Socialist parties in serious cooperation despite the political differences between Washington and the Socialists. Figures like Felipe Gonzales in Spain, Mario Soares in Portugal, Bettino Craxi and Pietro Longo in Italy, Pierre Jospin in France and Shimon Peres in Israel, to name just a few, had been given considerable information and had participated in a regular exchange of views with high administration officials. For the American government to give such a visible embrace to Vogel—who represented the more radical wing of the Socialist International—sent a new kind of signal to the moderates and undermined some of the work that had been done earlier.

Thus, by receiving Vogel before the German elections, the Reagan administration strengthened its opponents both in Germany and within the Socialist International. We would have been better advised to have told Vogel that we would be happy to see him but that we did not wish to involve ourselves in the imminent German elections. From the point of view of affecting the direction of international socialism, the United States should have invited someone like Soares to Washington instead of Vogel. That would have sent a clear message to all the Socialists and social democrats of Europe, and would have advanced our interests throughout the continent.

This question has been analyzed in some detail to show how the real choice facing the United States is *how* to have an

effect on the internal politics of other countries. We are simply
unable to remain piously outside the political struggles of the
free world. Consequently, it will be necessary to make our
choices realistically and effectively; of late, it seems we are unable to do so. To resolve our difficulties, we shall have to overcome some deep-seated problems, many of them rooted in our
national traditions.

THE ROOTS OF AMERICAN FOREIGN POLICY

The United States is the envy of much of the world and the
despair of many of our friends. Envied because of our wealth,
our freedom, and our vitality, we are despaired of because of
the often foolish impulsiveness of our international behavior.
As a Turkish general once put it, "The problem with having the
United States for an ally is that you never know when the
Americans are going to stab themselves in the back."[3] Our failure to conduct good foreign policy is the result of many things:
our history, our good luck, our ignorance, our political system
(particularly our method of choosing our leaders), and the me-
diocrity of our current elite.

American political culture has been shaped by two centuries
of material and civil improvement and by the security that comes
from rarely having had to face hostile nations close enough to
threaten American security directly. To be sure, we *have* had our
moments of great misery and despair in the United States and
we *have* faced serious foreign threats (for example, the burning
of Washington in the War of 1812 and the destruction of our
Pacific fleet at Pearl Harbor in 1941), but no other nation has
enjoyed the sense of security that has characterized two hundred years of American life. The long-term downside of this
relative good fortune is that only a nation with our history could
afford the luxury of conducting foreign policy on the basis of
abstract moral principles instead of the pursuit of our vital in-

terests; for less secure countries, the need to ensure survival is a more urgent consideration. But Americans—without the nearby foreign threats that so marvelously focus the mind of policymakers in other lands—have often pursued more grandiose but generally less realistic goals, with the results best described by the Turkish general.

The American diplomatic tradition thus developed through a long period during which two oceans protected us from our enemies, and during the century of American expansion, the British fleet gave us a strategic umbrella in case anyone sought to challenge us. As a consequence, we were relieved of the obligation to design and conduct strategically sound foreign policies. Even through the dawning of the age of intercontinental flight, Americans had little direct concern about foreign military threats. We could wait before entering wars, and we were generally disinclined to fight unless we were directly attacked. American involvement in the major conflicts of the first half of this century were largely the result of initiatives by our enemies rather than the consequence of deliberate American policy. Pearl Harbor, for example, was a Japanese decision that proved to be a great stroke of luck for the West, because it got the United States involved in the Second World War. When Hitler then declared war on *us*, it sealed the doom of the Axis.

This is not to say that the United States has only fought when attacked nor that we have always fought for admirable causes. Neither is true; the point here is simply that America, already favored by natural wealth, and unusually fair polity and society, and geographical location, had the additional good fortune of having been dragged into the great military conflict of this century in time to have a decisive effect, primarily because of mistakes by our enemies.

The strategic good fortune of the United States was viewed by many Americans as additional confirmation of the Puritan theory that this country had been singled out by Providence to be a "beacon light unto the nations" and, as such, could afford

the luxury of conducting foreign policy by force of moral example—a theme that has remained one of the mainstreams of
American political culture, even though our position in the world
is now such as to require a far more traditional approach to international affairs. But, given our history, it is understandable
that the United States should have failed to develop the sort of
geopolitical and diplomatic traditions that have normally accompanied national expansion. Predictably, some of the most distinguished American thinkers in the fields of geopolitics and
diplomacy have come from a foreign background or from the
military. These men and women were forced to address serious
strategic questions either because they came from countries that
had regularly experienced direct threats to themselves or their
vital interests abroad or because their profession demanded that
they do so. By contrast, many native Americans outside the
military grew up without any sense of national peril and did not
feel a sense of urgency to develop a coherent national strategy.
Such persons preferred to focus on the more idealistic side of
America's foreign activities. And having failed to appreciate the
extent to which other nations designed *their* foreign policies on
the basis of realpolitik, Americans often found themselves misunderstood, ineffective, or even in unwitting conflict with their
allies' best interests. That this generally occurred for "good"
(that is, morally laudable) reasons did little to mitigate the damage done or to enhance the long-term interests of the United
States.

I shall never forget the tongue-lashing I once took from
an Italian many years ago on the occasion of some moralistic
act on the part of the American Government. "Has no one in
Washington ever read Machiavelli?" he railed at me, "Do you
people *only* study the New Testament?" It often seems to foreign observers that our leaders conduct national affairs purely
on the basis of abstract moral considerations without due attention to the traditional, often amoral principles that govern the
survival of nations and peoples. Our friends—actual and poten-

tial—outside the United States may well be inspired by our moral principles and may even wish to follow our example, but they will not if by doing so they place themselves at risk. So, by one of those paradoxes that characterizes strategic thinking, our moral principles and our fine example generally suffer if our foreign policy is based *primarily* on abstract moral considerations. Our first obligation is to ensure that our geopolitical interests along with those of our allies are protected. To support a friend or thwart an enemy is to advance our principles. This, of course, requires that we be able to distinguish between our friends and our enemies—and there have been occasions on which we have been unable to make this distinction. Moral considerations should certainly enter the policy discussion, but they are most useful when they are concrete and comparative rather than general and abstract. In the largely lawless international environment in which we must attempt to advance our interests, to base policy on moral abstractions is to give our opponents an unacceptable advantage and to confuse most of our friends.

A classic case of such confusion came when the Soviets invaded Afghanistan and President Carter suddenly changed his entire assessment of the Soviet Union. Before then, Secretary of State Cyrus Vance had indicated that Carter and Brezhnev "shared common dreams" about international affairs. Rhetoric of this sort is not unusual in the world of diplomacy, but Carter and Vance appear to have really believed that Brezhnev and the other leaders in the Kremlin were "basically good people" who, in the end, "wanted to do the right thing." When the Soviets invaded Afghanistan, Carter decided that they were really bad sorts. In reality, of course, Soviet policy had always been made on the basis of calculations of interests and power, not on the basis of abstract (let alone Western) moral standards. Thus it was upsetting to our allies—as it was to many Americans—to discover that the president of the United States had been so confused about the motivating impulses of his primary adversary.

Carter's error rested on a typical American misconception:

that all persons in the world are essentially the same and that, with sufficient patience and good will, they can be made to do the proper thing. Carter's shock at the Kremlin's decision to invade Afghanistan reflected this misconception but did not entirely correct it, for Carter persisted in another, closely related conviction: if other countries were hostile to us, we must somehow have earned this hostility. Unaccustomed as we are to think in terms of actively defending our own vital interests and constantly striving, instead, to make the United States a moral example to the world, we listen carefully to criticisms of our practices, even when the critics are clearly biased. This tendency was particularly pronounced in the 1970s when the moral failure of the Nixon administration became generalized into an attack on the American government as a whole.

Carter believed that the United States under his two immediate predecessors had come to represent the major threat to peace and righteousness in the world. As he tells us in his memoirs, he had originally intended to quote in his inaugural address from a verse in Chronicles: "If my people, which are called by my name, shall humble themselves, and pray, and seek my face, and turn from their wicked ways; then will I hear from heaven, and will forgive their sin, and will heal their land."[4] The sins he had in mind were those he believed had been perpetrated by Kissinger, Nixon, the CIA and the Watergate crowd. "Instead of promoting freedom and democratic principles, our government seemed to believe that in any struggle with evil, we could not compete effectively unless we played by the same rules or lack of rules as the evildoers. I was deeply troubled," he noted, "by the lies our people had been told; our exclusion from the shaping of American political and military policy in Vietnam, Cambodia, Chile, and other countries; and other embarrassing activities of our government, such as the CIA's role in plotting murder and other crimes."[5]

Carter's approach to foreign policy thus began with a strong conviction that America had sinned and that without redemption there could be no proper policy. His administration worked hard to restrain the American "rogue elephant" by greatly limiting the activities of the CIA, by installing an activist group in charge of human rights at the Department of State, and by appealing to the good instincts of the Soviet Union in an attempt to reduce nuclear armaments (undertaking—unsuccessfully, to be sure—the unilateral withdrawal of American nuclear weapons from South Korea in the first weeks of the new administration).

These two confusions, which are held by some of the most influential writers and political leaders in America, produce some unfortunate foreign policy decisions. First, the conviction that foreign countries are basically similar to the United States and that foreign leaders share the same motivations as American officials makes it difficult for us to recognize real enemies when they appear. Second, the conviction that we are insufficiently moral to lead the struggle for our historic principles often prevents us from being properly aggressive when opportunities for democratic progress present themselves. The Carter period provides two excellent examples of the consequences of these misconceptions, though similar cases could be cited from other administrations. The first example, the Spanish transition from dictatorship to democracy, was a lost opportunity to support the kind of democratic revolution we should be working for throughout the world; and the second example, the fall of the shah of Iran to the Ayatollah Khomeini was a classic example of the American unwillingness to recognize the futility of trying to curry favor with those who are our sworn enemies for what they are.

THE SPANISH MODEL

When the Spanish dictator, Francisco Franco, died in 1975, it was widely feared that Spain would enter a period of intense internal conflict, perhaps even a second version of the civil war of the thirties. Instead, with a maturity and skill that hardly anyone had anticipated, Spanish leaders piloted the country through a remarkable transition from authoritarian dictatorship to democracy. Barely eight years after Franco's death, a Socialist prime minister—Felipe Gonzales—was elected with a solid electoral majority, and he governed the country with a broad-based consensus. How had this been achieved?

The key figure in the story is the king, Juan Carlos of Bourbon. Before being installed, Juan Carlos was the beneficiary of an almost universally accepted reputation for frivolousness. He was said to be a playboy, a mediocre political talent (if not an outright fool), and a most unfortunate choice for King. Rarely has an assessment been so wrong, yet the low esteem in which the king was held actually helped him because few imagined that he was capable of a remarkable behind-the-scenes operation to plan Spain's destiny. Two years before Franco's death, Juan Carlos had asked several potential prime ministers to submit to him, in writing, their plans for Spain in the period immediately following the dictator's death. After studying these written responses (of which there were at least five), Juan Carlos decided that Adolfo Suarez—the secretary-general of the Falange—was best suited to manage the transition to democracy.

From that point on, Suarez and Juan Carlos met regularly, updating their detailed transition plan so that when Franco finally died after a prolonged agony, they were in agreement not only on the general outlines of what they were going to do, but even on the specific measures and the tempo of change.

It is not known to what extent Franco himself was involved in the planning for this transition, but he cannot have been completely excluded from the process. Franco knew that Spain was going to change after his death, and he must have had at least some knowledge of the kind of planning that was going on. After all, he had selected Juan Carlos to lead the country after his own death, and he had elevated Adolfo Suarez to one of the key positions within the dictatorship. Thus, Franco's last years were, at least in part, a period of planning for a more liberal country. Following the dictator's death, the king and Suarez dismantled Franco's state from the inside (as only a man like Suarez, the archetypical insider, could), and then opened the political process to all contending forces, even Santiago Carrillo's Communist party.

What did the United States do during this exemplary transition from dictatorship to democracy in Spain? Despite their considerable enthusiasm for the process under way, the American leaders—from President Carter on down—failed for the most part to acclaim the Spaniards publicly for their courage and vision, let alone to give the sort of concrete support to Juan Carlos and Adolfo Suarez that would demonstrate steady American approval. Indeed, from the Spanish point of view, American desires were unclear, and Suarez himself came to suspect that Carter did not like the new Spanish system. He based his suspicions on three sound arguments:

First, Carter never invited Suarez to Washington for the kind of reception that demonstrates the strong support of one government for another.

Second, the United States never offered a significant aid package, leaving Spain to negotiate not only the transition from dictatorship to democracy, but also the equally difficult move from the protectionist economic system of Franco to a modern industrial society.

Third, the United States failed to provide meaningful assistance to the Spanish government in its struggle against Basque terrorism. As Suarez said to me in late 1977, there was only one real threat to Spanish democracy: the ETA (*Euskadi ta Askatasuna*) terrorists. If ETA were able to provoke a resurgence of Francoist repression, then democracy might yet perish in Spain. So Suarez turned to the United States, the leader of the West, and the one country able to provide Spain with the sort of intelligence and intelligence-gathering equipment that the Spanish government needed to infiltrate and dismantle the terrorist organization. To his consternation, the request was denied. Suarez could not have been expected to understand that the United States under Carter was more concerned about imagined threats to democracy from its own intelligence service than it was about international terrorist organizations. Indeed, Carter had introduced all manner of "safeguards" to prevent covert and clandestine action by the CIA: in the case of terrorism, there was a requirement that the president personally sign a "finding" that a given terrorist organization was "international" before the intelligence community could combat it. At the time of Suarez's request, no such finding regarding ETA had been made; hence no support was forthcoming.[6]

The Americans, then, were insensitive to the problems of Spain in transition; this was unfortunate in itself and bad for bilateral relations. American policymakers were also unaware of their own interests in the Spanish affair, and this was a far graver matter on a global scale. The successful transition from authoritarian dictatorship to democracy in Spain was the most graphic example of the sort of change the United States should seek to promote throughout the world, and Suarez and Juan Carlos had shown that it was possible. Carter should have made Spain the symbol of the vitality and viability of the democratic revolution, not only in Europe but throughout the developing world. Suarez was in fact the perfect ally for Carter, for he could have served as the point man for the democratic revolution in Latin America and in parts of North America. He spoke the language of Latin America, knew the problems firsthand, had a spontaneous understanding of the cultural conflicts, and did not carry the burden of Yankee envy and suspicion.

Instead of making Spain the symbol of American objectives, Carter directed his attention to more fashionable goals, seeking accommodation with Castro's Cuba and accelerating the downfall of Anastasio Somoza's corrupt regime in Nicaragua. The latter, particularly, demonstrated a fundamental disregard of international realities. Before the fall of Somoza and the triumph of the Sandinistas, Carter had met with the president of Mexico, Jose Lopez Portillo. At this private meeting, some months before the success of the Sandinista revolution, the American president had received an unusually explicit warning: Lopez Portillo told Carter that although he had contempt for Somoza, a triumph by the Sandinistas would make matters even worse because the prospects for democracy in Nicaragua would be worsened and other countries in the region (most notably Mexico) would be forced to make political changes themselves. Specifically, Lopez Portillo warned that a Sandinista victory in Nicaragua would compel him to shift Mexico's foreign policy to the Left, and he did not want to do that.[7]

Carter apparently did not understand the message being given him, as his response demonstrated: he asked Mexican assistance in accelerating the downfall of Somoza. The consequences were those that Lopez Portillo had promised. Carter was forced to recognize this at the end of his presidency when the United States restored military aid to El Salvador in a belated attempt to balance the Sandinistas' support for the Salvadoran guerrilla movement.

This kind of failure cannot be explained on the basis of provincialism and politics alone; there is a question of competence involved here as well. Carter was a visceral moralist in international affairs, but aside from his theological approach to America's role in the world, he had no fully formed world view. On actual policy decisions, he wavered between the aggressive anti-Sovietism of his national security adviser, Zbigniew Brzezinski, and the fashionably leftist views of his secretary of state, Cyrus Vance, which were reinforced by the even more radical views of U.N. Ambassador Andrew Young. Vance and Young were both products of the Vietnam period: the former had been deputy secretary of defense during the Vietnam War and came to regret his role in it; the latter had been an antiwar activist. Both suffered from an almost religious belief in the reasons put forward by the American New Left for the tragedy of Vietnam and often gained Carter's approval for policies based on these socially chic but never-questioned myths.

THE NEW LEFTISTS

Carter's view of America came to coincide in some respects with the dogmas of the New Leftists: like them, the president believed that America was a principal source of the world's problems and that one reason for America's aberrant behavior in the past was a visceral anticommunism that had on occasion led the United States to support some nasty dictatorships. Thus, his enthusiasm for the human rights campaign, which, through one of those ironies that frustrate those who try to reduce human behavior to orderly models, had apparently been dreamt up by Brzezinski as an ideological club to use against the Soviet Empire. But after an early rhetorical skirmish with the Russians, the human rights theme was almost invariably used against friends of the United States who failed to live up to the high standards the New Leftists demanded of rightist regimes.

So it was that a president who wanted to rein in the American "rogue elephant" ended by meddling in the internal affairs of many other countries—almost always speaking and acting in favor of forces hostile to the United States, though he tended to do so unwittingly. Many of Carter's advisers had a basic antagonism toward the sort of tyranny and corruption that Somoza incarnated—this required only common decency and was shared by almost all reasonable people who knew the facts about Nicaragua. In addition, some advisers were doubly enthusiastic, and also worked to end the dictatorship because the Sandinistas appeared to have impeccable revolutionary credentials. Many of the president's people believed that Nicaragua offered the chance to undo the imagined American sin toward Fidel Castro: we would embrace *Sandinismo* in Nicaragua and show that the United States could work successfully with a truly radical regime. Alas, the Sandinistas had no desire to accept the embrace of the Americans; they saw the United States as their imperialist enemy and devoted their energies to supporting similar-minded groups throughout Central America—the Cubans, the Russians, the PLO, and the rest of the support structure for subversive movements.

By the end of his term, Carter realized what had happened and restored military assistance to El Salvador. That willingness to reconsider the original policy was undoubtedly due in part to the great catastrophe that had occurred in Iran, where abstract moralism and ideological blinders were also at work, to the detriment of both American interests and the well-being of the majority of Iranians.[8]

THE FALL OF THE SHAH

When the shah came under attack by a mixed bag of reactionary religious fanatics, progressive politicians with little popular following, and frustrated middle-class entrepreneurs, engineers, and intellectuals, the Carter people sympathized with the opposition, even though, as events would demonstrate, they understood little of the issues involved and even less of the personalities in play—above all, the Ayatollah Khomeini himself. To be sure, they recognized that the shah was important to the United States, but they felt that the weight of moral value lay with his enemies. After all, the shah's regime kept political prisoners in jail, even tortured many, offered nothing like popular participation in government, and was moving slowly in granting women's rights. The leader of the opposition, the Ayatollah Khomeini, was a religious man who deplored the excesses of the shah's rule and spoke in the name of Islamic tradition.

If the American policymakers had looked at Iran in context, they would have seen that the shah, albeit an authoritarian ruler, was by our own standards by far the most progressive ruler in the Persian Gulf and that although there were political imprisonments and even torture in Iran, this was nothing compared with the practices in other Middle Eastern countries (with the exception of Israel). Yet Americans tended to deal with the Iranian question abstractly, focusing on the shah's sins in a vacuum and thereby ignoring the relative enlightenment of his rule compared to virtually all those around him. Despite the enormous importance of the shah to American interests in the region—along with Saudi wealth, Iranian military power constituted one of the two pillars of American Persian Gulf strategy—there were few in the American government and fewer still in the media and the academic community who argued forcefully that the United States should temper criticism of the shah—not only because such criticism was unfairly applied, but also because of the great catastrophe that his downfall would represent for American strategic interests.

Moreover, Carter along with Vance and the majority of the State Department experts—above all those involved in the human rights campaign—found it next-to-impossible actively to support the shah during street demonstrations in both Iran and the United States. Some in the Carter cabinet argued for vigorous support (Brzezinski and Schlesinger), but as time passed and support became tantamount to involvement in bloodshed in the streets of Iran's major cities, this option grew less palatable. In the end, nothing was done aside from enhancing the shah's own considerable confusion. *He* could not imagine that the Americans had not designed a serious strategy for the crisis; whatever option the Americans chose, he would bend with it. If the Americans chose to remove him, he would not resist; if they wished to fight for him, their strength was undoubtedly sufficient to prevail. This relatively passive attitude was almost certainly reinforced by his cancer, which was becoming more virulent during the final stages of the crisis. Because the shah was no more desirous than the American president of being involved in a major bloodbath and with his will sapped by his fatal disease, he waited for the signal from Washington that never arrived.

The fall of the shah was a major debacle for the United States, not only because nothing was done to fight for one of America's major allies during his time of troubles, but also because the disaster was compounded by the arrival in power of a regime violently anti-American, one that soon made the shah's crimes trivial by comparison.

If the Americans had looked at the Sandinistas through ideologically tinted glasses, they had drawn their conclusions about the Ayatollah completely blindfolded, for he had not even bothered to clothe his intentions in language acceptable to the West. But no one in the American government had read Khomeini's violent books, in which, with the compulsive veracity of the fanatic, he told precisely what he would do to Iran: restore the power of the clerics, destroy all vestiges of democratic progress, end the role of lay judges in moderating the religious courts, eliminate Jews and Bahais, disenfranchise women and drape them in long gowns and *chadors*, wage war on Arab neighbors held to be insufficiently fanatic, and work for the destruction of Israel and for the elimination of all American influence in the Persian Gulf area. When Stephen Rosenfeld of the *Washington Post*—one of three American journalists who had obtained translations of Khomeini's books and had published excerpts from them—suggested that Khomeini might be dangerous to both American interests and those of the Iranian people, he was accused by the head of the State Department's Iranian desk of disseminating material that was at best student notes, at worst a forgery. Thus, the American intelligence community, whose ability to gather accurate information is a crucial element in the policymaking process, failed to obtain the basic data on Khomeini.

With such bad information, the analysis was predictably misguided, and in the debate over Iran, whether within the government or among the broader public, it was rarely recalled that Khomeini's challenge to the shah came in the name of re-action, not revolution. The Ayatollah was the archetypical reactionary, as his pronouncements and writings demonstrated and as his later actions would confirm: it was precisely Iranian progress that Khomeini sought to destroy, along with the "satanic" forces that had contributed to the country's development— Bahais, Jews, Americans, and the rest.

Instead, Americans dreamt of a tyrant being overthrown by a revolutionary movement whose strident rhetoric represented an understandable reaction to the shah's excesses and to America's past sins. So strong were these dreams that even what *was* known about Khomeini was quickly forgotten. The first listing for Khomeini in the *New York Times Index* refers to a story in the early sixties describing Khomeini-led demonstrations *against* land reform and women's rights, but the journalists and academics who wrote about the Ayatollah in the late seventies told few such tales. Professor Thomas Ricks of Georgetown University denied Khomeini's anti-Semitism; Professor Richard Cottam of the University of Pittsburgh, the first American in years to meet with the Ayatollah (in An Najaf in 1978), granted there were some warts but, nonetheless, wrote shortly after the revolution of Khomeini's "Islamic humanist ideology" and maintained that Iranians supported Khomeini because they believed, with some reason, that Iran had suffered from "a rapacious American policy implemented by a puppet shah."[9] Professor Richard Falk of Princeton University wrote in the *New York Times* that "having created a new model of popular revolution based, for the most part, on nonviolent tactics, Iran may yet provide us with a desperately needed model of humane governance for a third-world country."[10] There were similarly optimistic views from Professor James Bill of the University of

Texas and from several members of the Center for Contemporary Arab Studies at Georgetown University.

The views of the academics were mirrored by those of many policymakers. The most outspokenly enthusiastic was U.N. Ambassador Andrew Young, who in a speech delivered in Washington argued that the Iranian revolution had been inspired and led by the tens of thousands of students who had studied in the United States and was thus similar to our own revolution and even to the civil rights movement of the sixties. Once his revolution had been thoroughly fulfilled, Khomeini— in Young's words—would be recognized as "some kind of saint."[11]

It was as if Carter and his friends reasoned that because they were sympathetic to the Ayatollah, Khomeini *had* to be friendly to them. If Khomeini railed against presumed past sins of the Americans, that was no cause for concern—the president felt the same way.

Carter's failures stemmed from a mixture of naive moralism and general ignorance about world affairs, but some of his advisers acted out of ideological conviction. They appeared to believe that the forces of the Left represented the wave of the future, and they were angered by America's past actions against communists in Cuba and Vietnam as well as against Communist-supported regimes in Africa. People with such a view of the world—and Andrew Young was perhaps the best known of this group—looked on the movement led by the reactionary Khomeini as revolutionary for the same reason they considered Castro and the Sandinistas to be revolutionaries—all three opposed traditional American foreign policy goals. They, therefore, combined a distaste for the shah's U.S. military alliance with a revolutionary zeal, all mixed with ignorance about Khomeini— a recipe for confusion that made inevitable the Iranian debacle.

The alliance between New Leftists and naive wishful thinkers produced a majority within the Carter administration who believed that although self-proclaimed revolutionaries might *appear* to be hostile to the United States, in reality they were good people whose only quarrel was with American imperialism. Committed as they were to revolution, the New Leftists felt that violent revolutionaries were more sincere in their desires for a purer world than those who argued for evolutionary change and a moderate course. They were able to prevail over those, like the president himself, who had no expertise in foreign policy and were unable to challenge the asumptions of the New Leftists. Finally, the search for a morally laudable foreign policy for the United States made it difficult for the American leaders to contemplate the notion that although the shah and Somoza were unattractive in many ways, their enemies might be even worse. In short, the choice of the lesser evil was excluded (proving once again that the search for the "best" is often the greatest enemy of the survival of the "good"); America's geopolitical interests were never the central focus of the analysis, but they were the immediate casualties of the Iranian debacle.

Given all of this systematic misperception, it was no accident that the Americans in Tehran did not prepare for the assault that seized the embassy there and held Americans hostage for more than a year. After all his self-abasing attempts to placate the Iranian zealots were met with scorn and greater abuses, Carter suddenly changed course. Just as he turned to military power to try to salvage the situation in Central America following the triumph of the Sandinistas, he felt impelled to launch a military force to try to liberate the hostages in Iran.

Carter's behavior upset America's allies because it demonstrated that the president did not understand the way the world works. Our friends around the world may not wish visibly to depend on us for their security, but they are shaken when they see our president confused about America's real interests. For example, Egypt's President Anwar al-Sadat was so worried at the suggestion that Carter wanted to reconvene the Geneva Conference in 1978 (thus bringing the Russians back into Middle East diplomacy) that he preempted the situation and went to Jerusalem himself. In 1983, when the United States moved to block a Libyan operation to overthrow President Nimeiri of the Sudan, the Sudanese and Egyptians denied the gravity of the situation and denied asking for American help, even though they had been gravely concerned and had—along with other moderate Arab countries—urgently sought American protection. These two episodes help explain the rules of the game: once America is seen to take the lead in a direction satisfactory to our friends, these same friends feel free to distance themselves from the policy (let the Americans take the heat, that's what leadership is all about). But if America doesn't understand what's really at stake, then drastic measures must be taken independently—in a life-and-death situation, don't let the United States sell you out. As the United States has shown such confusion over the past several years, more and more of our friends (not to mention enemies) are taking drastic action to improve their own national security.

The myths to which the Carter administration fell victim had often trapped politicians and intellectuals in America and elsewhere. But there was something new about the anti-Americanism of the New Left of the sixties and seventies: its rejection of anticommunism. Prior to the 1950s, many American liberals had routinely fought communism as a threat to freedom and democracy, but following the turbulence of the McCarthy years anticommunism became taboo within certain sectors of the Left. McCarthy not only gave anticommunism a bad name, he also gave it a right-wing label that endured for more than a generation. By the late sixties, the stylish view of the world—defined to a considerable extent by the New Left—held that American criticism of communism was hypocritical. The leaders of the New Left maintained that there was no substantial difference between the policies of the United States and the Soviet Union: the Soviets invaded Hungary and Czechoslovakia, and we invaded Vietnam and Cuba; they sent KGB agents through-

out the world, we did the same with the CIA; they had the
Warsaw Pact, we had NATO. Each side was seen to pursue its
interests with the same or similar methods. Given this symmetry
between the superpowers, the argument went, we had no moral
basis for systematic opposition to communism. Indeed, for many
self-styled revolutionaries, the Soviets appeared to back the more
attractive forces in the international arena.

With this reemergence of anti-anticommunism as a fashionable theory (it had had a brief vogue in the late forties around
the presidential candidacy of Henry Wallace), it became more
difficult for politically engaged people of a progressive bent to
make the traditional distinctions between democratic and antidemocratic forces on the Left. This went hand in hand with an
intensified radicalism in domestic matters, further reinforcing
the view that the United States was morally unworthy of leading
the forces of radical change in the world. Indeed, some of the
spokespersons for the New Left would argue that so-called radical forces (such as the Sandinistas and Khomeini) were morally
superior to American political movements and that those Americans who opposed such radical forces were held to be reactionary, antidemocratic or—in the debased political language of our
time—Fascist.

To be sure, many earlier American and European intellectuals had turned to the Russian Revolution of 1917, Mussolini's
early fascism, Castro's Cuba, and Mao's China as similarly superior to anything democracy had to offer, but prior to the sixties,
there was a strong element on the Left that fought such foolishness. By the late sixties and early seventies, the antidemocratic
New Left was generally triumphant. The last attempt to rejoin
the traditions of left-wing anticommunism and a progressive
social policy took place under John F. Kennedy and Lyndon
Johnson, and it failed along with the Vietnam War. Liberal anticommunism was defeated, first in the salons and the elite press,
then in the Democratic party with the nomination of George
McGovern, and finally with the defeat of Henry Jackson by

Jimmy Carter in 1976. The victory of the New Leftists meant that the slogans of the chic salons had become self-fulfilling prophecies: liberals henceforth felt uneasy in criticizing communism, either at home or abroad. Thus, in the mid-seventies when a brief boomlet for Eurocommunism developed in the United States, the Carter administration was at a loss in drafting an effective policy to deal with it. Indeed, as I have argued elsewhere,[12] the confusion in Washington was such that for a brief time it appeared that the Italian Communist party might actually gain entry to the Italian cabinet. But events—above all the murder of former Prime Minister Aldo Moro by the Red Brigades— imposed a sense of reality, and the Italian Communists were blocked once again. A similar confusion emerged from the Democratic party following the American invasion of Grenada in November, 1983 when the reflexive opposition to Reagan's move against the Communist regime on that Caribbean island led Democratic leaders to condemn the act at first. Then, when they realized that the American public overwhelmingly supported it, many of them shifted their position and supported the president.

THE RIGHT

The confusion in our ranks does not emanate from just one side of the political spectrum; the Right is similarly afflicted. If the New Left rejects democratic evolution, insisting that change be drastic and effected by groups and individuals with radical credentials and anti-American zeal, the Right tends to resist all social reform and fears mass movements. Conservatives have never quite understood revolutionary movements, and the Right's attachment to individualism naturally leads to a rejection of collective enterprises. In America, there was never a Marxist Left (one of the features of our history that sets this country apart from Europe) and, therefore, the anticommunism

of the traditional Right was of a less sophisticated nature than
that of the liberals, who saw in communism a corruption of their
own progressive values. The Right simply rejected communism—
and revolutionary movements in general—out of hand.

Yet, although the Right might agree with Alexander Hamilton that "the people . . . is a great beast," it nonetheless traditionally argues that successful principles can be taught and
transmitted from one generation to another and from one nation
to another. Thus true conservatives favor change, provided that
it is consistent with the best in national tradition. Yet, by the
late seventies, the most politically successful form of American
conservatism—the New Right—was endorsing extreme forms
of laissez-faire economics at home and a staunch refusal to
tamper with the status quo abroad (at least so far as friendly
countries were concerned). The New Right, quite in keeping
with conservative tradition, seems eager to challenge our opponents on the Left but quite unwilling to bring pressure for democratic change to bear on "friendly" governments to the Right.

The New Right suffers from a grave defect in the current
international scene: its distrust of mass movements prevents it
from playing an effective role with many of the turbulent forces
that now move the people of most of the world. Still, although
the New Right's reluctance to export the democratic revolution
to right-wing dictatorships parallels the Left's unwillingness to
challenge dictatorships of the Left, there is a notable difference:
for the most part, the dictatorships of the Left are enemies of the
United States, whereas those of the Right are often friendly to
us.[13] So, in terms of pure geopolitics, the Right's general instincts
are sound; the New Right wishes to focus our national energies
on challenging our opponents rather than on transforming our
friends and allies. Yet, matters are not so simple, for the East-
West struggle rarely takes place within the Soviet sphere of influence (aside from espionage and broadcasting); the main
battleground is in the Third and Fourth worlds. And in these
countries, the willingness and capacity of the United States to

promote democracy and greater social equity while ensuring national security are crucial to our long-term success and to the well-being of the people.

If we shore up dictatorships frozen in their repressive ways, we are not only abandoning our own revolutionary traditions, but we are also setting ourselves up for grave setbacks to our own international leadership. In many developing countries, we have helped educate and enrich members of an emerging business, intellectual, and professional class; in the process, they have learned the advantages of a free society. When they return to their own countries, they can make a decisive contribution if space is made for them, but if they are not given opportunities and a share of responsibility and power, they can readily become the nucleus of the opposition. To take the most recent example of this widespread phenomenon, many American-educated Iranians joined the National Front opposing the shah because of their frustration with a regime that refused to share power. When the reactionary forces of Khomeini seized control of the country, these reformers were shunted aside, if not exiled or killed. Had we insisted on the liberalization of Iranian government and society, these talented, educated people would have contributed to the development of a democratic state rather than become victims of a new repression.

Many on the Left—albeit largely the traditional Left, not the New Left—understand this, but they tend to forget the second part of the formula: the security of the developing country needs to be supported through the destabilizing transition to democracy. We need to tell the leaders of such countries that their long-term security depends on their willingness to liberalize, and we must also assure them that we will not ask them to commit suicide. This means that we have to be prepared to help them defend themselves against both external and internal enemies as we steadily urge them toward greater democracy.

Unfortunately, neither New Left nor New Right has been able to achieve this balance of policies. If the New Right prevails, we shall find it extremely difficult to challenge—and help change—the repressive anti-Communist governments in such places as the Philippines and Guatemala, thereby risking a repetition of the Iranian and Nicaraguan experiences. If the New Left is permitted to define our foreign policy, we shall simply abandon such countries to our (and ultimately their own) enemies, simultaneously diminishing both the long-range possibility for democracy within these countries and the short-range security of our own country. As Walter Lippmann wrote in 1961, after another period of largely conservative anticommunism:

> We cannot compete with communism . . . if we . . . place the weak countries in a dilemma where they must stand still with us and our client rulers or start moving with the Communists. This dilemma cannot be dissolved unless it is our central and persistent and unswerving policy to offer these unhappy countries a third option, which is economic development and social improvement without the totalitarian discipline of communism.
>
> For the only real alternative to communism is a liberal and progressive society.[14]

Lippmann's last line was incomplete. He should have said that a liberal and progressive society is the only alternative to communism that would be acceptable to the most vital elements in American politics. There are many acceptable alternatives to communism in other countries, where traditions akin to our own are either weak or nonexistent. Repressive dictatorships can be quite durable, so long as the dictators do not shrink from repression. Hitler and Mussolini were only removed from power when they lost the war, not by internal opposition. Contrary to the pseudoscientific "models" so popular nowadays, the processes that lead to fundamental change have much less to do with vast, impersonal forces than they do with qualities of leadership, strength of will, intelligence, and cynicism on each side of political power struggles. This means that countries where life is nasty, brutish, and short can continue that way for a long time if the leaders are intent on keeping things intact, but it also means that leaders can effect considerable change if they can be convinced it is in their best interests to do so. If the United States can convince friendly tyrants that they can *safely* experiment with change in their countries, then positive evolution can be brought about, and this meets the requirements of practical American politics as well as the demands of our own traditions of simple justice and the democratic revolution. As a practical matter, we find it difficult to justify a long-term alliance (or even a close working relationship) with a rigidly repressive regime; on a philosophical level, we find it hypocritical. It is sometimes possible to justify such an alliance on grounds of vital national interests (for example, the wartime alliance with Joseph Stalin's Soviet Union), but in the long run, the United States can only have stable alliances (or even good working relations) with countries that either live up to a certain democratic standard or can be seen to be moving in that direction.

Nonetheless, there are times when we must be able to enter into alliances of temporary convenience or choose between the lesser of two evils, and American public opinion—above all, Congress and the media—must be mature enough to understand the necessities for such choices, even when these choices seem to offend our national desire for universal social justice and American-style democracy.

The design and conduct of serious foreign policy is a difficult challenge, requiring leadership, diplomatic skill, knowledge of foreign cultures, a keen sense of strategy and tactics, and the ability to forge a political consensus within the United States along with an understanding or our own traditions. We have not had leaders with these characteristics for some time, yet the times, as politicians are wont to say, demand them. Why has our leadership been so poor, and how can we improve it?

3

THE FAILURE
OF THE AMERICAN ELITE

In the final days of Byzantium, the leaders of a once-great nation debated the finer points of theology while the enemy gathered his forces at the gates and finally removed the eloquent debaters from the halls of power. I believe that the American elite now alarmingly resemble those Byzantines, for American leaders frequently seem unable to define contemporary questions in terms of our national interests. Instead, foreign policy questions are invariably discussed in political and moral terms so abstract, narrow, and often transient that the strategic issues of survival and defeat are not properly raised.[1]

Blame for this state of affairs is of course most commonly—and fairly—laid on the shoulders of our elected and appointed officials, for they are supposed to lead the discussion of the vital issues. For many years now, our leaders have not adequately met their challenges, but in fairness to them, it must be recognized that they are hindered by those who are charged with communicating the information necessary for the public at large to make responsible decisions: the journalists and intellectuals. It is difficult for foreign policy experts to describe our international challenges if the television networks insist on presenting these questions in three- to five-minute blocks and with visual material that often distorts the real significance of events. Moreover, as will be shown, our journalists have now assumed an explicitly political role and have abandoned the notion that they are sometimes supposed to serve as simple "transmission belts" between the government and the people. Furthermore, such is the current confusion in our political culture that our news media often fail to distinguish between those people and governments who strain to be accurate and those who traditionally use the media primarily for propanganda purposes. In August 1983, for example, when the American government announced that the Libyans were involved in the civil war in Chad, Colonel Quaddafi—a man the media had often caught in self-serving lies—told American television news reporters that he was doing no such thing and that there was no Libyan role in the fighting. Thereafter, "CBS News" referred to the "alleged" Libyan role in Chad, as if the words of the Libyan dictator were worth the same as those of the American president—a leader who is under greater constraint to avoid lying than any other citizen on the globe.

The media will be discussed at length later on, but the point here is that many members of our own elite no longer have a clear sense of relative reliability and, therefore, are at a grave disadvantage in establishing the truth. In this manner, credibility becomes a matter of political chic rather than evidence and experience, and one person's opinion is considered as good as anyone else's. Lacking clear guidelines and untrained in the ways of the world our journalists act as if everyone reacted to conflicts precisely as they would. Both the phenomenon and its consequences have been elegantly described by Charles Krauthammer, writing in *Time* magazine:

> . . . If the whole world is like me, then certain conflicts become incomprehensible; the very notion of intractability becomes paradoxical. When the U.S. embassy in Tehran is taken over, Americans are bewildered. What does the Aya-

tullah want? The U.S. Government sends envoys to find out
what token or signal or symbolic gesture might satisfy Iran.
It is impossible to believe that the Ayatullah wants exactly
what he says he wants: the head of the Shah. Things are not
done that way any more in the West. . . . It took a long
time for Americans to get the message.[2]

Krauthammer well understands the risks of this "plural
solipsism," as he terms it: "To gloss over contradictory interests,
incompatible ideologies and opposing cultures as sources of conflict is more than antipolitical. It is dangerous."[3]

Yet, to see the world as it really is and to evaluate America's proper role in such a world requires both real understanding and good character, including a willingness to make hard
decisions for the sake of the nation, even if personal advantage
is sacrificed thereby. At present, we cannot expect such qualities from our leaders, for the political process by which they
acquire institutional power along with the educational system
that trains them produce too many individuals who are culturally unprepared for the world as it really is and unused to
thinking in terms of a real national interest. This is true of
many of the major segments that make up the policymaking
community: politicians, appointed officials, career diplomats, the
press, and academia.

I have already discussed the consequences of our lack of
clarity: the world has become a far more dangerous place because other countries are forced to guess about our likely reactions and, in the resulting uncertainty, often take actions of
which we disapprove and which we could have prevented—and
conversely, these countries fail to respond when we urge them
to act in harmony with our own interests. Thus, the aimlessness
and ineffectiveness of our political elite creates a new and major
threat to world peace. If we cannot address the great international questions while protecting our national interests, we will
contribute to stumbling into crises for which we, our friends,
and our adversaries will all be unprepared. Unfortunately, al-

though the Soviet internal crisis is far more serious than ours, the Soviet leaders are better prepared for international crises; their political leadership takes strategic questions more seriously than we do, their capability for covert action is far greater (and more secure) than ours, and their willingness to resort to all methods to achieve their goals gives them greater leverage over foreign leaders whose international conduct must meet standards established for the citizens of Western societies.

Therefore, we must address our internal political problems with a sense of urgency, not only because it is proper to do so, but also because our international survival may well depend on it.

If domestic politics are the primary determinants of foreign policy, no coherent foreign policy can be designed and executed in the United States. Domestic politics are now generally conducted by public opinion poll, leading to two deplorable consequences: the media have acquired a disproportionate influence because they both shape and measure the public's pulse and policy starts to resemble in its volatility those characteristics of public opinion least useful for the conduct of international relations. For public opinion, even under the best of circumstances, cannot be fully informed or up to date. Lippmann put it well a few months before our entry into the Second World War:

> If with their responsibilities and their means of knowing what is what, they sit around waiting for the Gallup poll and the fan mail, they will get a Gallup poll and a fan mail from a people that have not been able to know what men must know in order to judge wisely. They will have failed to give to the people the leadership which democracy must have—that is, to face their responsibility and to decide questions by consulting other responsible men and then to explain their decision, leaving to the people to judge whether the decision is reasonable and the results good.
>
> It is possible to run the affairs of a village by a town meeting. But the methods of the town meeting will not regulate the affairs of a great republic which embraces a continent . . . and is involved in one of the great crises of history.[4]

LEADERS

The definition of national policy objectives must come from the
country's leaders, in and out of government. Although there are
examples of countries continuing to function well for short periods without good leadership, these are rare instances; if we are
badly led, we shall almost always have bad policies. At this moment, our leadership is weak. This is not a matter of party; we
have not had a president with real experience in foreign policy
since Nixon; with the departure of Alexander Haig, the Reagan
administration had not a single cabinet member with adequate
foreign policy experience (the key players: Reagan, Weinberger,
Shultz, Casey, and Clark were all novices, and the situation was
not improved until McFarlane replaced Clark as national security adviser to the president).

To be sure, experience is not a guarantee. Cyrus Vance had
abundant experience and yet was one of the worst secretaries of
state in this century, thanks to the sort of cultural solipsism and
wishful thinking so charcteristic of recent American leaders
(perfectly expressed in Vance's heartfelt assertion that Carter
and Brezhnev "shared common dreams") and to a misplaced
conviction that the use of power in foreign policy is immoral.
But if experience in foreign affairs isn't sufficient for good policy, it is certainly necessary, if only to anticipate the foreign reactions to our moves. Alas, our political system now virtually
guarantees that the president will be out of touch with the world
situation.

Anyone who runs for the presidency must now devote
three to four years to the campaign, a period through which his
policy positions are dictated less by a careful study of the international situation than by the internal political debate in the
United States. Even on those rare occasions when a candidate
travels overseas, his trips are designed either to make news or to
reassure certain key domestic constituencies (Jews, Greeks,

blacks, Irish, or others), and his positions are more often based on the polls rather than on the actual situation. To be sure, he will have around him a variety of expert advisers, just as he will in the White House, but the really crucial advisers—in the campaign as in the oval office—are political, not substantive.

The world view of the president-elect is almost entirely structured by the internal American political debate of the preceding three or four years, and there is little time for him to catch up on the real state of affairs. If elected, he is faced with hundreds of personnel decisions, some of which will commit him to specific foreign policy positions for the next several years. Once the foreign policy officials have been selected and the new administration is in place, the president will rarely have time to reflect on his understanding of the world at large. For that matter, neither will the other top officials; Henry Kissinger observed at the end of his eight years in power that one leaves office with the same cultural baggage as one carried in, simply because of the great mass of specific decisions that must be made. Indeed, there is not even enough time to listen to all the voices one should hear on matters that require immediate attention.

We are consequently left with a president who comes into office out of date, with little prospect of quickly learning the subtleties of the world situation and with a time horizon of approximately three and one-half years. The best hope for a sensible foreign policy in the early years of such a presidency is that the president will largely delegate authority, even though on most important matters, it is he who must decide—the structure of the government is such that he cannot avoid these decisions, even if he wishes to. Were he to surround himself with extraordinarily talented persons in the foreign policy field and were such persons to be fully trusted by the president, it might still be possible to salvage the situation. But even here, his choice of advisers is subject to the same political constraints to which his ascendancy to the presidency was subject.

It might be thought that the president-elect would auto-

matically turn to those who had worked with him most closely
during the campaign, but recent history has not confirmed this:
Nixon chose Henry Kissinger as his key adviser, and Kissinger
had been a Rockefeller man; Carter took Brzezinski—one of his
own team—but also Vance, who was assuredly *not* a Carterite
(indeed, one of Carter's closest advisers—Hamilton Jordan—
said before the selection of the secretary of state that if Vance
were chosen it would be a sign that Carter had failed); and Reagan took Richard Allen—one of his own—and Haig, a survivor
of the Nixon years. All of this has the look of domestic politics
about it: unifying party ranks, giving rewards to all segments of
the political base, searching for broad consensus, and so forth.
Good, traditional politics, perhaps, but unfortunately not the
kind of process that creates strong, coherent foreign policy. Of
all these cases, the Nixon-Kissinger tandem was by far the most
effective, and the least typical of contemporary American politics. Nixon had extensive experience in foreign policy, and
Kissinger came from a European background (as did Helmut
Sonnenfeldt). Other leading figures in that remarkably talented
group had military backgrounds: Kissinger's top aide was Colonel
Alexander Haig, whereas his successor as national security adviser to the president was General Brent Scowcroft.

Even the minimal coherence of a campaign organization is
lost once the winning candidate moves into power; under the
best conditions, considerable time must pass before a new sense
of unity and mission can be created among the leaders of the
country. It is hardly surprising, then, that the most intense
struggles within the new administrations are those over turf:
who will control what? Although these battles are often masked
as debates over policy, they are in fact the preliminary skir-
mishes to the main policy event, for they determine who will be
in a dominant position later on.[5] Such items as which agency
will chair the various interagency committees, which assistant
secretary will be in charge of a specific question within a given
agency, and the like, are the objects of this competition. Pre-

dictably, the professionals are better at this kind of battle than the political appointees (professionalism means nothing if not skill at such activities), and this further restricts the ability of a new administration to shape foreign policy.

Most damaging of all is the carryover from the popular culture to the highest levels of government of the notion that there are no real standards of authority and, thus, that the premises of American foreign policy can be redefined with each new administration. Because foreign policy is put on the same level as domestic politics, the leaders of the country feel that they must respond equally to the demands of the true experts and to the hue and cry from below. This is a serious mistake because public opinion is always poorly informed on serious policy matters and also because effective policy and courageous leadership almost always produces its own consensus. Strong leadership for a just cause can alter the political universe.

Democrats seem to understand these principles better than do Republicans because leaders of the Left feel more comfortable with mass political action than do conservatives. For instance, Carter was not daunted by the polls that showed he had a poor chance of gaining approval of the Panama Canal treaties; he organized an effective public program, sent spokespersons from the State Department and the rest of the national security apparatus throughout the country, and debated with his opponents until he finally prevailed. Republicans rarely undertake such efforts, and insofar as they have tried to generate mass support for their policies, they have focused on domestic issues (tax cuts, spending reductions, and the like); they have been far less effective in actively promoting their view of the world. And such is the force of tradition that the Republicans under Reagan were initially reluctant to promote their foreign policy aggressively, even at a time—the first year of the administration—when they had every reason to expect public support.

Hobbled by the lack of adequately prepared leaders, poorly served by an educational system that has failed to provide the proper combination of understanding of the world and a rigorous commitment to the need of the nation to know and advance its vital interests, harassed by a popular culture that reduces international problems to abstract moralistic issues, the American government cannot design and execute a serious foreign policy. Instead, it must improvise day to day, hoping only that international catastrophes will not occur at moments when they can be exploited electorally.

When someone with real expertise and the desire to advance our geopolitical interests reaches a top position in our government, he is often regarded as a nuisance by the amateurs around him, for he is forever demanding that they face up to their responsibilities in a timely fashion. Haig's is the most dramatic recent case, for he alone in the original Reagan cabinet came with a rich background in foreign policy. And from the first day, he preached a sermon that his colleagues did not want to hear: America's international position was precarious, therefore, we needed to act, and needed to act *quickly* if the trend were to be reversed. Haig knew that unless basic initiatives were taken within the first year of the new administration, it was unlikely they would be taken at all, for the second year brings congressional elections and narrowed options. Moreover, in addition to these general considerations, there were specific situations that demanded speedy action. Haig accordingly pushed hard for strong action within the first six to twelve months, particularly in the Caribbean, where he felt it was possible to deal the Cuban/Russian alliance its first serious setback in many years. To his dismay and mounting frustration, Haig found that the White House—and the Pentagon—were not ready for such steps. There were many understandable reasons for this reluctance, including a desire to concentrate national attention on economic issues and a reluctance to appear overly belligerent early in the administration, but Haig—who had been through it all before—insisted that if the moment of early consensus were squandered, it would be far more difficult (and costly) to achieve positive results in the future. Moreover, Haig knew that America's friends and allies were waiting for evidence that America had emerged from its post-Vietnam torpor and was prepared to advance its and its allies' vital interests. Delay would discourage potential friends and encourage enemies.

This sense of urgency could be properly sensed only by persons with a mature feel for foreign policy issues, and, with the exception of U.N. Ambassador Kirkpatrick, who had years of study and work with such questions, was not shared by Haig's colleagues. One can well imagine the mounting irritation at the White House with the one cabinet member who insisted on bringing bad news to the president and who demanded timely action that would invariably incur domestic political costs without any guarantee of swift success. So that, although there were plenty of personality conflicts and no lack of political errors by the secretary of state, the "Haig problem" grew from the inevitable frustration of the serious policymaker who realizes that the clock is running out on a vitally important project.

Timing is almost everything in foreign policy, which is one of the reasons abstract moralists and other ideologues have such a hard time with it. What is "right" at one moment can be disastrous at another time and sometimes only a matter of days divide a successful policy move from failure. Haig's conviction that it was necessary to move *quickly* against Castro was based on many different elements, most of them pointing in the same direction. First was the conviction that the Communist world was in 1981 deeply concerned about Reagan, believing that he would seek some sort of foreign policy victory in the first few months of his administration. Combined with this concern was the sort of fear that used to be associated with Nixon: the fear that he was capable of drastic and unpredictable action. And as did Nixon, Haig cultivated this image, believing (correctly, in my opinion) that such an image worked to the advantage of the nation in dealing with our foreign adversaries. Reagan had acquired a similar reputation—whether or not such considerations ever played a role in the president's calculus—for his forceful handling of the air controllers' strike early in his administration. This had an enormous effect on the world at large, for it projected an image of a president capable of decisive action, even in the face of domestic political pressure.

In part because of fears of Ronald Reagan and Alexander Haig and in part because of the logic of the situation, Castro soon became convinced that he would face a major American challenge from the new administration. In private conversations with various friends and associates, he predicted that the United States would move against him once the Russians had committed themselves in Poland. He did not know precisely *where* the American move would come—it might be in the Caribbean or in Africa (Ethiopia or Angola)—but come it would. Finally, Castro was certain that the Russians would not lift one mailed finger to save him from Washington.[6]

From Haig's perspective, this was a useful situation: our enemies were frightened of us and unsure of the reliability of their own defenses. The Carter administration had identified the Cubans and the Russians as the controlling hand behind the guerrilla movement in El Salvador, therefore, the Reagan administration could challenge Cuba on the basis of information and analyses developed by a prior administration that had supported the Sandinistas against Somoza. Finally, given Soviet concerns in Poland and Afghanistan and their parlous economic condition, the moment would never be better. Thus Haig called for a visible show of military power in the Caribbean combined with a vigorous public exposé of Cuban activities in the region so that once the Russians moved in Poland, Castro would be convinced that he would have to face the United States in isolation. Under those circumstances, there was every reason to believe that Fidel would come to terms with the United States rather than face certain defeat.

For this strategy to work, however, two things were required: the military threat had to be palpable (Castro had to see the movements of ships, planes, and manpower in the region), and the political atmosphere had to be hot (so that the Cubans and the Russians would be convinced of the intensity of the American determination to inflict damage on Cuba). In the event, neither requirement could be met. The Pentagon did not wish to squander its recently acquired monies to sail ships and fly airplanes (the funds were earmarked for acquisitions), and the White House did not then want a supercharged domestic debate on Central America.

A year passed, the Russians moved against Solidarity and America did nothing. The net effect was to convince Fidel that he was safe. In the spring of 1982, when General Vernon Walters was sent to Havana to see if there were any real prospects for peace in Central America, a relieved Castro reread the situation and delivered his real answer shortly thereafter—the guerrillas in Central America dramatically increased their activities. Now, to demonstrate to the Cubans and the Russians that he was indeed serious, Reagan had to undertake a demonstration of military power far greater than what would have been necessary two years earlier: the 1983 military maneuvers, although underlining the seriousness with which we took the Central American crisis, achieved far less than could have been obtained in 1981.

Haig had been unable to convince his colleagues in the cabinet that a special opportunity existed in 1981. A proper sense of timing cannot be quickly taught to those who have not lived through years of foreign policy challenges; it comes only with firsthand experience and the accumulated effect of past errors and subsequent reconsideration. With the departure of Haig, there was no one in the cabinet with such a background.

Reagan would almost certainly have done better if there had been more expertise in the cabinet, for he certainly understood that something needed to be done in Central America. By contrast, his predecessor assembled a team with plenty of actual knowledge and experience, but the president himself—along with his most important political friends and advisers (Andrew Young, Hamilton Jordan)—typified the combination of abstract moralism and cultural solipsism that bedevils our policymaking elite. Carter had great confidence in his own instincts, and his instincts told him that his mission was to save America from its worst tendencies.

These convictions, as passionately held as they were misguided, led Carter into a thoroughly erroneous line of policy. When the shah's time of troubles arrived, Carter was paralyzed by his own moralism, even though he recognized the terrible dangers to American interests that the fall of the shah represented. With Andrew Young terming the Ayatollah Khomeini "a saint" and with most of the fashionable Left in America and throughout Europe denouncing the tyranny of the shah, Carter's passions worked against strong American action to shore up what the American public had been convinced was a terribly repressive regime.[7] Only two members of the Cabinet—Brzezinski and Schlesinger—had the courage to tell the president that, distasteful though it might be, American support for the shah was preferable to the vengeful whirlwind that Khomeini would bring. Schlesinger, though secretary of energy, was respected by the president for his knowledge of foreign policy. Schlesinger and Brzezinski originated the notion that Carter should dispatch a high-level emissary to the shah to urge him to defend himself as actively as was necessary. And it was Schlesinger who proposed that a carrier be sent into the region, both to "show the flag" to the shah and his minions and to remind the Soviet Union that the United States would not put up with mischief along the Russo-Iranian border.[8]

It was to no avail; the paralysis in the White House was mirrored in Tehran. Carter and the shah remained immobile throughout the long melodrama, each waiting for the other to make a decisive move. In the end, the only person with a clear vision of what he wanted—Khomeini—triumphed.

The crucial point here is not that policy errors were made

(committing errors is the most typical human activity) but rather that the kind of leaders we select for ourselves are bound to commit errors of a particular sort. The most recent example of "error as by-product of abstract moralism" is the sad performance of the United States during the Lebanese tragedy of 1982–83.

In the summer of 1982, the PLO's military base in Lebanon was smashed by the Israeli armed forces; dozens of terrorist organizations that had used the country as their training and operational center were now dispersed around the globe. The Syrian army was also defeated, throwing into question the efficacy of Soviet weaponry and Arab fighting capacities. The Soviet Union's influence in the Middle East—based as it was on support for radical Arab regimes and movements in the region— was substantially weakened. Lebanon itself, after seven years of internal bloodshed and terror, looked forward to a more peaceful future under Bashir Gemayel, unanimously elected by the leaders of the various factions in the country's Parliament and vigorously supported by the government of the United States. Less than two years later, the situation was almost totally reversed. The terrorists had returned. Syria, thanks in large part to Soviet support, had again become the dominant power in Lebanon. Bashir was dead and his brother Amin was forced to obey his Arab neighbors, trying to carve out some margin of independence between Syrian military might and Saudi money. The Soviet Union acquired new influence in the region; the internecine slaughter started anew; it was America, and to a lesser degree France, Britain, and Italy, who had hundreds of fighting men killed and suffered a loss of face and power.

To be sure, Leganon in and of itself was not a vital strategic interest for the United States. One can reasonably argue that the Israeli invasion was a mistake, that we tried our best to be evenhanded and to shore up a Lebanese government that simply did not have sufficient popular support and military wherewithal to prevail against its various enemies, and that we were well rid of our involvement there. But even if all these claims were true, they are beside the point; although we did not want the Israelis to invade Lebanon, once the deed was done, the United States had a lot at stake in the outcome. Yet, after the first week or ten days, we had no serious, durable policy to match the stakes in the region. Wandering from one worthy objective to another, trying to behave honorably, alternately catering to pressures from the moderate Arabs, from Israel, from the hapless Lebanese and from the American Congress, our policy changed constantly, baffling our friends and encouraging our enemies. In the end, as so often happens, the one country in the area that knew what it wanted—Syria—prevailed.

THE INVASION AND ITS AFTERMATH

The invasion of Lebanon had been opposed by the United States, but as on so many other occasions, American advice was rejected. Not only was the invasion launched, but it was a most ambitious one. Its aims were the total destruction of the PLO presence in Lebanon, driving the Syrian armed forces out of the country (or, at a minimum, eliminating Syrian military control over significant areas of Lebanon), and the creation of a stable Lebanon under a government headed by the Christian groups around Bashir Gemayel. The wisdom of the Israeli action is not at issue here; our attention must be drawn to the American interests in the fighting and the outcome of the conflict. Having failed to prevent its outbreak, what did he want from the Lebanese war?

First, it was necessary to recognize that most of the world considered this *our* war. I was in Amsterdam a week after the invasion and witnessed thousands of Dutch marching through the center of town to condemn the *American* invasion of Lebanon. This was symptomatic of much of world reaction; most people and most governments could not believe that the Israelis had undertaken such an ambitious campaign without our approval. They most probably believed that the invasion plan had been drafted in Washington—even some Israeli journalists and analysts, who should have known better claimed that the United States gave Sharon a green light.[9] Thus, the results would be credited or debited to our international account.

In retrospect, the perception of the war, as at least in part, an American affair was not so far from the mark. Our ally was fighting with our weapons against our enemies, and the ease with which the Israelis removed the Soviet SAMs* from the Bekáa Valley along with the astonishing Israeli victory in the air war (100 Soviet aircraft destroyed to none on the Israeli side) was widely viewed as demonstrating American superiority over the Soviets. Second, the rout of the PLO quite clearly advanced our interests in the entire region, for it struck at the heart of international terrorism, removed a deadly threat to the moderate Arab countries with which we preferred to deal, and delivered a blow to the various Libyans, Iranians, South Yemenis, and Syrians who constituted the radical Arab bloc that had opposed American goals in the Middle East for years. Third, the Soviets were not only embarrassed by having two of their principal clients soundly defeated, but they found themselves unable to react effectively, even when the Israelis overran their embassy compound in Beirut.

It was in our interest to have the Israeli victory as complete as possible, both because a clear-cut win would lessen the chances of a comeback by the Syrians, the PLO, or both and because a thorough defeat of the Syrians along with the departure of the PLO and their allies from Lebanon might make possible a strategic realignment in the region. The Israeli victory was, after all, a clear repudiation of the military strategy of the Soviet-backed radicals, from the PLO to the Syrians. The United States had thrown its economic, military, and diplomatic weight behind the

* Surface-to-air missiles.

peace process as embodied in the Camp David accords, and the leading rejectionists had just been swept away on the battlefield. Under the circumstances, we were entitled to drive home the basic point that those who made peace with Israel had gained territory and American aid, trade, and technology, whereas those who sided with the radicals and with the Soviet Union received only battlefield defeats.

Specifically, the United States might seize the opportunity to point out to President Hafez al-Assad of Syria the facts of recent life in the Middle East: Syria had tied herself to the Soviet Union and had been thrashed in every war. Sadat had tired of this cycle, had gone to Jerusalem, and came away with the entire Sinai, spanking new American weapons (instead of the rather more outmoded variety the Russians tend to send to their clients), and $2 billion a year in aid. Wouldn't it be wise for the Syrians to attempt a similar maneuver?

The idea of an approach to the Syrians was also attractive in the more limited context of Lebanon, for—as events would demonstrate—without Assad's agreement, no Lebanese settlement could be considered durable. If, however, the bitterness of Syrian defeat could be sweetened with magnanimity from the victors, not only Lebanon but the entire region might take a step toward peace. The kind of indirect accommodation, if not de facto cooperation, that might develop between Israel and Syria under such circumstances could lay the basis for more ambitious initiatives later on, after each had seen that the other was willing to behave reasonably and after the Syrians had tasted the advantages of closer cooperation with the West.

Finally, the notion of weaning Syria away from the Soviets and the Arab radicals made sense with regard to the issue that had heretofore been held to be the central problem of the Middle East: the Palestinian question. The events of early June had shown this claim to be without foundation; not a single Arab country had rallied to the side of the PLO, and Libya's Colonel Qaddafi—the self-proclaimed leader of the rejectionists and vig-

orous supporter of international terrorism—invited Arafat and
his men to commit mass suicide. There was no talk of oil em-
bargoes, no threat of reprisals against the West, no volunteers
from the Arab world. Indeed, the only men who arrived in Lebanon to assist the PLO came from a non-Arab country: Khomeini's Iran. When the PLO came face-to-face with its mortal
enemy, the Arab world did not lift a finger for Arafat.

In any case, Syria was no advocate of a Palestinian state.
Given the Syrians' insistence that their country was historically
entitled to be the dominant force in the Middle East, there was
no room on Syrian maps of the region for Lebanon, let alone for
yet another tiny Arab country. Thus, if the United States could
engage the Syrians in the peace process, it might be possible to
address the central conflicts in the region rather than debate
endlessly the Byzantine intricacies of the Palestinian issue.

To be sure, such an imaginative diplomatic approach is
easier to describe than to conduct, and each of the issues is more
complicated in diplomatic practice than in analytical theory.
Nonetheless, for a brief period, a window of opportunity had
opened, providing the United States, Israel, and the rest of the
Western world with a chance to explore the possibilities of real
progress toward peace. These possibilities were never tested. Instead, the United States acted as if the Israeli invasion had been
contrary to American interests, that the real obstacle to peace in
the area was Israel, and that if the Israeli forces would only return to their country, the Lebanese situation could be satisfactorily resolved and chances for broader progress in the region
would be enhanced.

This American approach to the conflict in Lebanon was of
course not new; often in the past, the United States had prevented Israel from pressing a military advantage to the point of
decisive victory. But the most recent example of that pattern—
to save the Egyptian army from destruction in the waning days
of the Yom Kuppur War—had permitted Nixon and Kissinger
to separate Anwar al-Sadat from the Soviet Union. In the Leba-

nese war, there was no such objective. So far as one can tell, the prime actors in Washington at the time—the president and his political advisers, National Security Adviser Clark, Defense Secretary Weinberger, Vice President Bush, the State Department Middle East experts led by Assistant Secretary Veliotis, and Special Representative Habib on the spot in Beirut—acted on bad information and misguided principle. Their view of the war fundamentally shaped by the highly misleading pictures and words of the news media. Under pressure from every Arab capital and from numerous West European allies to end the fighting and tempted by illusions of quick diplomatic fixes, the Americans acted to halt the Israeli advance just when thorough military victory was within days or even hours of achievement. This limited damage to Syria. The Americans then put out the story— first in private to Saudi diplomats, then in a public statement from the White House—that the Israelis would not invade Beirut. This proved to be another grave mistake, perhaps even more serious than demanding that the Israeli armed forces stop their advance. For the White House announcement came at a time when Arafat was desperately searching for a haven, convinced as he was that only the departure of the PLO from Lebanon would prevent its total destruction. But the promise that the Israelis would not invade Beirut, coming as it did from Washington and reinforced as it was by the Saudis, encouraged him to stay and await developments. The military and political momentum of the Israeli advance was thereby broken, the Syrians and the PLO were given time to regroup, and the siege of Beirut was paradoxically rendered inevitable, for it became necessary to convince Arafat all over again that he would not be permitted to remain in Lebanon. This was something that should have been obvious to everyone. Whatever one's assessment of the Israeli actions, it was clearly unthinkable that Begin and Sharon would go so far, only to stop short of achieving their fondest hope at the gates of the Lebanese capital.

Significantly, it was at this time that the United States

briefly obtained agreement from the Syrians to withdraw their troops from Lebanon and to accept the PLO in Syria, an agreement that fell through as the Israelis were reined in and American marines were sent to Beirut.

Had the United States done nothing at that crucial moment, two useful things would almost certainly have happened: the Israeli army would have taken control over the Beirut-Damascus highway, thus sealing off the vital East-West corridor from Syria into central and western Lebanon; and the PLO would have been routed out of the country, without the bloody siege of Beirut.

Why did we intervene to impose a cease-fire at the crucial moment of the Lebanese war? There were many reasons, including the intense internal conflicts between Secretary of State Haig and other members of the cabinet, but one principal and enduring cause of the decision was an attentiveness to the pleas coming from moderate Arab governments and a belief that anything that was clearly good for Israel had to be bad for the moderate Arabs. It seemed impossible to the Americans—especially once Haig, one of the few American officials who did not take the Saudis literally, had left the scene in late June—that the Saudis and other Arab moderates could be delighted by events in Lebanon, even as they condemned those same events from every available pulpit. Yet, the Saudis certainly should have been pleased with the broken power of the PLO and the severe setback dealt to the Syrians, for both contributed mightily to Saudi security. On the other hand, no Arab government could afford to admit publicly to such views, not even the Egyptians, whose policy of seeking peace with Israel was clearly vindicated by the developments in Lebanon. Any Arab leader who failed to condemn the Israeli invasion would automatically become a target for terrorists and radicals in the region, and it was clearly preferable to deplore the invasion while taking private satisfaction at its results. However, for the positive trend to continue, the United States would have to recognize what had *really* happened, and the Arabs probably presumed that the Americans were fully aware of this (after all, had we not coordinated the invasion with the Israelis?).

A second reason for the American-imposed cease-fire was the widespread belief that there could be no major steps toward a Middle East peace unless the Palestinian problem was solved; for most of our experts, this meant the creation of some sort of PLO-led entity, whether independent or linked to Jordan. With the total failure of the PLO's military strategy in Lebanon, the Palestinian problem had now taken on decidedly diminished importance, at least for the moment. The immediate issue was Lebanon—and any conceivable regional realignment needed to be resolved between Israel and Syria, two countries that were opposed to the creation of a Palestinian State. Significantly, the most imaginative diplomatic initiative of the summer was a "secret" trip to Jordan by Assistant Secretary of State Veliotis in an effort to enlist King Hussein's support for a joint initiative with Arafat. No such attention was lavished on Assad, and the Israelis were not fully informed about the details of this initiative, which was the basis for the American peace plan announced in the president's September 1 speech.

The third reason was the powerful effect of the media's shameful misdescriptions of the fighting in Lebanon. Casualty figures of unbelievable dimensions were reported and repeated without challenge; accounts of Israeli violence were presented ad nauseam, while the story of years of systematic PLO terror in Lebanon took months to emerge; American television and print commentators portrayed the war in language hitherto reserved for the Nazi assault on Western civilization, and accounts of Israeli atrocities, almost all of which turned out to be fabrications, were recounted uncritically.* All of this weighed heavily on American officials, who were in any event straining to counter widespread portrayals of the Reagan administration as bellicose. The president and his advisers were afraid to be identified with

* For more on press distortions, see Chapter 4, especially note 1.

the Israeli juggernaut, especially because the PLO had been so often misdescribed as a moderate, peace-seeking organization. The longer the war went on, the greater the pressure on the administration to dissociate the United States from the invasion and to take steps that would be considered peace seeking.

The fourth reason was the by now deeply ingrained reflex among the professional policymakers that held Israel responsible for blocking the peace process. After some initial uncertainty, this reflex dominated all American decisions. It first took the form of blind faith in the Syrians willingness to leave Lebanon if only the Israelis would agree to do so. It continued with opposition to *all* Israeli positions: first to Israel's desire to remain in Lebanon, later to Israel's desire to leave; first to Israeli willingness to engage in joint military operations, later to Israeli refusal to do so. Significantly, the only time the American marines confronted another armed force face-to-face in Lebanon was when Captain Johnson stopped the movement of some Israeli tanks in Beirut.

The reflexive opposition to Israeli military success dovetailed with another American attitude, this one firmly entrenched in the Pentagon and widely shared in other bureaus of the executive branch: the belief that, in the end, American interests in the Middle East are basically linked with those of the Arab nations. Our biggest clients in the region are the Arabs (principally Jordan and Saudi Arabia), and in military matters as in diplomacy years of familiarity have bred comradeship. This is probably the underlying reason for Secretary Weinberger's widely reported reluctance to put American soldiers in a position where they would have to "fire on Arabs."

FROM THE SIEGE OF BEIRUT TO THE ARRIVAL OF THE MARINES

Despite the opposition to Israel's invasion, we in essence adopted the Israeli political plan for Lebanon: a new government would be formed led by Bashir Gemayel, and this government would preside over the country. Within a very few weeks, however, the linchpin of this strategy, Bashir himself, was removed by Syrian-sponsored terrorists, thus setting the tone for what would follow. In an emotional reflex, the Lebanese installed Amin Gemayel in his brother's position, but Amin and Bashir were two quite different men. Where Bashir's charisma and courage guaranteed a certain energy and imagination, Amin was more a creature of maneuver, compromise, and uncertainty. Bashir could command the forces of the Phalange; but the Phalangists did not fully trust Amin and could not be expected to commit themselves entirely to his side. Finally, Bashir's close working relationship with Israel over the preceeding few years would have ensured a smooth channel of communication and a minimum of trust. Neither existed with Amin, whose basic foreign contacts ran from Paris to Riyadh.

With Bashir dead, quick action was required to chart Lebanon's course, but no such action was forthcoming, either from the presidential palace in Ba'abda or from the presidential oval office in Washington. Instead, Habib and his deputy, Morris Draper, in Beirut and the galaxy of officials in Washington (now including George Shultz) strove mightily to arrange for the long-promised PLO exodus from Beirut. After weeks of false promises, Arafat and his men finally began their exit from the capital in August, protected by American marines. By then, the symbolism of the PLO withdrawal had shifted from the initial picture of a shattered organization to that of defiant men and women (no longer called "terrorists," they were now "fighters"). Having lent our prestige and power to protect the PLO from Israel, the marines departed, only to return shortly thereafter to protect Palestinian refugees from their Christian enemies, following the massacres at Sabra and Shatila. Once reinstalled, and flanked by military contingents from France, Italy, and Great Britain, the marines became hostages to Lebanese fortune and eventually to Syrian revenge.

The Syrian recovery and eventual victory was the result of a systematic misreading of Assad. There seems to have been a widespread conviction that Syria, suitably grateful for American moderation and evenhandedness, would be only too pleased to cooperate with our overall objectives by withdrawing from Lebanon once we had arranged for the Israelis to leave. Assad, however, viewed the situation in more traditional terms, and he had a far more serious approach to foreign policy. He was beaten, but had not been expelled from Lebanon, and there was no sign of any force willing and able to do that. He had lost battles, even wars in the past, but he had not altered his fundamental objectives, and the loss of hundreds or thousands of his fighting men was hardly a major strategic concern. Just a few years before he had ordered the slaughter of somewhere between ten and thirty thousand of his own people when the Islamic Brotherhood in the city of Hama dared challenge his rule; nothing approaching that number fell to the Israelis. Once the Russians replaced his tanks, airplanes, and antiaircraft missiles, he was prepared to take his revenge.

From the beginning, it was necessary to convince the Syrians that the Israeli victory had fundamentally altered the Middle East. If we were determined to restrain the Israelis, we would have to show a willingness to use our own power in Lebanon. Otherwise Assad, who had no compunction about killing *his* enemies, would inevitably reassert his own interests. This was not properly appreciated in Washington, where Habib, supported by others in the State Department, was clearly convinced that the Syrians had in fact promised to withdraw from Lebanon once the Israeli departure had been arranged. The Syrians had apparently agreed to withdraw at the end of June, but that was at a time when the balance of power was held by Israel. As time passed and the situation became more favorable to Assad, this alleged guarantee would inevitably be reconsidered.

By late summer, American diplomacy was firmly committed to the search for a broader Middle Eastern "solution," as em-

bodied in the president's September 1 speech. Promised by Veliotis that Jordan was ready for a deal with the PLO and by
Habib that Syria was prepared to leave Lebanon, Reagan challenged all the parties in the region to take chances for peace.
The initiative was a worthy one, but none of the basic players in
the region had reason to believe the United States was firmly
committed to an active policy, and the only way any of them
could take a major risk was if the American commitment was
taken to be irrevocable. Paradoxically, the American effort to be
evenhanded undermined chances for an equitable settlement, for
it deprived the other countries of clear guidelines. The United
States had been considered Israel's main source of strength, yet
we had prevented the Israelis from finishing the military job
and were engaged in some heated public exchanges with Israeli
leaders. Our rhetoric seemed balanced, yet we were not dealing
with the Syrians, who held the key to a Lebanese settlement and
to Jordan's ability to reach an agreement with Arafat. In short,
we had not made the basic choices, and no one in the region
knew precisely where we would come down.

Predictably, no one in the Middle East proved equal to the
challenge. With the abrupt lack of subtlety that characterized
so much of his foreign policy, Begin rejected the call for broad
negotiations out of hand; after first acting as if a PLO-Jordanian
federation had been achieved, Hussein and Arafat had to admit
that the PLO was unwilling to abandon its rejection of any negotiations with Israel; the Saudis could not possibly take a clear
position and hedged their bet by financing all the contending
Arab parties; and the Syrians were not even in the game. Mean-
while, the Lebanese and the Israelis struggled to reach some sort
of agreement. Israel quite naturally wanted normalization along
the lines of her agreement with Egypt; Amin, unsure of his own
position and undoubtedly baffled by America's attitude toward
Israel, tried to have the best of all worlds: a promise of Israeli
withdrawal along with the stability that only Israeli troops could
provide; good working relations between Beirut and Jerusalem,

but no formal normalization that would antagonize the Arab world.

Without strong American guidance and guarantees, Amin could not take the risks associated with a formal peace treaty with Israel, and without Syrian participation, no stable Lebanese arrangement could be made at all. The window for strategic breakthrough was closing and the instrument that had opened it in the first place—Israeli military power—was no longer available. The siege of Beirut and the Sabra and Shatila massacres were too much for Israeli public opinion, coming as they did on top of more than four hundred dead soldiers, and for the first time in Israel's history, the consensus in favor of the IDF* came apart. The Minister of Defense, Ariel Sharon, and even generals of the army were widely held to have lied to the cabinet, the Knesset, and the country and to have contributed through their negligence to the massacres. With mounting intensity, the Israeli public made plain their insistence that there be no further fighting in Lebanon, and this insistence was strengthened with each new report of an Israeli death. If further military force were required to impose a settlement in Lebanon or generally advance Western interests in the region, it would have to come from other sources, barring a direct threat to Israel itself.

The Americans hoped that the Lebanese could eventually defend themselves and that while we trained the mixed Christian and Muslim army, the multinational force would deter any substantial advance by Syria and her Druze, Shiite, and PLO proxies. Here again, optimism overcame good judgment. Despite warnings that the ethnic and religious tensions would undermine the cohesiveness of the Lebanese army, American officials believed almost until the very end that it would be possible to create an effective fighting force that could withstand any likely challenge. And there was also an unspoken conviction that once the Syrians, the Druze, the Shiites, and the PLO had experienced

* Israel Defense Forces.

the effects of the guns of the *New Jersey* and the "smart bombs" of our navy fighter-bombers, they would desist. There were even some who believed that the mere presence of the marines would suffice to stabilize the situation. All these predictions proved false because our enemies in Lebanon learned that although we might occasionally respond to attacks against us, we were not prepared to fight seriously to advance our diplomatic interests.

The significance of these developments was not lost on the Syrian leader. His missile defenses rebuilt with newer Soviet SAMs, his fallen airplanes replaced with newer Soviet MIGs, Assad slowly tested the Lebanese terrain and found it agreeable. He took control of the broken military units of the PLO and turned them against the remnants of the forces loyal to Arafat north of Beirut. A variety of terrorist bands—some sent from the Ayatollah Khomeini, some ordered up by Assad's brother Rifaat—wreaked vengeance against their Lebanese opponents, thereby bringing Shiite and Druze armed bands in line with Syrian strategy. Druze leader Walid Jumblatt was reminded that his own father had been murdered by Syrians and that his own fate—as Jumblatt candidly admitted to some of his friends in private conversation—could well be the same if he did not co-operate with Damascus. While all this happened, the Americans awaited a response to the president's call for regional peace, and the American secretary of state, still believing that the Syrians would leave Lebanon once the Israeli withdrawal were arranged, patiently negotiated a treaty between Beirut and Jerusalem that was signed in May.

THE DEFEAT OF THE WEST

The events of the spring and early summer serve to demonstrate that good deeds do not always produce good results, and that brilliant negotiations may be useless if they do not serve a realistic objective. In the first half of 1983, we launched a worthy

peace initiative and orchestrated a noble agreement between Israel and Lebanon. Both failed in less than a year, victims of terrorism against Lebanese civilians and of acts of guerrilla war
against the United States and her European allies.

The Reagan plan was rendered inoperative when King Hussein announced that he could not obtain PLO approval for his
proposed negotiations with Israel regarding the disposition of
the West Bank and Gaza. Arafat was in no position to save his
broken prestige because his own military men were either under
siege or annexed by the Syrian army, and Assad was bent on
expanding Syrian power, not handing Arafat and Hussein the
right to deal for Arab territory.

The May treaty was abrogated by Amin the following
March for the same reasons; by this time it had become clear
that Syria would dictate the Lebanese settlement, all other forces
having been murdered, demoralized, and driven from Lebanese
soil. The Syrian maps turned out to have been accurate, at least
for the moment.

Most telling of all, the Syrian reconquest of Lebanon was
achieved in direct conflict not only with the American-trained
Lebanese army, but also with three of the most powerful countries on earth: the United States, Israel, and France. Once the
fighting ended in the summer of 1982 (or, to put it differently,
once the marines landed), there was only symbolic response to a
crescendo of Syrian-sponsored attacks against us, the French,
and the Israelis. First came the murder of Bashir, and there was
no response, even though the Syrian hand in the assassination
was announced on Lebanese radio and television. Then came the
summer bombing of the American Embassy in Beirut, and there
was no response, even though it was unthinkable that the attack
could have occurred without Syrian assistance and even though
the Iranian involvement was well enough documented for Secretary Weinberger to announce it publicly. Having failed to respond to these assaults, we were then predictably subjected to
the devastating bombing of the marine barracks in Beirut in

October 1983, an attack that was coordinated with a similar one against the French barracks, and, a few days later, yet another attack against an Israeli position further south. This time there were some token responses, quite limited actions from the air and sea. A few shells and bombs could not be expected to impress, let alone deter, a country that had experienced far worse the previous summer and lived to fight again.

Why did we not respond? Once again, there is no simple answer, but the crucial point is that the problem consists of a systematic pattern of inaction and not an isolated case. The pattern consists of a widespread reluctance on the part of American officials in both the executive and legislative branches to use military power to support and advance our diplomatic objectives. This opposition to the use of American fighting men generally goes under the name of the "Vietnam syndrome"; paradoxically, this disease has proven most virulent in the Pentagon. There does not seem to be a single case in the past several years in which the military leaders of our country enthusiastically supported a military action or recommended it among a choice of options. In those cases where American officials felt military power was needed, it tended to be civilians who urged its use, and they almost always came from buildings other than the Pentagon in Washington. More often than not, Pentagon officials have argued that unless there were a strong national consensus for such actions, they preferred not to undertake them. In making this case, they ignored the basic rules about the domestic politics of foreign policy: successful policies generate consensus, and failure is never popular. The issue to be addressed should be whether the national interest can be advanced, not an attempt to predict public reaction to the use of military force in the abstract.

On the other hand, there are indeed many powerful and influential people oposed in principle to the use of American military power, even when it might advance our interests. Secretary of State Vance, it will be recalled, resigned on precisely this issue, and many members of Congress, many writers and broadcasters, and virtually all of the Democratic candidates for the presidency seem to share Vance's view. Furthermore, there are strong political figures around the president who are similarly opposed to military action, apparently believing that the main danger to Reagan's reelection is public fear that he is a threat to peace. Like the military leaders, these political advisers and assistants to the president have evidently forgotten that he was elected in no small part because the American people were alarmed by a foreign policy based on abstract principle instead of on national interest, and that the political consequences of failure are far graver than those of the effective use of all instruments of national policy.

The key word here is *effective;* as Carter learned to his regret, the worst of all policies is to use military power half-heartedly and fail. And yet, for many years now, successive American governments have opted for this formula and achieved this result. It began in Vietnam with the cost-efficiency theory of military power: escalate bit by bit until you find the precise level at which might achieves the national objective. Thus we seek at all costs to avoid overkill and try to achieve a reasonable compromise between the use of power and the conduct of diplomacy. This accountant's and lawyer's approach to conflict also leads us to ask others to do our work for us: in one theater after another, we have gone in for military training programs, studiously avoiding the commitment of our own power. This was the heart of the Nixon Doctrine in Southeast Asia, as it is the basis for our actions in Central America and in Africa today, where we are training various countries to resist Cuba, Nicaragua, and Libya.

These theories have been demonstrated false on one battlefield after another, and they are unlikely to prove correct now, for in essence they turn over initiative to our opponents, who can react to every measured increase in our actions with an escalation of their own. To take the Lebanese case, the Syrians and their proxies were able to probe our intentions until they discovered that the Western forces would not fight on the ground. At that point, their only problem was the Lebanese army (and to some extent the Phalange), with which they were able to deal. As one member of Congress wryly observed, if the marines were in Lebanon to fight, they were too few; if they were there to die, they were too many.

There is one last point about the use of miiltary power: even our much-vaunted ability to strike from the air and the sea seems to have been overstated, in part because of an unwillingness at the Pentagon to turn over decision making to the officers in the field. The air strikes in the Shouf Mountains, for example, were ordered from Washington, down to the last detail—numbers of planes, the precise hour of the actions, and so forth. Thus, bureaucratic habit and jealousy over turf have extended from the corridors of the government to distant battlefields—to the detriment of our national interest.

But even if our armed forces were properly prepared and the commanders in the field were given suitable autonomy to conduct their operations, we would still be unable to design and execute serious foreign policy without a change in outlook. As things currently stand, any president who ordered a military action would be subjected to terrible denunciations and would be hamstrung by congressional demands to fine-tune the fighting from the halls of the Senate and the House. Thus, at least for the moment, quick actions are conceivable, but prolonged combat or hazy engagement (as with guerrillas, whether in Lebanon or El Salvador) creates grave political problems for any administration.

Nonetheless, until at least late in the summer of 1983, there were worthy military actions that could have been undertaken in Lebanon had we been serious about our support for Amin and our opposition to the Syrian reconquest of Lebanon. Such actions could—and should—have been aimed at clearing the Druze and Shiite forces out of the area immediately south and southeast of Beirut and off of the Western slopes of the Shouf Mountains. This would have permitted the Lebanese army around Beirut to link up with other mixed and Christian armed forces south of the city and, at least, would have given the new government a substantial zone of the country to manage. Such operations might have been conducted in conjunction with other elements of the multinational force and/or the Israelis. Indeed, such operations were proposed, discussed in the White House and in other Western capitals, and rejected. The resulting Western inaction gave the Syrians the opportunity to design and time their actions carefully, picking their targets and judging their effect.

THE PAYOFF

It has been said, by Secretary Shultz among others, that the outcome in Lebanon did not represent so much a failure of American policy as it did an unhappy ending to a fine effort by the United States and its European allies to bring about positive developments. Unfortunately, most of the rest of the world inevitably saw the matter in quite different terms. We had thrown our support firmly behind Amin Gemayel and his government. The president said so; our armed forces were sent to Lebanon to train Amin's army; and the multinational force was supposed to maintain order in Beirut, at least in part to give Amin a chance to mobilize his forces and stabilize the country. The effective collapse of the Lebanese army was, therefore, an American failure, and so was the Syrian-imposed abrogation of Secretary Shultz's hard-won Lebanese-Israeli treaty. More serious still, Syrian domination over Lebanon sent a chill down the spines of other pro-American leaders in the Middle East, for once again they saw a friend of the United States challenged by radical forces lose. The comparison that immediately springs to mind is the fall of the shah.

Unlike Amin Gemayel, the shah was a close American friend and ally of long standing and the shah's Iran occupied a crucial position in American geopolitical strategy. Yet, when he was challenged by the radical forces around Khomeini, we did not fight for the shah, and this frightened our allies around the world, who reasoned that if we were not prepared to fight for one of our most important allies, all other American friends were at risk. Reagan made much of this point when he defeated Carter, as he did of America's failure to take on the forces of international terrorism, and he promised that we would be more reliable and more vigorous in the future. Lebanon provided the first Middle Eastern test of American resolve, and it confirmed the fears generated by our behavior at the time of the shah's fall. As in Iran, we firmly committed ourselves to a government and then saw that government overthrown by its (and our) enemies without making any effective effort to save it. As in Iran, Americans were directly challenged and ultimately humiliated by radical anti-Western forces. As in Iran, there seemed to be no way effectively to use our military power to advance our diplomatic objectives.

To be sure, there were major differences. Our commitment in Iran was far deeper and the challenge to our interests was far greater than in Lebanon. Yet, anxious leaders around the world look for patterns in our behavior, and Lebanon recalled Iran and other American defeats in the recent past.

Our defeat in Lebanon encouraged our enemies in the Middle East and elsewhere. Those who form the rank and file of international terrorism inevitably concluded that if you kill enough Americans, you can get the United States to do what you want. Libya's Colonel Qaddafi, one of the mainstays in the terrorist international, said as much in a speech in early March 1984: the Americans do not have staying power, he announced to his followers, and if we continue to attack them, they will yield to us. There was a surge in terrorism directed against

Americans, both overseas and even at home, where multinational corporations reported a striking increase in bombings and terrorist threats in the first quarter of 1984. Furthermore, the Soviet-supported guerrillas in Central America took heart from the Lebanese example and were encouraged to continue with their own "Syrian strategy": keep fighting and wait for the American will to wane.

The most grateful of all for our failure in Lebanon were of course the Soviets, for they had suffered a most humiliating defeat in the summer of 1982. They were delighted to find themselves in the position of a boxer who has been saved by the bell and then finds his opponent exhausted at the start of the following round. They did not hesitate to push their advantage, both through the terrorist groups that they train and encourage and through the radical Arab nations with whom they work in the region.

As our enemies were cheered, our allies and potential friends were discouraged. It was no accident that President Mubarak of Egypt, no pillar of moral strength in any event, publicly warned that the American retreat from Lebanon would be a grave setback for the Middle East. No one knew more than he; for a brief moment, Sadat's strategy of making peace with Israel seemed to have been totally vindicated. But with the American defeat, the Egyptians increasingly distanced themselves from the Camp David agreements, and, as the slogan of the moment had it, reentered the Arab world.

The Saudis were similarly discouraged, although they were directly responsible for no small part of the fiasco. Considered by many a major power, Saudi Arabia in reality is a power vacuum, a rich prize for the bands of marauders that inhabit the Middle East. The Saudi government adopted a traditional policy of paying its enemies, hoping they would direct their energies against other countries. But they knew that eventually their turn would come and that our failure to fight, first for the shah and

then for Amin Gemayel, made it more likely that the royal family would flee to their already well-prepared luxurious exiles
rather than stand and resist.

The discouragement of our friends and allies was not limited to the Middle East; we can be certain that the Afghans
fighting against the Red army in their country were dismayed,
as were the Nicaraguan *contras* attempting to stop the totali-
tarianization of their land.

Thus, the Lebanese debacle, although it occurred in a country that did not represent a crucial challenge to our interests,
ended by affecting our vital national interests around the world.
This aspect of geopolitics—by which events in one corner of the
world influence the behavior of distant countries—is one of the
hardest for the strategically unskilled to appreciate, and it is one
of the reasons that the American leaders failed to take appropriate action in Lebanon. Perhaps the final irony of the story
lies in the figure of George Shultz. Brought in to replace the con-
troversial Alexander Haig, Shultz at first rejected Haig's approach to the Middle East, only to embrace it a year later. He
found himself confronted with the same opposition Haig had encountered, fought the same battles within the administration
that Haig had fought, and lost to precisely the same coalition in
Washington that had brought down Haig in the first place. At
the end of it all, Shultz had learned a great deal about foreign
policy—indeed, he may well have been the exception who proves
the rule about the impossibility of learning on the job. But he
was unable to reshape the administration's basic approach to
policy. He was simply outnumbered by colleagues who lacked
his understanding.

THE POLICY PROFESSIONALS

When leadership at the top is fundamentally flawed, we cannot
expect the prudent bureaucrats who execute policy to produce

miracles. In fact what we want from the professionals in the Department of State and the Department of Defense, in the intelligence community, and on the National Security Council staff is tough-minded objectivity, challenges to policy ideas from the top when they seem misguided, but then disciplined obedience to policy instructions once the decisions are made. These objectives are difficult to achieve, and those civil servants and professional foreign service officers who do them best often find themselves attacked by the party out of office in the misguided conviction that the professionals who best follow orders do so because of political zeal rather than out of respect for duty. During the 1980 campaign, for example, candidate Reagan and many of his supporters often attacked the "Carterite State Department" for the various policies of which the Reaganites disapproved. To be sure, Carter appointed some of his supporters to high State Department posts, but most of the members of the department were career people and the overall criticism was not only unfair, it was misguided: Carter was entitled to loyal support from the professionals, just as Reagan was when he became president. The expertise of the professionals is as important to a proper functioning of the government as is the vision of the political appointees. Conflicts develop when the professionals take it upon themselves to ignore the political mandate of the administration or when the political appointees attempt to remake the principles of American foreign policy overnight. In the best of worlds, the two groups would generate a creative symbiosis but, at present, neither performs particularly well. The politicians suffer from lack of understanding, and the professionals are afflicted with lack of vision.

THE BASE: BUREAUCRATS AND TEACHERS

The basic decisions about America's international behavior are made at a high level, but the information on which the decisions are made, the options that are brought forward, and many of the bits and pieces that make up our leaders' view of the world come primarily from the policy professionals in Washington.

The best of the professionals are well educated and move comfortably along the Washington cocktail-party and banquet circuit. Like their peers in the press, the business world, and the academy, they tend to respect the conventional wisdom that is reflected in the fashionable press and transmitted through the fashionable universities. And the conventional wisdom these days, as has been seen, is morally abstract and strategically amateurish. Furthermore, it is difficult for the professionals to think in terms of long-range American interests. First of all, they are expected to be loyal to the administration currently in power, and this requires them to adapt to changes in world view from one president (or secretary of state) to the next. Second, the professionals spend a lot of their time trying to understand the point of view of foreign countries and to communicate *that* point of view to Washington. This is the origin of clientitis, the systematic distortion of the world to favor the interests of a particular foreign country or group of countries that so often afflicts our professionals. Clientitis is as understandable as it is unfortunate, and only persons with solid culture and personal convictions can overcome it. But our professionals come from the same popular culture that produces the people at the very top; furthermore, these professionals soon learn that career advancement goes smoothly provided they do not take unnecessary risks. Consequently, they have every reason to follow the line of least resistance. Rare indeed are the products of the system who can transcend the conventional wisdom, think for themselves, express their own ideas, and still manage to carry out the policies of a current administration.

One must, therefore, sympathize with the policy professionals, but only up to a certain point, for in many ways, the shortcomings of these very professionals encourage the amateurism of so much of U.S. foreign policy.

Much has been written of late about the plight of American education and attention has tended to focus on the scientific and technological costs of declining standards in our schools and universities. The price is just as high in the area of more generalized education, out of which must come an understanding of international affairs. A person who has not been measured against proper standards during his or her years of training is unlikely to perform satisfactorily in the policy process. Can a person with poor language skills grasp the subtleties of diplomatic exchanges? And if someone has not been taught to think rigorously and precisely, how can we trust the analyses he or she sends forward through the bureaucracy? Finally, there is the unfortunate tendency in the United States to stress engagement at the cost of objectivity. Although academia once tried to impress on its students that to come to a true understanding of any problem one had to stand back and observe, all too many educators today seem to believe that one ought instead to jump in and feel. Emotional detachment is often replaced as the badge of the academic with commitment to fashionable causes.

Given the clear evidence in the decline of educational quality in this country, it should surprise no one to learn that the quality of thinking and writing in our foreign policy establishment is not good enough. In time, when word processors replace typewriters in the State Department, the CIA, and the Department of Defense, spelling errors will be eliminated; but the egregious grammatical mistakes, the omnipresent logical confusions, and the startling lack of understanding about the history and culture of foreign countries will persist. Unless the government is prepared to undertake a remedial culture program for its foreign service officers and other officials, these problems can be corrected only if our educational system improves and provides a better educated pool from which to draw our foreign policy experts.

Many will say that Americans have never been particularly good at studying foreign cultures, and it is a commonplace that the study of history has traditionally been given short shrift by our schools, but until recently our elite universities regularly graduated extremely well-trained professors of foreign language, foreign literature, and even foreign history and law. But these areas have fallen under the common curse; with salaries increasingly noncompetitive with other fields, and with grants disappearing and entire departments closing down, study of such problems is far less attractive. Consequently, our universities are producing fewer really well-educated generalists from whom our best foreign policy minds are traditionally drawn.

A few years ago, the *Washington Quarterly* commissioned a series of articles on area studies programs in leading American universities in order to understand the political worldview of the emerging elite of this country. Resources for the serious study of foreign areas are slim, the quality of research is generally low, and the worldview of the "experts" is as abstract and divorced from reality as that of the opinion makers. It turned out, for example, that Latin American studies programs were unusually low in quality and that, for the most part, the conceptual model used to "explain" the history and sociology of the Latins was a sort of pidgin Marxism copied from nineteenth-century Europe and transposed willy-nilly onto Latin America.[10] This quite understandably distorted the picture, with unfortunate results for scholarship and more serious drawbacks for policy. It should come as no surprise that our Latin American experts in the State Department are among the weakest of all the regional specialists and that intelligence assessments about Latin America are similarly low in quality.

The conventional wisdom in Latin American studies accounts for some of the incoherence surrounding the American government's long-standing inability to design and conduct wise policies because the professionals were unable to compensate for the ignorance and lack of proper sense of timing at the top. Most administration officials were unfamiliar with the history of El Salvador and were not aware that the Duarte government—the one in office at the time of Reagan's election—was quite radical in the context of Latin America. A group of progressive generals had seized power in 1979 from an oligarchic group that had long ruled the country. This coup constituted a moderate revolution: some thirty thousand of the old ruling class left El Salvador, and much of their land was appropriated for redistribution in one of the most radical land-reform programs in the history of Latin America. In 1980, the generals brought Napoleon Duarte in to head the government, and Duarte and his colleagues promised constitutional reform, democratic elections, and a continuation of the redistribution program. All of these promises were maintained—an achievement in itself.

It was only after this progressive coup that a unified guerrilla movement came into being. Fidel Castro—who in El Salvador as elsewhere in Latin America has insisted on a centralized movement before supporting it—appears to have been particularly disturbed at the success of El Salvador's pluralistic and bloodless revolution, for supplies and advisers (many of them based in Nicaragua) soon poured in to those committed to the overthrow of the new government. There was no such support for those opposing the oligarchs.

The guerrillas—as they always do—fought in the name of social justice against a regime that was admittedly far from perfect. But had the guerrillas been in good faith, they would have supported the Duarte government, for his goals were a necessary first step for the kind of egalitarian and equitable society the guerrillas claimed to be their goal. Instead, the guerrillas (based in Nicaragua where their Cuban advisers could give them logistical support and strategic instructions) attempted to split the country and to destroy much of its productive base, the most common "military" action of the FMLN* being the destruction of roads and electrical systems.

Furthermore, the guerrillas proved to be part of an inter-

* Farabundo Marti National Liberation Front, the largest guerrilla organization.

national movement rather than an indigenous, homegrown protest. There never was much domestic support for the FMLN—
by giving them the benefit of every doubt, one might guess that they might have had something like 15 percent of the electorate in the 1981 elections had they participated.[11] And the guerrillas' operational base was outside the country: Nicaragua in the first instance, and behind that, Cuba. So compelling was the evidence that even the Carter administration recognized the external threat to El Salvador and accordingly resumed military assistance to that country in 1980. This was the situation that the Reagan administration inherited in 1981.

Despite the evidence (and the classified material made matters far clearer than the information that was released to the public), the professionals in the Department of State and the Department of Defense were reluctant to get involved in a public debate on behalf of Duarte. In fact they were occasionally quite cynical of the men in El Salvador who were risking their lives to preserve a democratic revolution. At one high-level meeting in the fall of 1981—with experts from all agencies present—one of the top State Department professionals argued against any effort to promote our policies publicly because, in his words, "They have their bastards and we have ours; there isn't a lot of difference between them." Those who challenged him were by and large political appointees.

This official's simple-minded view of the war in El Salvador as one between "their bastards and ours" showed not only a lack of understanding, but a lack of belief in the basic principles of the United States. If Duarte and the progressive military won in El Salvador, one could reasonably expect steady progress toward democratic institutions and practices; if the guerrillas won, the Salvadorans would experience a tyranny at least equal to, and probably far worse than, that which they had endured under the traditional oligarchs. But the Latin Americanists, having acquired a view of social transformation from eighteenth- and nineteenth-century Europe, reflexively saw the generals as reactionary and the guerrillas as progressive. The experience with Castro and then with the Sandinistas had not shaken their belief in this model.

Moreover, the cynically "balanced" view of the struggle in El Salvador is the one affected by the current media elite: war is hell, and all warriors are bad. It takes real strength of character and confidence in one's own knowledge and understanding to go counter to what the media can present as the current dominant consensus, and few bureaucrats possess these characteristics. Those who can resist the imposition of the manufactured consensus are either firmly politicized or soundly grounded in their own expertise, and they are few in number.

A comparison of the various regional bureaus in the State Department during the past few administrations confirms several of these themes. In most cases, aggressive and intelligent leadership has overcome the residual inertia of the "system," and accomplished significant results. Thus, for example, Assistant Secretary of State for African Affairs Chester Crocker achieved distinguished results with virtually the same personnel that had acquired a distinctly lackluster reputation during the Carter years, and Hugh Montgomery, the director of the bureau of intelligence and research, produced fine results from a bureau that had been considered one of the weakest in the entire system for many years. Richard Holbrook, the assistant secretary of state in charge of Southeast Asia during the Carter presidency, was extremely effective (although I don't care for the results), and two consecutive assistant secretaries for European affairs— Richard Vest and Lawrence Eagleburger—had distinguished tenures. But individual leadership was not the whole story.

By and large, the areas that can draw on strong academic traditions are those with the greatest diplomatic expertise (thus, the European Bureau in the State Department is the strongest regional bureau), and they are predictably those whose national traditions most closely resemble our own political culture: Western Europe, Israel, some of the ASEAN countries, and the other

scattered democracies. But here, too, the effects of the demorali-
zation of American national purpose and the controlling influence of a chic group that is not motivated to fight anywhere for
any principle have made themselves felt. To be sure, those who
are steeped in Western traditions—along with some of those
who devote their lives to the study of our totalitarian enemies—
are less susceptible to the intellectual fads of the moment. But
in the academy as in the government, rare is the individual who
maintains his integrity in the face of consensus.

To be sure, the academics have one great advantage over
the bureaucrats: they can devote an entire career to specializing
in one area, whereas the professional foreign service officers
jump back and forth from one area of focus to another. The
same, astonishingly, is true of intelligence officials. Whereas
once upon a time the intelligence community could boast of individuals who had devoted a lifetime to the careful study of one
area of the world, today one rarely finds such expertise. This
was one of the principal reasons for our failure to respond adequately to crises in such crucial areas as Iran, where there was
no full-time, adequately specialized Iran analyst available to the
Carter administration at the time of the shah's time of troubles.[12] But because the scholars rarely understand the real problems faced by government officials, even when there is profound
understanding of a foreign culture, this is usually not translated
into useful policy recommendations or even into policy-relevant
analyses. Despite the theoretical advantages that the academy
offers over the bureaucracy, as a general rule scholarly assessments contribute to the problem rather than help to solve it.
At the time of the Iranian crisis, the vast majority of American
academic experts misdescribed the nature of the shah's regime,
typically measuring it against the highest Western standards
rather than in its own regional and historical context, and they
were grotesquely optimistic about the consequences of a Khomeini victory. Most of the experts whose words filled the op-ed

pages of American newspapers on this subject hailed the fall of
the shah and supported Khomeini's "revolution," imputing to
Khomeini their own reasons for disliking the shah. As a consequence, Americans were led to believe that the shah had been
overthrown because he was too reactionary rather than, as was
the case, because he was too progressive.

The consequence of this sorry state of affairs is that the
scholars and the bureaucrats inbreed their common confusions.
Ideally, the foreign policy professionals ought to be able to get
away from their work for an extended period (a sabbatical year
for example) in order to stand back and view the broader picture. But with things as they are, such periods would probably
be better spent living and studying abroad rather than in American universities, which are often part of the general problem.

But even if the policy professionals were far better than
they are, they would be unable to make good policy without
proper leadership. Overall policy must come from the top—
above all, from the White House—and if the vision at the top is
flawed, policy will suffer accordingly.

IS GOOD AMERICAN POLICY POSSIBLE?

To take stock: our problems spring from a national elite insufficiently prepared to represent us and our interests. The principal
danger derives not so much from policies that are themselves
perilous, but rather from incoherence and lack of constancy and
understanding among those who formulate and conduct policy,
and these characteristics of our international behavior in turn
stimulate other countries to take drastic action on their own.

If we are to remedy this dangerous state of affairs, we will
need better leaders, and they in turn will have to convince the
public of the rightness of their policies. I am convinced that this
is possible, but it is becoming more difficult as the tempo of con-

fusion and danger increases. Our current problem was well described by Walter Lippmann in 1935, in an address to the Phi
Beta Kappa fraternity at Harvard:

> For us the point at which the malady is most ominous is
> when young men come asking us what tradition we possess
> by which they can confront this contradictory world. The
> older generation who sit in the seats of authority, and in the
> nature of things determine the answer, do not have an an-
> swer. They do not know what to say when they are asked
> what ideas they possess which offer the new generation valid
> purposes and noble duties.[13]

The task would be daunting enough without the urgency
that our international obligations and risks impose on us; and it
would be herculean, even with means of communication between
government and the public that functioned honestly, without
constantly trying to advance their own—media—interests. But
to develop an elite capable of leading us through the great East-
West crisis into which we have entered, we shall also have to
deal with the problem of the Fourth Estate, composed of journalists and their allies, who have seized a share of governmental
power for themselves.

4

BARRISTERS, JUDGES,
BROADCASTERS, AND JOURNALISTS

One day during the Lebanese War in July 1982, I got a telephone call at the State Department from Leslie Stahl of "CBS
News." "How can it be," I was asked, "that Begin and Sharon
are continuing to bomb Beirut after everything we've put on
television?" I speculated that maybe Begin didn't make policy
on the basis of American evening news broadcasts, but this
hardly slowed down Ms. Stahl. "But look at the pictures, and
they're going worldwide."

She had a point of course; after the systematic distortion
of the war by the media throughout the West (and the distortions were even worse in most of Europe than here), the public
outcry against the Israelis made it certain that strategic goals in
Jerusalem and Washington would be overridden by the need to
respond to the images on the evening news. Indeed, so potent
were the pictures that President Reagan eventually based much
of his own policy on them (particularly one of a Palestinian
child with his arms apparently blown off that turned out to be
false—his arms had been deliberately bound to his body in order
to produce the illusion).[1] Afterwards, it was widely observed
that no democracy can wage a lengthy war anymore as war is

supposed to be waged unless it stumbles into a lucky situation—
like the Falklands, where the British were able to keep the journalists out or under military censorship, or like Grenada, where
the combination of an extremely rapid operation and a delay of
a couple of days in journalistic coverage made it possible for the
military planners to conduct their operations with relative calm.

War is a special case of politics, and politics in the United
States, as throughout the Western democracies, is often defined
by the media. Every morning in Washington our leaders begin
their day by reading the Press Summary. That this generally
precedes the reading of the classified Intelligence Summary
speaks volumes about the power of the press, for the Press Summary, for the most part, establishes the agenda for the government during the next dozen hours.

The media, along with their allies, the lawyers and judges,
have truly become the Fourth Estate, an integral part of the daily
functioning of the government. The leading practitioners—both
in the media and in the older branches of government—know it
full well. Journalists have abundant space in all major government agencies, except the CIA, and even there a "public affairs
office" has been established. It is no accident that journalists
often have better access to leading government officials than do
their immediate subordinates, close friends, and even members
of their families.

PROBLEMS AND POWER OF THE PRESS

The practice of journalism hasn't changed much since the days
of clay tablets and styli; although journalists in earlier genera-
tions made just as many mistakes as our modern exemplars, it
didn't matter so much. There were many different newspapers,
and by and large the impact of the printed words was much less
than that of highly centralized television networks. The political
weight of the media was tolerable (although each advance in the

popularity of the printed word was passionately deplored by political and intellectual leaders, who dreaded an inevitable debasement in quality). Today, top government officials, including presidents and cabinet members, spend a disproportionate amount of time trying to avoid open conflict with the media, thus permitting the members of the media to impose their views on those of elected and appointed officials. Our officials behave this way because of the great damage the press has been able to inflict on one administration after another.

The very nature of this problem points to the basis of media power. Just as the Third Estate earned its formal rights when it demonstrated an ability to destroy leading members of the other two estates, so the media entered its current golden age after impressively creating and destroying a series of national leaders. The first to fall was Johnson, the victim of a vast outcry that was in large part driven by the media against the Vietnam War. Then came Nixon in Watergate; then Carter was first built up and subsequently destroyed by the Washington press corps. The media had demonstrated that it possessed the power to create and destroy a politician; henceforth, it would play a major role in defining the rules of the game in Washington. Without a demonstration of such real power, the media would not have been taken so seriously; it never had had this power before the 1960s. Since then, the Fourth Estate has taken on all the trappings of other elite institutions: big salaries, luxurious perks, high status, top billing on the society pages. Its offices are side by side with those of other government officials. (When some of Johnson's top aides suggested that the press corps might be moved out of the White House and forced to rent their own space in nongovernment buildings, they were quickly advised to drop the matter . . . by other government officials!) And like all other nouveau riche classes, the media have brought along with them a new style and a new mythology to protect their privileges.

The media's mythology generally goes under the name of

the First Amendment, which in the interpretation of most journalists amounts to the right to print or report most anything
about most any event or anyone—regardless of the cost to the
individuals involved or to the national interest. The version of
the First Amendment actively promoted by the media and their
lawyers gives the media all the prerogatives of a secret intelligence agency: they decide what constitutes evidence, they protect (or expose) the nature of their sources and methods, they
decide when to pay for information, and they carefully control
the declassification procedures to suit their own interests. There
is no Freedom of Information Act for the media (or the legal
profession); journalists (and the lawyers who work with them)
want the government's secrets to be accessible, but *their* secrets
are to be withheld from the public. When the executive branch
wishes to protect itself against inquiries, it invokes executive
privilege, arguing that it cannot conduct its business unless certain things remain secret. The media invariably challenges the
government's right to secrecy, while claiming that the revelation
of their own sources and methods would have a "chilling" effect on freedom of the press, access to information, and the like.
Both invoke the national interest on behalf of their own desires.
That there is a substantial difference in the legitimacy of their
respective claims (no one elected a newsperson, nor have journalists sworn an oath to uphold and defend the Constitution) is
often forgotten by First Amendment advocates, along with the
judges and lawyers who have argued and upheld the press position. As Leslie Stahl's call during the Lebanese War shows, many
of the current media stars fully believe that *they* should define
the national agenda—the polling data, most dramatically the
polls published in *Public Opinion* magazine in 1981, confirm
this emphatically.

The power of the media comes from the centralization of its
operations and the remarkable ideological coherence of many of
its leading practitioners. Many media watchers like to claim that
there is a real difference between the content of television news

and that of newspapers and magazines. Perhaps so; certainly, print media are able to do more serious analyses. But in practice, it is one big fraternity, and the members define each other's tasks: the morning news programs are almost always based on the first editions of the *Washington Post,* the *New York Times,* and, to a lesser extent, the *Wall Street Journal.* That is why the government's morning news summaries determine so much of the day's activities: the journalists in town will be following up on these stories, whereas the officials will be trying to get the best possible treatment on the evening news broadcasts.

To a certain extent, this is a positive development, because it forces government officials to look at their own decisions from a different perspective. Furthermore, a good journalist will some-times obtain information and understanding that the government does not have itself. Yet over the past several years, a certain uniformity has emerged among major media, suggesting that free inquiry does not abound. Indeed, the most recent studies of the attitudes of media leaders indicates a disappointing con-formity.

Apologists for the press generally explain the relative uni-formity of news coverage by referring to the mechanics of the news business: the requirements for photographs, the nature of deadlines, the common training of producers and editors, and so on. But the facts are otherwise. As S. Robert Lichter and Stanley Rothman wrote in *Public Opinion* in the fall of 1981:

> In 1972, when 62 percent of the electorate chose Nixon, 81 percent of the media elite voted for McGovern. This does not appear to reflect any particular personal aversion to Nixon, despite the well-publicized tensions between the press and his administration. Four years later, leading journalists pre-ferred Carter over Ford by exactly the same margin. In fact, in the Democratic landslide of 1964, media leaders picked Johnson over Goldwater by the staggering margin of sixteen-to-one, or 94 to 6 percent . . . over the entire sixteen-year period, less than one-fifth of the media elite supported any Republican presidential candidate. In an era when presiden-

tial elections are often settled by a swing vote of 5 to 10 percent, the Democratic margin among elite journalists has been 30 to 50 percent greater than among the entire electorate.[2]

It should be noted that by "journalists," the authors mean writers, producers, editors, and directors. This means that we are dealing with a group of striking ideological homogeneity, and the ideology documented by the *Public Opinion* poll is recognizable in much of our news coverage:

> In most instances, majorities of the media elite voice the same criticisms that are raised in the Third World. Fifty-six percent agree that American economic exploitation has contributed to Third World poverty. About the same proportion . . . find America's heavy use of natural resources to be "immoral."[3]

Theirs is a view of the world in which the United States is a major problem, not a major contributor to solutions. Moreover, they object to some of the traditional ways in which countries have tried to solve international problems. A solid 55 percent in the poll would prevent the CIA from operating secretly against foreign governments hostile to us, a media attitude that was subsequently adopted by Congress when it decided in the spring of 1984 that, although it was all right to defend Salvadorans from weapons being shipped from Nicaragua, it was not permissible to attempt to bring down the Sandinista regime.

The media, then, are a largely homogeneous political class with the usual overriding class interest: increasing their own power. (According to the *Public Opinion* research, the media elite believe that they are today the second most powerful group in American society—second only to the business community—and that they *should* be the most powerful.) In the pursuit of greater power, the media have adopted an ideology that serves their own interests and weakens their opponents within the United States. Because much of their activity is aimed at weakening the American government, on occasion the media ideology even strengthens opponents of the United States.

The keystone of the media ideology is the claim for unlimited free speech that goes under the name of the current reading of the First Amendment and grants an absolute right of free speech without any requirement for responsible use of that right. In practice, of course, the only real dispute among persons of intelligence and good will is where to draw the line and to determine what obligations the citizenry must fulfill in exchange for the right to free speech. Thus far, the line has been drawn around a community of people that the courts term "public figures." Regarding such persons, the courts have in essence granted the media unrestrained assault, save in those exceedingly rare cases where a person can show that he or she was damaged by the media *because of malice* in articles or broadcasts that were false (the truth is always a defense against libel and slander charges). In practice, malice proves quite difficult to establish in court; hence, the media have rarely had to pay off for their attacks on reasonably well-known individuals. Furthermore, the media usually have many advantages in court cases because the major media can afford to pay lawyers—or get free legal help— and because they have managed to use the First Amendment both to protect their sources and to keep control over their "evidence." Thus, a plaintiff asking to see unpublished notes or unbroadcast videotapes may be told that the media will not produce these because of alleged tampering with press freedom.

Students of the class struggle will recognize what is going on: the new class is taking for itself the privileges that previously adhered to the old ruling classes while stripping them of their traditional rights and privileges. Like the Lewis Carroll character who knew what true revolution is all about, the new journalists and lawyers insist that a word means what *they* say it means. Thus, "privacy" is what defends citizens from "government snooping," and it is good. But attempts by people in the government to protect themselves from press snooping is *not* "privacy," it's called "censorship," and it is bad.

In the increasingly intense conflict between media and gov-

ernment, the journalists portray themselves as the true representatives of the public. This, too, is in keeping with the growing political pretensions of the Fourth Estate because in our
system, "the public" is the source of political legitimacy. The
media—as befits a rising political class—is seeking to legitimize
its power at the expense of its competitors in government. The
Fourth Estate accordingly portrays its rights and privileges as
absolute, whereas those of the government are held to be limited and at the mercy of the media. This is intolerable, both on
philosophical grounds and in the practice of government.

The right to free speech carries an obligation to try to use
it responsibly, for the First Amendment does not give anyone
with a typewriter or a microphone license to go about malign-
ing other citizens, in the government or out. Lippmann, who
was enraged by claims that free speech meant license, put it this
way:

> If there is a dividing line between liberty and license, it is
> where freedom of speech is no longer respected as a proce-
> dure of the truth and becomes the unrestricted right to ex-
> ploit the ignorance, and to incite the passions, of the people.
> Then freedom is such a hullabaloo of sophistry, propaganda,
> special pleading, lobbying, and salesmanship that it is diffi-
> cult to remember why freedom of speech is worth the pain
> and trouble of defending it.
>
> What has been lost in the tumult is the meaning of the obli-
> gation which is involved in the right to speak freely. It is
> the obligation to subject the utterance to criticism and de-
> bate. Because the dialectical debate is a procedure for attain-
> ing moral and political truth, the right to speak is protected
> by a willingness to debate. . . .
>
> [I]n the absence of debate, unrestricted utterance leads to
> the degradation of opinion. By a kind of Gresham's law the
> more rational is overcome by the less rational, and the
> opinions that will prevail will be those which are held most
> ardently by those with the most passionate will. For that
> reason the freedom to speak can never be maintained merely

by objecting to interference with the liberty of the press, of
printing, of broadcasting, of the screen. It can be maintained
only by promoting debate.[4]

But how can the country have a serious political debate
when the medium in which the debate is supposed to take place
is itself an interested party? Most journalists these days consider
it beneath their dignity to simply report the words of government officials—and let it go at that. Indeed, it is virtually impossible to find a single distinguished television correspondent who
limits himself or herself to simple reportage. Yet if the public
never gets a simple transmission from the media, receiving instead the journalists' interpretation of what has happened and
what it means, then an honest public debate cannot take place.
As things stand today, not only do we get our news filtered
through politicized reporters, but the correspondent's own comment is often disguised and presented as the remarks of an
anonymous "government official."

For a while, some members of the press developed a technical gimmick to gain additional authority. This was known as
the two-source rule and meant that nothing was printed or
broadcast on the basis of a single source; some kind of confirmation was required from a second "reliable" person. The
two-source rule had its heyday during the Watergate scandal,
when everything in the press that was damaging to the Nixon
administration was subjected to violent criticism from the White
House and the journalists conducting the campaign against the
president had to find a procedural shield to hide behind. Once
the elevation of the Fourth Estate had been achieved, however,
the two-source rule was quickly shelved; once again, we hear
from "a high government official, who asked that his name not
be used."

The two-source rule was simply another of the subterfuges
used by the media to do what they want to do (increase their
own political power) without having to meet standards of evi-

dence or propriety. That it was purely a gimmick was demonstrated one day in 1981, when the *Washington Post* carried a story citing an anonymous official, and alongside the story was a picture captioned, "High official who asked not to be identified." In practice, you can almost always get someone in Washington to confirm a story for you. The issue is not whether some number of persons believes a story, the issue facing serious journalists and editors is whether the story is true. To ascertain this, however, is difficult and often takes longer than journalists' deadlines permit.

The two-source rule, and others like it, provide editors and journalists with a procedural fig leaf behind which they can hide if the story turns out to be wrong. They can always say, "We played by the rules." But "playing by the rules" isn't too reassuring when the rules themselves are made by one of the contending teams and when the referees are also interested parties. Indeed, the Watergate affair itself demonstrates the conviction of the media that they are above the kind of standards they insist upon for public servants.

Early in the investigation, Carl Bernstein of the *Washington Post* obtained a list of telephone calls made by Watergate burglar Bernard Barker to the Committee to Re-Elect the President (CREEP). Here is what Bob Woodward and Carl Bernstein said about the event in their best-seller, *All the President's Men:*

> Bernstein had several sources in the Bell system. He was always reluctant to use them to get information about calls because of the ethical questions involved in breaching the confidentiality of a person's records. It was a problem he had never resolved. . . . Why, as a reporter, was he entitled to have access to personal and financial records when such disclosure would outrage him if he were subjected to a similar inquiry by investigators?[5]

Bernstein got over his ethical dilemma with minimum anguish and went on to obtain other confidential records and even tampered with a grand jury before Nixon finally fell. (The section of *All the President's Men* dealing with the jury tampering caper—ending with Judge Sirica letting Woodward and Bernstein off with a verbal slap of the wrist, even though it was clear he knew they had tampered with his grand jury—should be required reading for anyone who wants to see how judges, lawyers, and journalists work together to restrain their opponents while permitting themselves all necessary license.)

In the autumn of 1972, the *Washington Post* published an article by Woodward and Bernstein that claimed that Hugh Sloan—treasurer of CREEP—had told a grand jury that Bob Haldeman had been running the committee's secret slush fund. This turned out to be false, and the *Post* went through some bad hours as the White House counterattacked. Like Bernstein with the telephone company records, Ben Bradlee, the executive editor of the *Post*, faced an ethical problem. Should he admit error? Again, *All the President's Men* shows that the media stars quickly saw the central issue: "I was up the river with these two reporters. I can remember sitting down at the typewriter and writing about thirty statements and then sort of saying, 'Fuck it, let's go stand by our boys.' "[6] Like any governing class, the Fourth Estate judged it better to lie than to lose face.

THE MEDIA AND FOREIGN POLICY

The leaders of the Fourth Estate suffer from the same lack of understanding of the world that besets the other members of our policy elite as well as from the abstract moralism that permeates our popular culture. Like the others, they are rarely forced to meet proper standards. Their careers depend on getting published as close to the front of the newspaper or magazine as possible or on "making air," and this in turn depends on catching the eye of the editor back in New York, Washington, or Los Angeles. The best place for an ambitious media personality is Washington; the worst fate is to be shipped off to some

remote corner of the world, left to file stories about lands and
peoples that do not interest the evening television viewer or the
morning commuter on the train or the bus. This produces exag-
gerations of the stories that do get attention because calm, dispassionate accounts of foreign developments are not usually
exciting enough in and of themselves.

With rare exceptions, our foreign correspondents are looking for "angles" that will enable them to get foreign news into
the American media. This is difficult because Americans aren't
much interested in foreign news, except insofar as it affects
them directly and dramatically. The best way to succeed is to
find some scandal involving the United States (in government or
in the business community) or something that will make life
difficult for the American government. The natural ally of the
journalist is often the American bureaucrat who is stationed
overseas and watching for developments that will cause problems. The alliance can work well indeed. First, there is no need
for the journalist to learn a foreign language, master a foreign
political culture, or evaluate the reliability of foreign sources. It
should be noted, in defense of all but the most powerful American newspapers, that officials of foreign governments are generally not eager to talk candidly with American correspondents
or stringers; if they have something important to say, they will
work with their own national press most of the time. Second,
like the journalist, the embassy official is looking for the "American angle." Third, the embassy and the correspondent may
have a common interest in hyping a story (or a given embassy
official, either alone or in tandem with someone back in Washington, might wish to do so). It is hard to learn the ins and outs
of any society, and harder still in a country and culture not
one's own; with the career inducements pointing back toward
Washington and the line of least resistance leading straight to
American officials, rare indeed is the foreign correspondent who
develops real foreign sources and develops real insight into the
country or region he is covering. Our news thus often remains

locked in an American context complete with the chic radical ideology that dominates the media, and the debate we need does not take place. This lack of serious reporting of foreign news was well demonstrated by the case of "The Plot to Kill the Pope."

One might have expected that the attempted assassination of Pope John Paul II in the spring of 1981 would have produced a frenzy of activity from our leading investigative reporters. The story had everything: a photogenic and exotic Turkish assassin (Mehmet Ali Agca) with a violent and romantic background (including an escape from a prison in Turkey held to be escape-proof); one of the world's most charismatic and powerful men (the pope himself) shot at one of the most dramatic moments in postwar history (the struggle for the destiny of Poland and perhaps that of the entire Soviet Empire); and strong suspicions that Agca might not have acted alone. Yet, for nearly a year, only two American journalists took the time and effort to dig out the details that pointed an accusing finger at the Kremlin, and one of them—Claire Sterling—has lived in Italy since the 1940s. Almost all the rest bought the convenient "cover story" offered by the would-be assassin; and as the evidence for the Soviet connection mounted, they generally looked the other way.

Within days of the shooting in St. Peter's Square in Rome, a team of *New York Times* correspondents in the Middle East, Europe, and the United States had concluded that Agca was associated with a "xenophobic, fanatically nationalistic, neofascist network steeped in violence,"[7] namely the National Action Party of Turkey and other related right-wing groups. Although the reporters from the *Times* were not able to account for the source of the money with which Agca traveled throughout Western Europe for months before the shooting in Rome, they did find some "hints" that it had come from "drug sales or robberies" (this theme—Agca as common criminal—would be repeated over and over again, and it seems to have come from East European sources).

Most of the other leading newspapers, weekly newsmagazines, and television news organizations followed the lead of the *Times* until the account was revised in August 1982 by Claire Sterling, in September by Marvin Kalb's essay on NBC, and then by Italian magistrates who ordered the arrest of a Bulgarian airlines employee in Rome and asked the Bulgarian government to lift diplomatic immunity for two of their diplomats in order that they might be arrested as well. Much of the information that led four separate Italian magistrates to the conclusion that Agca was part of an international conspiracy based in Eastern Europe was available to our journalists within days of the shooting. Yet, as late as January 1983, the *Washington Post's* stringer in Rome was writing that the accusations against Bulgaria made by Italy's defense minister "were at least partly related to domestic Italian politics,"[8] and the *New York Times* man in Rome scoured the Western world to find high-ranking officials who would give him statements sceptical of the Soviet/Bulgarian connection.

FIRST REACTIONS

Within two weeks of the shooting, the American press had effectively taken the position that Mehmet Ali Agca was either a "lone nut," or was part of a fanatic right-wing international network. With rare exceptions, nobody was inclined to follow the logic of the assassination attempt: Who could expect to benefit from the murder of the pope? What motive could be ascribed to the attempt (as different from the possible motives of the man who pulled the trigger)?

Not a single American newspaper or network looked carefully toward the East; for the most part they were content to speculate about Agca's character, and occasionally they hinted darkly at a Fascist conspiracy. The *New York Times* reported that Italian police investigations had failed to turn up any evidence for an "international conspiracy," even though the *Times* stressed Agca's connections with a neofascist network. Writing from Turkey, *Times* correspondent Marvine Howe described a "Rightist Web of Intrigue"[9] in some detail, suggesting that the international network might well have provided Agca with the money and assistance necessary for his lengthy travels prior to his arrival in St. Peter's Square on May 11.

This was the pattern for much of the comment on the assassination. Thus, Georgie Anne Geyer: "Ali Agca is a cold-eyed fanatic—a Turkish ultra-nationalist and religious zealot who hates the West and Christianity and sought the most effective way to attack them."[10] Thus, Joseph Kraft: "Ali Agca . . . went after the pope as a living symbol—indeed, the most prominent example—of the spirit that breaks down the barriers the islamic fundamentalists seek to rebuild." Kraft concluded that this sort of fundamentalist revolt "is not an organized terrorist conspiracy that can be stamped out by more police and vigilance."[11] Thus, Joseph C. Harsch: "There is every indication that the man who fired at the Pope was a criminal psychopath. If he had accomplices or an organization background it was apparently of a right-wing variety. There is no serious suggestion that the deed was motivated from Moscow or the man trained by Moscow or by its agents."[12]

These stories were written against a precise political background: the charges of Secretary of State Alexander Haig that international terrorism, actively supported by the Soviet Union, was a major issue for the United States and required strong action by all the countries of the West. Thus, whether implicitly or explicitly—for example, Joseph C. Harsch, writing explicitly in the *Christian Science Monitor*, which by the way would turn out to be by far the best American newspaper on this subject— the shooting of the pope inevitably constituted a sort of test case for Haig's claims.

Information was at first hard to come by, but for those who spoke Italian and who had some decent contacts in Rome, the matter was far from impenetrable. George Armstrong, writing

in the *Christian Science Monitor* just five days after the shooting, observed that "the more that is learned of Agca, the more
unlikely it seems that he could be a lone killer stalking the Pope
in Italy for most of the last six months." According to Armstrong, "the hottest theory circulating in Rome today" took as
its starting point the fact that "the two Poles the Soviets most
fear are Stefan Cardinal Wyszynski and Karol Wojtyla. The
former is believed to be near death in Warsaw, and the latter,
who became Pope John Paul II in 1978, was felled by bullets
last Wednesday."[13] According to this theory, Agca was trained
and assisted by Libyans.

David Ottoway of the *Washington Post* also heard whispers
about a plot coming from the East, although he didn't give it
much credence:

> "It could be a Moslem group in opposition to the Catholic
> Church," remarked a high-ranking Italian official, "or there
> could be a Polish connection," he added, noting Agca alleged
> he was in Bulgaria after his escape from a Turkish prison in
> November 1979.
>
> The Bulgarians might be upset enough by the alternative to
> communism evolving in Poland and the strong backing of
> the Catholic Church, as well as of the Polish pope, to the
> Solidarity independent union movement to encourage Agca
> in his endeavor, according to this "hypothesis."
>
> One Western diplomatic source, however, called this theory
> "off the wall," together with that holding some extremist
> Moslem group responsible.[14]

One need not be a genious to figure out the nationality of
the diplomat who termed the Soviet connection "off the wall,"
and this remained a near-constant refrain throughout the story:
American officials strove mightily to discourage the notion that
the KGB might have had something to do with the shooting of
the pope.

In mid-September, the Rome court that sentenced Agca to
life imprisonment published its verdict, and it somewhat unex-

pectedly stated that Agca had not acted alone. Although the court admitted that no evidence had been unearthed as yet to "uncover the identity or the motives of the conspirators," it nonetheless stated that "Agca suddenly appeared among the crowd to execute, with almost bureaucratic coolness, a task entrusted to him by others in a plot obscured by hatred. . . ." So far as I know, this was not reported in our major publications nor by the television networks. So far as they were concerned, the Agca case was closed.

THE SECOND PHASE: FROM READER'S DIGEST TO NBC NEWS

Unlike the "elite" press, *Reader's Digest* was not inclined to drop the matter. Claire Sterling was asked to look into the case in detail, and her careful article was completed in all major respects by spring 1982. The editors at the *Digest* then devoted months to checking, cutting, and rewriting with her (a process almost unknown to most of our major "news" publications) before publishing it in the September issue. In the same period, similar conclusions were reached by Marvin Kalb, whose "NBC White Paper" on the "Plot to Kill the Pope" was broadcast in September 1982. Both Sterling and Kalb (along with some unpublished research by former CIA and National Security Council staff official Paul Henze) managed to establish that Agca was involved in a network of Bulgarian and Turkish officials, smugglers, and mafia characters; that Agca had lived in one of the most luxurious hotels in Sofia long enough to remove any reasonable doubt that he was "protected" by the Bulgarians; that Agca had opened secret bank accounts as early as 1977 and that after his escape from Turkey he spent over $50,000 in a year without ever cashing a check; that Agca's network of Bulgarians and Turks (some of whom lived in great luxury—normally reserved for high Bulgarian Communist party officials—in Bulgaria and traveled on Bulgarian passports) provided Agca with money, with the gun he fired at the Pope, and with other forms of organizational assistance; and that the network extended to Bulgarians in Rome. Finally—and this was Marvin Kalb's "scoop" (although at least some American government officials knew it earlier)—the pope had sent a message to the Kremlin saying that if the Russians invaded Poland, the pope would stand with his people and take a leading role in the resistance to the Red army.

The Claire Sterling article attracted a fair amount of popular attention, but it did not generate much in the way of follow-up from our journalists. Sterling had already been the subject of a considerable campaign of debunking for her earlier work on international terrorism in which she had documented the substantial role of the Soviet Union. For her pains, she had been attacked in the *Village Voice* week after week and even subjected to a particularly nasty piece in the same issue of the *Washington Post Sunday Magazine* that carried an excerpt from her book. At least one ABC News executive was so exercised about Sterling that he issued an internal memorandum suggesting that ABC run nothing on the air that would tend to substantiate the "Sterling-Haig theory" of international terror.

Thus, it was predictably easy for journalists and editors to ignore the original piece, both because its author had already been declared tabu and because *Reader's Digest* itself is considered a low-class source for our elite media folks (Herblock had devoted a particularly savage cartoon to the president when Reagan cited another *Digest* piece in connection with clandestine Soviet involvement in the peace movement). On August 17, the *New York Times* ran a brief Reuter's News Agency story on the Sterling article on page 12; and two days later carried the predictable Soviet denial on page 7. There was no special investigation, no follow-up of their earlier five-man research project.

It was somewhat harder to downplay the story when Marvin Kalb—one of the leading media stars in Washington—embraced the same theory a month later on national television. Yet, according to friends of Kalb, he was surprised when many of his colleagues in the Washington press corps expressed shock and dismay that he would embrace such a view of the Soviet Union.

I was working at the State Department when the NBC show was screened, and many of the State Department correspondents were openly hostile to the notion that the KGB might have been involved in the plot. This was not simply a matter of questioning the evidence—the material that Kalb and Sterling uncovered, although powerful for those willing to follow the logical and circumstantial trail, might not convince an American judge and jury "beyond any reasonable doubt.") Rather, it took the form of a philosophical objection: they doubted that "the Russians would do such a thing." Several of our most celebrated correspondents simply refused to admit the possibility that the Russian government had authorized the assassination of the pope. When I pointed out the considerable number of political assassinations throughout the world that appeared to have been Soviet-directed (from Trotsky in Mexico to Bulgarian dissidents in London to the late premier of Afghanistan and to the late president of North Yemen), they granted those cases, but insisted that the pope was something qualitatively different. Moreover, some of them found Kalb's program overly "cold warriorish."

Thus, Sterling was discounted in advance, thanks in part to the desire to weaken the "Haig theory" of international terrorism, and Kalb was criticized for failure to obtain the decisive proof of Russian involvement. No matter that one almost never obtains decisive proof of clandestine operations—even in the United States where the Freedom of Information Act provides a great amount of information of a sort we shall probably never read in the Kremlin archives—and that even when we finally discover hard evidence of Soviet clandestine activity, it comes some years later, and usually thanks to defectors. No matter, either, that anyone who spoke to high Vatican officials would have found that many of them believed in a Soviet connection.

On November 26, the *New York Times* announced the arrest of Sergei Ivanov Antonov—a Bulgarian airlines employee in Rome—for complicity in the shooting of the pope. The next day, the *Times* carried an interview with an Italian judge who announced that the available evidence did not justify any theory of an international conspiracy. This would establish a pattern of sorts, whereby the actions of Italian magistrates were reported, but the *Times* would carry a goodly amount of opinion from other Italians and (invariably unnamed) Western government officials tending to diminish the credibility of the charges against the alleged conspirators.

On December 17, the *Times* man in Rome, Henry Kamm, filed a story from Jerusalem claiming that "Israeli and West German intelligence and security sources with a special interest in international terrorism are skeptical of charges of a Bulgarian connection in last year's attempted assassination of Pope John Paul II by a Turk."[15] Kamm made a good deal of this alleged Israeli skepticism, especially as his Israeli sources provided him with abundant evidence that the Communist bloc was deeply involved in international terrorism, even to the point of revealing that three of the most radical PLO leaders were currently in the same Bulgarian hotel in which Agca had stayed for fifty days.

I asked Israeli officials if they could confirm Kamm's account of their government's skepticism, and they responded after several days by denying that any Israeli intelligence official had made such a statement. Indeed, within a few weeks—on January 2, 1983—a top Israeli military official was quoted by the Associated Press: "Israel believed Italian assertions that there had been a Bulgarian connection—and a link to the Soviet Union—in the attempted assassination of Pope John Paul II." This story, curiously enough, appeared *only* in the early edition of the *Times;* subsequent editions did not carry the AP story, nor, so far as I know, was there any follow-up.

On December 30, Kamm wrote that the evidence available for the Bulgarian link was insufficient to tie the Bulgarian secret police or the KGB to the shooting. And then in January, on a trip to Bulgaria, he gave a remarkable picture of that country:

> In addition to its unusual political stability and absence of dissidence and factionalism, Bulgaria basks in a reputation for economic progress rare in a time of recession and crushing foreign debt in other Communist countries. Its people's standard of living has risen. Food and a broad range of consumer goods are in better supply than they have ever [!] been before, and Sofia today, even at the height of winter, presents a more relaxed and prosperous appearance than it has in this correspondent's 18 years of acquaintance.
>
> The foreign debt stands at a manageable $2.3 billion and is declining as payments are routinely made. From being an almost exclusively agricultural country, Bulgaria has become industrialized with a specialty assigned to it by Comecon, the Communist economic grouping, in electronics. Major Western concerns in the field cooperate with Bulgarian manufacturers and speak of their accomplishments.[16]

How could such a bucolic and progressive country possibly have been involved in an assassination attempt? For the next several weeks, it seemed as if *Times* reporters (and a total of five was put on the story) could not find anyone in the Western world who believed that the evidence was convincing. At the State Department, Bernard Gwertzman got the official line: "United States intelligence officials remain intrigued but unconvinced by allegations in Italy that Bulgaria instigated the attempted instigation." Moreover, Gwertzman surfaced another subtheme in the story, thanks to State Department officials: the whole thing was simply an internal Italian debate. "Italian leaders are divided on the case. The Socialist Party . . . has accused the Bulgarians, and by implication, the Soviet Union of instigating the plot against the Pope as well as in gunrunning, drug smuggling and cooperation with Italian Red Brigades terrorists.

But the dominant Christian Democrats have been more restrained."[17] The same point was made by the *Washington Post*'s Rome stringer, Sari Gilbert.

Finally, there was the *Times* editorial position, published on December 18. First, the "moral point": "when it comes to assassinations of state, Americans have reason to test the evidence soberly, and to avoid excessive sanctimony." That is, in the matter of state assassinations, we are presumably primary practitioners. Second, the logic of the situation: "If any nation was implicated, it erred foully and foolishly. Killing a Polish Pope would not have made Poland less rebellious; relying on the silence of a deranged zealot risks devastating exposure. Scruples aside, the command to eliminate a statesman is the last resort of a bankrupt diplomacy." Finally, the whole thing may well be a misunderstanding:

> [W]hen the Congo was in turmoil in 1960, [Eisenhower's] angry words were taken by aides as an order to assassinate President Lumumba. In this and other cases, notably Fidel Castro's, the C.I.A. acted on murky authority that would preserve official "deniability" and came up with harebrained plots that, mercifully, failed. . . .
>
> In a world of murderous bureaucracies, crimes of state are not so much ordered as implied. That Yuri Andropov willed an attack on John Paul II is possible but hardly proven. That his people became mired in a sleazy conspiracy on imagined authority is a likelihood Americans should be the first to understand.

Crimes of state are certainly ordered. In the United States, with our legalistic fetishism, not only an explicit presidential order, but congressional approval is required for any covert action, and even back in Eisenhower's day, an explicit order would have been necessary. In fact, because there is only the flimsiest evidence on which to hang the claim that the United States wanted, let alone attempted, the assassination of Lumuba, those who claim it have to resort to the expedient of suggesting that Eisenhower somehow "implied" his wishes. Furthermore, the *Times*—along with a surprising number of others—had the wrong culprit; a decision of such magnitude in the Kremlin would have to have been made at the Politburo level, not by the head of the KGB. Thus, it was Brezhnev and company (Andropov included, of course) who would have had to make the decision.

What about the strategic considerations? The Polish crisis threatened the entire Soviet Empire (as it still does, albeit not with the same immediacy), and there were three crucial figures in the Solidarity phenomenon: Cardinal Wyszynski, Pope Wojtyla, and Lech Walesa. The first was dying in Poland (and had been given six weeks to live as of the time of the Agca operation); both of the others appear to have been targetted by the Russians for assassination. The *Times* might believe that a movement deprived of its leaders remains as threatening as before, but few others would agree. From the Kremlin's standpoint, a pope who might go to Poland to lead the resistance was a dangerous man, indeed, and was better off in history than in the Vatican.

But more to the point, neither the *Times* editorialists nor their correspondents realized that the Agca case was only one among many and that the weight of evidence in the hands of Italian judges was growing almost daily.

The information came from several independent Italian judges, not from the activities of the secret services or the police. The Italian judiciary is exceedingly independent, and often keeps its own counsel, even in cases with delicate international implications. Thus, even officials of the Italian government, including the secret services, were not abreast of the cases, and had to depend on the judges for what little they did know. One of the results of this state of affairs was that American officials—almost always the basic sources for American correspondents, whether at home or abroad—could not provide the journalists with any hard information.

Thus, throughout December, while the Italians issued one

charge after another, and the Italian press was filled with information about Bulgarian subversion in Italy, the readers of the *New York Times* along with those of most leading dailies and weeklies and, of course, television viewers, were unaware of the considerable body of evidence in the hands of Italian judges. They did not realize that the Italians had arrested a Bulgarian agent and an Italian working at a high level in the socialist trade union who had contacts with Solidarity in Poland, nor had they heard that the Bulgarians had been caught deeply involved in an enormous drugs- and arms-smuggling operation in northern Italy. Nor did they realize that the Bulgarian agent in question (Luigi Scricciolo) was providing information that matched what Agca had been saying under interrogation, thus giving the Italians further confirmation of the existence of a Soviet-inspired "Plot to Kill the Pope."

RECONSIDERATIONS

During the very week that the *New York Times* was urging Americans to refrain from thinking the worst of the Soviet Union, the mood of the elite press began to change. Of the three major networks, only CBS systematically ignored the story or gave it short shrift late in its evening news broadcast. At the same time, the weeklies *Time* and *Newsweek* visibly began to change. In the last edition of the year (published December 27 but dated a week later), *Time* revealed that the pope himself believed that Agca was part of a KGB plot and went on to deal with the growing evidence. The following week, both *Time* and *Newsweek* gave considerable space to an investigation of the new information; *Newsweek* made it its cover story and moved a giant step toward accepting KGB involvement:

> . . . there is reason to believe that the Bulgarian secret police recruited Agca, through Turkish intermediaries, into the ranks of its hired guns, and that he was armed and supported by the Bulgarians when he shot the pope.[18]

Time came to much the same conclusion that week: "the normally cautious Italian politicians exuded confidence that they possessed the evidence to incriminate, at the very least, the Bulgarian secret service."[19] What had changed the minds of the weeklies? First, there had been the presentations to Parliament by Italian ministers, above all Defense Minister Lagorio's strong statement that the shooting of the pope was "a true act of war in a time of peace." This did not, however, sway Henry Kamm, who wrote in the *New York Times* on December 21 that "a Government official said that [Lagorio's statements] reflected a desire by the Socialists to exploit the present public concern over Bulgaria for political advantage by assuming positions in defense of Italian security harder than those of their Christian Democratic partners in Government." Second, the interlocking evidence was beginning to be appreciated, and more information about Agca's Bulgarian connections was available.

Bit by bit, the logic of the case began to assert itself, and even some columnists who had previously been skeptical changed their minds—Joseph Kraft, for example, and Georgie Anne Geyer. The latter explained that the pope represented a systematic challenge to the Soviet Empire: "a brilliant and sophisticated kind of infiltration—and it terrified and enraged the Soviets, for whom murder has historically been a normal tool of diplomacy."[20]

Furthermore, as *Time* had observed, the "normally cautious" Italians were taking a hard position on the case, and this required some explanation. Historically, Italy has been quite soft on international terrorists; the normal treatment of Arabs caught in flagrante delicto on Italian soil preparing a terrorist attack has been to book them on a private flight to Tripoli or, in the good old days, to Beirut. All of a sudden, here we have several judges of impeccable reputations taking a hard line, refusing to drop charges, and even holding firm in the teeth of some quite violent language coming from Sofia and Moscow. Would they act in this fashion without compelling evidence? Would they jeopardize Italy's national interest (which includes, at a minimum, good commercial relations with the Soviet Empire) without something approaching solid proof? Would they risk their reputations on the basis of flimsy, circumstantial evidence? It seemed most unlikely. And as the columnists thought it over, it seemed that even the Americans' reluctance to accredit the Bulgarian connection represented a sort of confirmation. Flora Lewis wrote in the *New York Times:*

> The sinister aura of this spy story too fantastic for fiction is enhanced, not diminished, by the remarkable caution of Western governments. Even President Reagan . . . is ducking the question of possible Kremlin complicity now. That is obviously because it is so dreadful to contemplate the consequences if more damaging facts do emerge.[21]

Flora Lewis, thus, launched a new theme: the Russians may well be guilty, but it's best for us not to say so. She noted that the assassination of Archduke Ferdinand of Austria-Hungary at Sarajevo had been instrumental in kicking off the First World War, and she warned that we must "prepare against impetuous action and an emotional response that could make St. Peter's Square comparable to Sarajevo."

In the weeks that followed throughout January and February, this theme was reiterated over and over again: tracing the assassination plot back to the Kremlin might endanger world peace (or a possible summit between Reagan and Andropov, or arms control talks, or "good relations"). Indeed, by the end of January, Robert Toth of the *Los Angeles Times* was told that "the CIA believes that Bulgarian officials knew in advance of a terrorist's plans to kill Pope John Paul II but never thought they would be carried out." And Toth noted later on that this theory would "remove at least one stumbling block in the way of a summit meeting" because, in the words of an American official, "Reagan could never meet Andropov if it was proved unequivocally that the Bulgarians, and therefore the Soviet KGB, was behind the plot."[22]

The elite press had fallen victim to its usual double standard. It is inconceivable that the *New York Times* would urge the Kremlin to downplay evidence of American involvement in clandestine activity, even if no murder were involved; it is virtually imposible that an American journalist would take at face value a statement from an *American* intelligence official along the lines of "please take it easy on this story because it's bad for our relations with the Russians" if there were abundant evidence of American plotting to murder a foreign leader. In such a case, our journalists would be bravely waving the banners of "the people's right to know," would demand an end to "official cover-ups," and would insist that "the truth must out, and let the chips fall where they may." No such cry was heard from CBS (in fact hardly anything about this story was heard from CBS), the *New York Times,* or even those publications—like *Time* and *Newsweek* of late—that came to take the evidence seriously.

In the story of the "Plot to Kill the Pope," our journalists weren't practicing journalism; they were trying to conduct policy. First, they made an assessment: it would be crazy for the Russians to do such a thing (or, a major variant, it was done so sloppily, it couldn't have been the Russians); therefore, it wasn't them. Then, when the evidence became too great to ignore, they shifted gears; yes, the Russians were involved, but we don't care for the consequences of this discovery, so let's "limit the damage" (this was the point of trying to stop the trail at the Bulgarians' door rather than following it to Moscow) or, if that fails, deny its significance. As a last resort, we can invoke real-politik: national interest demands détente; therefore, don't bother us with these James Bond-type stories.

At the beginning of the pope story, many journalists were hostile to the KGB connection because it would give added credibility to Haig's claims that the Russians were behind a good deal of terrorism in the world. But in several stories in early 1983, it was casually revealed that most knowledgeable people in the West are thoroughly convinced of this Soviet connection, particularly in the case of Italy. When Henry Kamm quoted his unnamed Israeli intelligence source to undermine the Bulgarian connection, he went on to provide considerable proof of Communist bloc involvement in international terrorism. Sari Gilbert, the *Washington Post*'s stringer in Rome, revealed on March 20 that the Italians were quite convinced of a long-standing connection between Eastern Europe (primarily Czechoslovakia) and the Red Brigades, a point also made by *Time* and *Newsweek*. Thus, those of us who for years have been arguing for such a connection—and were subjected to the most remarkable scorn from our colleagues in the elite media—have been vindicated. But the acceptance of these views is done in such a way as to deprive it of any political impact. It is quite difficult for there to be a serious reassessment in the elite media, for it would necessitate explaining why the many leads were ignored for so many years and why so many stories were spiked. Instead, as part of the "damage limitation" campaign waged around the "Plot to Kill the Pope," the truth is admitted without searching for its consequences.

THE POLITICS OF THE MEDIA

As the Bulgarian case shows, our journalistic elite suffers from some of the same defects as our political elite. This is only to be expected because journalists, diplomats, and politicians go to the same schools and universities and assimilate the same popular culture. In many ways, they reinforce each other (nor could it be otherwise because they depend so much on each other: the journalists on the government officials for their stories, the officials on the journalists for their glory). Yet, familiarity with American officials has reinforced the media's contempt for our leaders, whereas foreign countries—including some of our enemies—receive surprisingly gentle treatment. The tradition of investigative journalism that has led to so many exposés of American behavior has rarely been applied to other countries, except for some friends and/or allies of the United States: Israel, Iran, El Salvador, and Argentina are perhaps the most obvious examples.

In part, the investigative zeal directed against the American government and those of our friends and allies can be explained on purely operational grounds: our totalitarian opponents do not open their archives to journalists, nor do they leak as do officials in America and other democratic (or inefficient authoritarian) countries. In the Warsaw Pact countries, leakers are treated as traitors, and even the release of routine economic information can be punished by death. Yet, notwithstanding this important difference in the conduct of journalistic investigations in various countries, the elite media have developed a double standard for reporting about foreign governments.

The United States and its allies are held up against standards that are not applied to the Soviet Union and *its* allies. Relatively minor human rights transgressions in a friendly country (especially if ruled by an authoritarian government of the Right) are given far more attention and more intense criticism than far graver sins of countries hostile to us. Accusations against our enemies are often treated more skeptically than those directed against us, even though our own government, along with those of most other democracies, strains mightily to tell the truth, while the Soviets, along with many other totalitarian regimes, have entire government agencies to spread systematic distortions of the truth (the most celebrated example being the KGB's Disinformation Directorate).

To be sure, there are some excellent American journalists (the word "reporter"—which suggests a suitably modest view of the profession—is hardly found any more), and there are many first-rate articles. Yet, as Walter Laqueur has rightly observed, it is virtually impossible to get an accurate picture of the world from the American press. And even when the real story is written, it is often years late, as in the case of the conspiracy of silence among Western correspondents stationed in China during the last years of Mao. Once a moderate liberalization had set in under Deng Ciou Peng, the horror stories of the cultural revolution appeared in the West, but not at the time.

Stories that appear well after the fact do not have the same political impact as those that are written while events are in progress; so, the massacres at the Palestinian camps of Sabra and Shatila in Lebanon in the summer of 1982, where between *four* and *six hundred* persons were murdered, got hundreds of times as much space and infinitely more outrage when reported at the time they occurred, than did the murder of between *ten* and *thirty thousand* persons in the Syrian city of Hama a year earlier, which wasn't reported for several months. Most of the outrage over Sabra and Shatila was directed against Israel, which was indirectly responsible for the massacres, whereas little outrage was devoted to the Lebanese Christians who did the act. In like manner, the Israeli invasion of Lebanon was violently denounced, whereas the Syrian/Druze/Palestinian occupation of Lebanon a year later was not condemned (indeed in many newspapers and magazines it was written off as a return to Lebanese "normalcy"), and reports of massacres larger than Sabra and Shatila were frequently not carried at all in the American press.

It is hard to escape the conclusion that much of this writing and broadcasting rests on political conviction rather than investigative difficulties alone. In the case of the attempt to kill the pope, the American press would have deluged us with stories had there been the slightest indication that the CIA was involved in it. Similarly, stories about the alleged ill effects of Agent Orange, a chemical defoliant used in the Vietnam War by our armed forces, far outnumber those about Yellow Rain and other poisons used by Soviet proxies in Laos, Cambodia, Afghanistan, Eritrea, and elsewhere.

The ideological nature of the double standard can also be seen in the relative authority given statements from Western and non-Western governments. As mentioned, a denial by Qaddafi leads "CBS News" to speak of "alleged" Libyan involvement in Chad (after all, it was only alleged by the American government, and thus it was somehow suspect), while the same network ran, without properly identifying it, a Cuban-made film to challenge a claim by the president that the Soviet Union was shipping weapons to Nicaragua. And no less a figure than Seymour Hersh, a Pulitzer-prize-winning correspondent from the *New York Times*, actually wrote that the Vietnamese "re-education" camps created after the North overran the South, were rather well-liked by the South Vietnamese who were sent there. Hersh's article appeared in 1979,[23] at a time when the seas of Southeast Asia were filled with boat people desperately fleeing Vietnamese repression. Finally, Loren Jenkins of the *Washington Post*, who won a Pulitzer Prize for his coverage of the Israeli invasion of Lebanon, claimed on a National Public Radio broadcast that he believed the Israelis had actively assisted and had watched the massacres in Sabra and Shatila.[24] This turned out to have been false.

Most of the distortion of reality comes from the political goals of the Fourth Estate and from the weaknesses journalists share with the other members of the American elite. But some of the themes come from our enemies. The large disinformation apparatus of the Soviet Union and the bloc countries is aimed at discrediting the United States, dividing us from our friends, and disconcerting us at home. Numerous journalists in foreign countries have been identified as Soviet disinformation agents; some are in jail (the most famous such case occurred in France a few years ago when the heir to the Pathé movie empire was convicted as a Soviet agent of influence and sentenced to a substantial jail term. The story was not carried by any major media outlet in the United States). It would be amazing if there were no similar agents in the American media.

Few people enjoy discussing this subject, and it is generally misunderstood. Disinformation is not simply spreading lies; it is a systematic misrepresentation of the world that portrays the Soviet Union as peaceloving and the United States as aggressively expansionist. In this campaign, elements of the truth, half-truths, and outright lies all play a role in the Soviets' attempt to turn people against us.

One will rarely find the complete disinformation "line" in any publication or broadcast, but elements of it certainly are present with some frequency. Perhaps the greatest success of Soviet disinformation is the constant cynicism about American *motives* that characterizes so much of contemporary journalism. Thus, many people tend to forget that if the United States prevails in a conflict, we will strain to support democratic forces and a peaceful evolution toward a more equitable system. If the Soviet Union prevails, the totalitarian curtain falls over the victims. Yet a surprising number of journalists act as if Soviet support for terrorists and guerrillas were based on some sort of humanitarian impulse, whereas our opposition to such forces were the result of unqualified support for any and all anti-Communist regimes. "One man's terrorist is another man's freedom fighter," a slogan oft repeated, suggests that condemnation of terrorism depends on whose ox is being gored. In reality, significant terrorism *only* occurs in relatively open societies (the efficient dictatorships quickly clamp down) and always drives the government to greater restrictions on individual and group freedom. The fight for freedom is against regimes that are unfree, not against the Western democracies and inefficient dictatorships that have been the targets of most of the terrorist attacks in the past decade. But these points are rarely made by the media, and it does not much matter whether our journalists have accepted disinformation or simply forgotten the fundamental differences between East and West; the effect is the same, and it makes it harder to design and to conduct good policies.

Two final points: the double standard, the intense suspicion of everything done by the American government, and the insistence on absolute license for the media, all lead journalists to become collaborators with the terrorists, who depend on the media for much of their effect. Serious editors and journalists are aware of this, but refuse to sit down and design a responsible policy of cooperation with the government.

Suspicion of American intentions and the increase in media power that comes about when American officials and policies become the object of press scandals drive many journalists to seek out the secrets of the American government. The phenomenon of "leaks" is intensely bothersome, for the damage it does extends far beyond the particular story in question. If leaking becomes endemic, reasonable policymaking becomes even more difficult. First, it makes serious discussion almost impossible, for people are understandably afraid to speak their mind if anything they say may appear in print. This applies equally to our own government officials and to foreign leaders. In the real world (as opposed to the one described in the press and in most of our textbooks), leaders often say one thing in public and something quite different in private. Some Americans consider this immoral and delight in exposing such hypocrisy (particularly when Americans do it), but it has been a legitimate form of political behavior for centuries, and it will not change. It is vitally important for the leaders of the United States to know the real state of affairs, and this can occur only if our own officials and foreign leaders feel free to speak their minds. But they do not like to see their private thoughts in the newspapers, and they will not share their private thoughts (or their secrets) unless they can be certain that confidences will be respected.

The same holds for intelligence matters. In many areas of the world, our enemies' societies are closed to normal ways of gathering information and our only hope of finding out what is going on is to gather information by secret means. To put the matter bluntly, citizens of those countries have to commit treason so that our security can be protected. And if we are going to receive such information, the identity and activity of such persons must be protected. In this area, leaks can mean death. But even if the sources survive the leaks, the repeated appearance of "secrets" in the media eventually convinces sensitive sources to cease sharing information with the American government.

You would think that government officials would not leak such information and that newspaper people would think twice before publishing it, yet although such reasonable requirements are often observed, every so often something happens to demonstrate that this is frequently ignored.

In 1981, the American government received information indicating that Libya's Muammar Qaddafi had recruited a team of terrorists to murder President Reagan. This information reached the press in garbled form, and at a certain point—before any stories had appeared—several leading journalists called me about the story. I pleaded with them not to publish anything about the matter. I put it this way:

> I shall have nothing to say about the substance of this story, now or later. But I believe that you will not know whether it is true or false, and I also believe—very strongly—that you should publish nothing, regardless of the truth of the story. If it is false, you risk provoking hysteria over nothing, thus forcing the government to appear to respond to a threat that does not actually exist. If it is true, then you risk both preventing us from catching these assassins and drying up future sources of information. In the worst case, both the President and some brave person in Tripoli may die, just because our press could not behave responsibly.

Stories came out in a torrent. But some months later, a leading *Time* magazine correspondent told me bitterly that he felt "he had been had" on the story, that *Time* had printed a lot of nonsense about it (as indeed it had), and that he was going to get even with some of his sources. The *Time* man thereby introduced yet another element in the ongoing conflict between media and government: the media make their own standards, but woe to the government official who does not tell the truth, the whole truth, and nothing but the truth to a journalist, even if the official is discussing something he should have been silent about in the first place.

On the other hand, there are times when American journalists swallow the most remarkable nonsense about foreign governments when the source is an American who the journalists like. In 1975, when the Lockheed scandal broke in Washington—thanks to the activities of the Senate subcommittee headed by the late Frank Church—it had a devastating effect on the Italian government. Leaks from the Church committee indicated that the defense minister of the time, Luigi Gui, had taken bribes from Lockheed representatives. Church himself confirmed these leaks to Italian journalists, who understandably raised such a hue and cry that Gui resigned his position. Yet I had an unusually good reason to believe that Gui was in fact innocent in this matter, for within a few days of the scandal in Washington, Gui called me and the *New York Times* correspondent in Rome, Alvin Shuster, to his office. On his desk were documents from the Church committee. Gui said to us, "I do not speak English, so I am not in a position to understand these documents. But I know I have not taken any money from Lockheed, so I would be grateful if you two would read these documents and tell me how it is that the U.S. Senate has come to the erroneous conclusion that I have taken bribes." We read the material—apparently everything the Senate had gathered on the case—and could find nothing that incriminated Gui, and we told him so. Gui then asked us whether it was possible for him to sue Senator Church, and we said we thought it was impossible. He then traveled to Washington and submitted his case to the SEC, from which he received a clean bill of health. But he could never get Church to admit there was no evidence against him, nor could he get the case raised in an American court. An Italian investigation similarly cleared him, but his career was destroyed. He was one of many innocent victims of this and other scandals, for by the time all the evidence was in, no one was interested in it; yet, at the time of the scandal, few were inclined to accept Gui's word against that of an American Senator on a moralistic rampage.

Leaks are of a piece with the other ways in which our ability to conduct foreign policy is weakened by the growing power of the Fourth Estate. The leak is almost always a gambit in the Washington political game as well as a part of the policy process. The leakers may be currying favor with the media or may be planting information to influence a specific decision. In the first case, they are helping themselves by enhancing the prestige of a journalist; in the second, they are using the media as a stage for their preferred policies. Interestingly, the most damaging leaks traditionally have come from a high level, not—as might be imagined—from frustrated bureaucrats unable to get a hearing within the system. According to former Director of Central Intelligence Richard Helms, the really damaging leaks—those that have enraged President Reagan and produce serious internal investigations—almost invariably come from high-level officials and more often than not from the White House itself.

Helms recalls times when the FBI was asked to track down the leaker and was usually able to do so. But the leakers turned out to be at the very top of the government pyramid, and in the end, the president took no action. This closes the circle: leaking begins with a political motive and continues because of politics. If the president wants to end this practice, he can do it; but he will have to fire some of his own appointees, endure a political firestorm, and insist that the White House itself become a model of behavior.

THE LAWYERS

The lawyers were part of the Third Estate and actively participated in its rise to power in the eighteenth and nineteenth centuries. We find them again in the ascendancy of the Fourth

Estate, sometimes in the role of protagonists, on other occasions as accomplices of the ascendant media.

Without vigorous legal defense of the absolutist interpretation of the First Amendment, the media could never have achieved their current share of political power. The insistence that government should not have secrets from the press but that the press can keep secrets from everyone else is so paradoxical and preposterous that it is better explained by reference to political struggle than to principle. It is clear that a free press is a useful check on arbitrary political power, but if the press is not held accountable, then arbitrary political power will flow there, with unfortunate consequences for American government.

By and large, this threat is downplayed, both by media spokespersons and by the lawyers and judges who are sympathetic to them. Indeed, the political role of the press is rarely admitted by such persons, even by those who should know better. One of the smartest and most elegant legal writers in America, Judge Richard Neely (author of *How Courts Govern America*) argues that "the media are crusaders because it is profitable, not because they are civic charities. Since unearthing corruption, treachery, and incompetence in government brings an audience, all news media and all elected officials are usually portrayed as natural enemies."[25]

Unlike the rest of his book, in which he is unusually balanced and full of sympathy for public officials, Neely comes out solidly on the side of the media in their struggle with the other branches of government and with private citizens. Not a word is spent in behalf of those who might be libeled; instead, we hear of the dangers of libel suits to the media:

> With the right laws and sufficiently high punitive damages for injury to reputation, papers can quickly be put out of business. This process of putting newspapers out of business when they are negligent has been characterized by the U.S. Supreme Court as creating a "chilling effect on First Amendment rights," and in fact there are few things more

chilling than the prospect of bankruptcy. If this . . . were permitted, papers which are currently energetic in pointing out political problems [Note the careful understatement!] would become like most small-town rags and would be reduced to carrying noncontroversial national news, local social events, sports, and the lonely hearts column, because they could not afford to risk the consequences of their own negligence. . . . Thus we have *the miracle of the First Amendment defense* and the expeditious, cheap device of the summary judgment, by which the trial court can dismiss a complaint before the defendant has to mortgage the family farm to pay his lawyer. (Emphasis added.)[26]

These days, however, it is the libeled and not the libeler who have to worry about bankruptcy. The big papers and the big networks have money and lawyers (and they have insurance against big libel decisions), and they hardly need to worry about bankruptcy stemming from their "negligence." The greater concern today is the unregulated, unaccountable activities of media to expand their own power.

Just as the lawyers have worked to give the media unprecedented power, so they have expanded their own role in the formulation and conduct of government policy. The lawyers' importance in domestic policy is well known, to the point where a modest best-seller is entitled *How Courts Govern America* (although its author, a judge, stresses that it is judges, not lawyers who really count . . . to which it may be replied that if there were fewer lawyers, the judges wouldn't count so much). Depending on which source is considered most accurate, we have one lawyer for every four or five hundred people in the country, a ratio that in turn is either twenty or twenty-five times that of Japan, ten times that of France, and three times that of England. Both critics and supporters of the growth of the legal profession agree on the meaning of this trend (which has seen the number of lawyers in the United States go from 269,000 in 1960 to 590,000 twenty years later): consensus is breaking down, and the public is searching for new sources of authority. But even if one accepts this diagnosis, one is hard pressed to account for the willingness of the judges and lawyers to permit certain matters to reach a courtroom. From the *New York Times* on October 21, 1982 comes the following bit of evidence:

> Huntington, W. Va., Oct. 20 (AP)—A 5-year-old boy haled into court by school officials was cleared today.
>
> A circuit judge dropped charges against the child, whom school officials had accused of disrupting his kindergarten class. But the judge ordered a Welfare Department hearing to determine "what to do with the child." In the meantime, Judge D. B. Daugherty ordered that the child be accompanied by an adult if he returned to school. . . .

A year earlier, a seven-year-old in Florida was sued when he hit a friend, and the case actually was tried. The president of the American Bar Association in 1981 wrote of children taking to the courts to sue their parents, of jilted lovers suing for broken dates, and of ministers purchasing malpractice insurance, and he pronounced these characteristics of "a society suffering from fundamental ills of which hyperlexis is a symptom."[27] Maybe so, but they are also characteristics of a legal profession that is all too happy to bring such questions to trial and of a judiciary that orders adults to accompany five-year-olds to kindergarten. In short, the lawyers and the judges are pleased to acquire greater power at the expense of those who used to hold it, whether families, legislatures, or presidents.

It should come as no surprise that the lawyers play a very active role in the day-to-day conduct of foreign policy, in areas where one would hardly expect them. In November 1983, for example, I was asked to help read and organize the thousands of pounds of documents that American armed forces captured on the island of Grenada. Late one afternoon, I came across a carton that contained hundreds of unmailed letters written by Cubans in Grenada back to Havana. The letters had uncanceled Cuban postage stamps, suggesting that they would have been pouched back to Cuba and mailed there; I offered to help read

them, only to be told by a Defense Intelligence Agency official
that they had to remain sealed until the Pentagon's lawyers decided whether they could be opened, or whether they had to be
sent to Cuba to be posted. (I do not know the final decision, but
if the lawyers ruled that the letters be sent to Cuba, I would be
inclined to mail the lawyers along with the envelopes.)

On another occasion, in 1982, two Nicaraguan pilots had
flown an airplane to Costa Rica and asked for political asylum.
Some time later they arrived in Washington, and they had such
interesting and important stories to tell about the Sandinista
regime that many of us at the State Department felt that they
should testify before some congressional committees. Once
again, one of the lawyers came forward. "Just a moment," he
said, "these men made off with a Nicaraguan airplane. That constitutes a prima facie case of grand larceny. We have an extradi-
tion treaty with Nicaragua. If these men go public in Washington and the Sandinistas ask that we send them back, we might
have to extradite them." Some of the State Department officials
present at the meeting expressed the sentiment that the Nicaraguans would be extradited over the lawyer's dead body, but, of
course, he eventually prevailed, and the Nicaraguans never testi-
fied.

All these cases—domestic and international alike—show
that the concepts of traditional authority, including the centuries old notion of *raison d'état,* have lost their sway in the United
States. They also show that the courts are trying to claim authority for themselves. In the last year of the Carter administration, some of the most powerful lawyers in America secretly
worked on an agreement between the United States and Iran
that would "unfreeze" Iranian assets in American and European
banks and, at the same time, lead to the release of the American
hostages in Iran. At a certain stage in the discussions—in which
American government officials worked hand-in-glove with lawyers representing American banks—the lawyers asked Secretary
of State Muskie and his colleagues to leave them alone so that

they could, in the words of one of the lawyers, "have a little dogfight" over interest rates. After the private discussion among the lawyers a new element of anxiety was introduced into the negotiations because "the debate over the interest rates was the first crack in the united front that had been maintained by the bank lawyers—a reminder that the public interest was not necessarily foremost, and that the client's was. Even the fate of the fifty-two hostages had not obscured that fact at the meeting."[28]

Yet, these same lawyers were considerably put out some time later when the Algerians, who were negotiating on behalf of the Iranians, refused to deal with the American lawyers. "For some reason [the Algerians] didn't trust anyone who was not a U.S. government official, so [the American lawyers] were excluded from the ensuing negotiating sessions."[29]

The brilliant Harvard sociologist David Riesman has observed that excessive litigation in domestic affairs erodes American productivity and the strength of our society and, in the end, makes it harder for us to compete with other nations,[30] and the same applies to the excessive use of lawyers in international affairs. At a minimum, decision making is slowed below acceptable tempos; at worst, the lawyers foment a "fear to act" that further centralizes power in the hands of the lawyers and judges. By the late 1970s, many Americans were rightly worrying about an "Imperial Judiciary."

The rise of the lawyers, judges, and journalists is part of the decline of the traditional American elite as new groups strive to acquire the power that has become available because of the default of the older ones. The phenomenon is politically understandable, but it has the gravest consequences for the national interest—for the new groups are unqualified to do the work of the government, much as they would like to. If most American foreign editors and foreign correspondents are insufficiently cultured and informed to make policy, the lawyers are even less qualified to play such a role. And like the journalists, they will continue to seek greater power unless our leaders in government reassert their own prerogatives and manage to lead the country. If this does not happen, our incoherence and unpredictability will increase, along with our risk.

THE NEW CLASS VERSUS THE GOVERNMENT

In their quest for greater power, the legal and journalistic groups—what might be termed the "new class"—have predictably concentrated their political guns on the holders of traditional positions. Anyone who has had to fill out the seemingly endless "disclosure" forms prior to accepting a moderately high position in the American government has undoubtedly asked himself, "Is it worth it?" I know one current ambassador who was fortunate enough to reach a ripe age with considerable assets, and it took him and his lawyers a full month to provide the information required. Furthermore, he knew that if he ever became a target for the press, all of his activities over his many years would be carefully scrutinized for any sign of suspicious goings-on and that even if he had behaved properly throughout his life, his reputation would be badly damaged by such an investigation. This man proved to be an excellent ambassador, as was to be expected, but, like every other high government official, he lived with a kind of sword of Damocles over his head throughout his service.

The point here is not that we should drop ethical requirements for our public servants; far from it. But this is not the Kingdom of God, it is the Kingdom of Man, and our standards have to be appropriate to the human race and not those required for entry to Heaven (indeed, those utopian experiments that have demanded saintly credentials for their leaders have generally ended badly). Impossibly high standards and relentless examination of every detail of our leaders' lives will produce less interesting leaders, not necessarily more gifted ones.

We the people are entitled to know a good deal about our leaders, but when things reach the point where worthy and good men and women refuse to come to work for the federal government because they do not wish to see every detail of their biography laid out before a hostile press, we need to restore some semblance of balance. As Friedrich Dürrenmatt has devoted a lifetime to demonstrate, no human being can stand up to a minute examination of his biography. Everyone is guilty of something, whether a sin of omission or commission. It follows from this that any time the media decide to zero in on a public figure, eventually enough will be uncovered either to bring about the figure's political demise or—in the case of a person whose skin has not been sufficiently thickened for such an ordeal—his "voluntary" departure from the scene. In another of the paradoxes by which the media have gained so much power, there are many restrictions on the FBI, making it very difficult for them to investigate a person without solid grounds for suspecting criminal activity; but the media have no such restrictions. They can snoop around simply because they suspect that they will find something interesting (of course, sooner or later, they always will). This simply has to stop, for eventually persons of quality and sensitivity will refuse to accept positions of importance in this country. There are many good people who do not wish to have every detail of their lives exposed to public analysis . . . and they are right. Not only are they likely to be damaged, but they have virtually no chance of equitable redress, even if the "accusations" against them in the press are false.

I have myself been "accused" of having worked for the CIA, and I feel strongly that this represents at least some threat to my personal security, especially when I travel abroad. Having never been in the employ of the Central Intelligence Agency, I once tried to bring libel charges against a publication, and was lucky enough to find a good lawyer who was willing to take the case *pro bono*. But he told me I would have to put up at least $10,000 to cover expenses because the publication would make

us travel overseas, interview "sources," and so forth. Finally, he
said, we would not be able to collect any money, even if we won
the case, because the publication in question was structured so
as not to have any assets worth mentioning. Thus, to respond
effectively to these allegations, I would have to go into debt.
There is a remedy for such matters: a law requiring an automatic, stiff fine for publications that *incorrectly* accuse someone
of being a spy. This would quickly put an end to most such
libelous activities because editors can rarely be confident of such
"evidence" as they are given. At the same time, the law would
protect accurate publications (as it should).

But whatever the specific remedy for such grievances, it will
not greatly improve the general problem of an unaccountable
media structurally opposed to the American government. If the
media are going to be given the same powers and perquisites as
a government agency, then they should be subjected to the same
checks and balances and held up to similar standards of accountability as other government agencies. If, on the other hand, they
are going to be considered a special interest with privileges and
prerogatives greater than those of any other special interest (remember that the First Amendment has to do with freedom of
religion as well as freedom of speech), then they should be
firmly relegated to the private sector. Either way, we should
strive to encourage competition among the media and some sort
of "watchdog" body for the media should be established—*not*
the so-called ombudsman, who is paid by the news media and,
therefore, treads lightly on their exposed warts, corns, and cal-
luses—with authority to require prominently placed corrections
and apologies (and perhaps even authority to recommend com-
pensation for damaged parties) for erroneous or grossly misleading stories. Finally, there should be a clean separation between
government and media: no more government offices for journalists (they should make appointments with government officials and check in and out of buildings along with all other private citizens). This will not end leaking, nor will it eliminate the

close personal relationships between journalists and policymakers that make "scoops" possible, but it will ease the media pressure on the government and make it possible for officials to concentrate more on their policy problems and less on their public image.

If a more reasonable arrangement is not made, we are faced with two possible outcomes: either there will be a violent anti-media reaction, leading to government regulation of the media and real damage to freedom of the press, or else the media will eventually prevail, thus producing a kind of government-by-public-opinion-poll. Such an outcome—which might be called electronic mobocracy—is precisely what Alexis de Tocqueville feared, seeing that the egalitarian tendencies of American democracy might degenerate into the "tyranny of the majority." These days, the pollsters—increasingly in tandem with the journalists—define and, on some occasions, present themselves as the true representatives of that majority.

Either of these possible outcomes—a runaway press or a suppressed press—would be very damaging to the country, and it would make an intelligent foreign policy virtually impossible to design and conduct. But institutional "solutions" cannot save an elite that is incapable of leadership. A free, generally unrestrained press is useful, precious, and sometimes invaluable; but an efficient, clear-minded government is far more important.

Although it is necessary to make the media accountable, that is only one step toward better policy—but by no means the most important one; it is also necessary for the government to lead the country. Every president in memory has complained about leaks and about the unfairness and inaccuracy of the media, yet with the exception of a handful of issues, no administration since that of John Kennedy has enthusiastically attempted to present its case—with vigor, as they used to say—to the public. There have been exceptions, and they suggest that if the government accepts the rules of the game and takes its case to the people, it will do very well indeed. Thus, Carter overcame considerable hostility and got the Panama Canal treaties passed and Reagan beat back a major challenge to his second-year budgets. These victories—in the face of intense domestic opposition and, in the case of Reagan, media hostility as well—show that the government can achieve many of its objectives if it defends itself with passion and continuity. But most of the time, our officials content themselves with single media "events" rather than conducting extended campaigns. It is the latter that work, whereas the former simply play into the hands of the media by providing them with a single event that they can then place in a broader context. But an ongoing public policy and educating the public about the real geopolitical interests of the United States and the true options available to the nation cannot be conducted by persons who themselves lack such a vision. In the end, we are back to the basic problem: the creation of a policymaking elite with a proper understanding of the American tradition and its proper place in the world.

5

THE SOVIET EMPIRE

Any discussion of the Soviet Union must begin with a warning: there is much we do not know about the U.S.S.R. Even the most experienced Kremlin watchers are groping in the dark much of the time. Our knowledge of the inner workings of the Soviet elite is severely limited; we are woefully ignorant of the relations among the various factions contending for power, of the internal debates about the economic system (including the crucial role of the military in economic planning), and, above all, of the discussions of strategy within the Politburo.

On the other hand, we do get to know a great deal about the results of the Kremlin's secret deliberations, both domestically and internationally. Moreover, from the actions taken by the Kremlin we can make some fairly well-educated guesses about the objectives of Soviet policy, the dreams that underlie their actions, and the vision of the future on which their policies are based. There seems to be little doubt that the underlying drive for their policies is the belief that theirs is a revolutionary society destined to provide the model for the future of the rest of mankind. Like us, the Russians (and here it is necessary to distinguish the Russians from some of the other nationalities in the Soviet Empire) consider themselves the initiators of a new era in human history, the founders of an international movement

that will inevitably prevail over its opponents. It is fashionable—above all among cynical Western intellectuals who have
no deep political convictions to sustain their own visions of the
future—to say that the leaders in the Kremlin no longer believe
in communism or that they use it merely as a method of maintaining and expanding their political power. In reality, the leaders of the Soviet Empire apparently continue to believe intensely
in communism—as a method of extending Soviet power and also
as a vision of the future of humankind.

At the same time, the Soviet leaders along with their subjects know full well that things have not worked out well in the
Soviet Empire. As will be seen, they recognize the failures of
their society more clearly than do most American leaders, and
no leader in the history of the Soviet Union had a keener appreciation of the discontent and discouragement of the populace
than did Yuri Andropov. After all, his fifteen years atop the
KGB gave him intimate contact with public opinion, especially
with the dissidents he regularly sent to the *gulags*. The death
of Andropov has not removed this knowledge from the Kremlin,
for he elevated many of his old KGB associates to key positions
in the Communist party and the government (but Andropov's
desire to rectify some of the historic structural flaws in the Soviet system is apparently not shared by Chernenko, whose
Brezhnevian conservatism and lack of physical energy have
greatly slowed the tempo of action in the Politburo). But such
recognition of reality has not undermined the belief in the superiority of communism, nor confidence that in the end communism will prevail throughout the world.

One recent event may serve to confirm this apparently paradoxical state of affairs. When American and East Caribbean military forces removed the Communist regime of Grenada in the
autumn of 1983, a vast archive was captured and brought back
to Washington for analysis. This archive constitutes the first
case study of a Soviet takeover of a foreign country that we have

ever had. It is a remarkable body of evidence, for it shows that the first priority set by the Russians (and carried out by their Cuban proxies) was the communization of the island. An enormous quantity of money and manpower was committed to the task of indoctrinating Grenadians in Marxism-Leninism (or, rather, Stalinism, for there was far more of Stalin than of Lenin in the ideological courses on Grenada). This indoctrination took place both at home and overseas as selected Grenadian comrades were sent to Havana, Moscow, East Berlin, Prague, Sofia, Ho Chi Minh City, and even Tripoli, Libya, to study and train. When the New Jewel Movement and the Cuban Communist party drafted a secret agreement for the exchange of personnel, the bulk of the exchanges was in the field of mass propaganda and indoctrination: journalists, experts on church affairs, editorial cartoonists, experts in the use of sound systems for mass rallies, and so forth. Grenadian journalists were sent as far as Angola for meetings with other Communist correspondents and trained in techniques of "third-world journalism."

To be sure, Grenada was not communized; four years did not suffice for such an ambitious project, and the Grenadians were neither culturally sympathetic to the ideology nor receptive to the finer points of Marxism-Leninism. But it was clear that the Russians and their proxies were quite prepared to stay the course and persist in their programs until a new generation of Grenadians had been raised with a Communist catechism. One may presume that the Grenada enterprise was based on the Cuban experience and that a similar program continues in Nicaragua, even though the communization of Eastern Europe has not succeeded.[1] The Chinese seem similarly tempted to reject their commitment to communism.

Through all of this, the Kremlin leaders have continued to demonstrate both a genuine dedication to Communist methods and Communist ideas *and* a capability for split vision that permits them to believe in the eventual success of communism, even while they rush about the world shoring up its failure in virtually every place it has been installed. The mounting signs of the failure of communism makes the Soviets potentially dangerous policymakers, for if the contemporary realization of communism is unsatisfactory, those who have emotional as well as professional investments in its eventual success will take enormous risks to see it expand, simply to justify their lifelong faith. If the rulers of the Kremlin were truly cynical, this risk would not exist, for their primary concerns would be the traditional goals of the leaders of nation-states: maintenance of personal power and the success of their respective countries. These are certainly important to Chernenko and others in the Soviet leadership circle, but a palpable international demonstration of the success of communism is also of great concern, the more so as the system within the existing Empire reveals its structural defects.

In short, the Soviet Union is a revolutionary regime and, like all revolutionary regimes, international success—in this case the ability to export communism—is a fundamental measure of its legitimacy. Thus, the intrinsic, structural expansionism of the Soviet Empire, so well analyzed by Edward Luttwak,[2] is catalyzed and enhanced by the revolutionary dynamic of communism and given greater urgency by communism's mounting difficulties at home.

Soviet policy reflects the inevitably conflicting tendencies within such empires. In the best short treatment of the Kremlin's international strategy, Soviet foreign policy is closely linked to the nature of the Soviet system. And the system is characterized by forces and trends that often head in opposite directions:

—The system appears fragile in many ways, yet it is ruthlessly maintained by totalitarian rigidity;

—The system is in the throes of a grave economic crisis, but it is also the beneficiary of great military efficacy;

—There is great internal stress, but the Western world frequently appears to disintegrate in the face of the Soviet challenge;

—The Kremlin views the external world with great anxiety, yet conducts its foreign policy with the arrogance characteristic of a superpower;

—There is a rebirth of Russian nationalism alongside a continuing dedication to the internationalist ideology of Marxism-Leninism;

—The leaders in the Kremlin appear to be increasingly isolationist, yet the basic weapon of their diplomacy is the international Communist movement.[3]

THE STRUCTURAL CRISIS I:
THE FAILURE OF MODERNIZATION

No society is without its problems, but the difficulties of the Soviet system are far greater than those facing Western countries. It is now evident that the Soviet Union today is facing a structural crisis that along with its unprecedented military might must constitute one of the two basic elements of any serious analysis of the Soviet Empire.

We begin with an assessment of the Soviet crisis, for it lies at the center of the Kremlin's vision of itself and of the world it wishes to create:

> [T]he major source of tension in our economy is not only the missing harmony but also the real contradictions in interest between vertically dependent groups: workers and group leaders, group leaders and managers, managers and Ministers. The centralized system of rules and norms which has for decades ruled the economy has become unbelievably compromised and antiquated.

These words come from a confidential economics memorandum written at the Novosibirsk Research Institute in 1983. It was leaked to the Western press by "informed sources" in Moscow, and was duly reported outside the Soviet Union; domestic readers saw nothing of it (the memorandum was "for internal use only," reserved for the Kremlin elite). Some (for example,

William Safire in the *New York Times*[4]) read it as part of an
ongoing internal debate between the Andropov faction and the
Chernenko crowd; others (for example, Leo Wieland in *Encounter*[5]) saw it as yet another feeble effort to generate some
sort of internal reform, with a thinly veiled threat of purges as
a side feature. I do not believe that we know enough about the
internal politics of the Kremlin to be able to evaluate the political purposes of such a document; the undeniable importance of
the memorandum is that it accurately describes the structural
crisis of the Soviet Union, and it shows us that the Soviet leadership is aware of the crisis.

By any reasonable standard, the Soviet system has been a
profound failure; if any administration in the West had a record
like that of the rulers in the Kremlin, it would be quickly removed from office. Food is in short supply, in large part because
of the chronic failure of an agricultural system that has managed
to ruin one of the formerly great agricultural producers of the
world and that cannot efficiently distribute what it does produce;
consumer products approaching the quantity or quality of their
Western counterparts are nonexistent; housing is inferior and
severely limited; wages are low and working conditions harsh
and often dangerous; uniquely among industrialized nations, in-
fant mortality is rising and both the birth rate and the rate of
industrial growth are falling. Several recent studies[6] have shown
that the demographic trends of the Soviet Union will greatly de-
crease the percentage of Russians in the Soviet population in the
near term, thus adding to the already present ethnic abrasive-
ness.

Not only does the system not "work" well on its own, it
fails even to exploit fully those demonstrably successful technological systems it imports from the West. The most accurate
data available suggests that the Soviets manage to achieve only
60 percent of the productivity of the West when using identical
equipment (and sometimes the same plant structure), and this
only gives the crudest measurement of the inefficiency and un-

imaginativeness of the Soviet system. The most interesting and, in the long run, perhaps the most threatening failures of the Soviet economic system are its inability to master Western technological and managerial know-how and the intensifying conflict between the pampered elite in the Kremlin and the working class—Russian and non-Russian alike—within the Empire.

Of all the Soviets' internal problems, the failure to master productive skills is perhaps the most alarming. Although the Soviet Union has managed effectively to convert a high percentage of its gross national product into military power (indeed, Edward Luttwak[7] argues convincingly that no Western country has achieved anything like Soviet efficiency in this field), it has done so despite chronically low levels of productivity, even in sectors with the most advanced technology. Although most of the information we have comes from the so-called civilian sector of the Soviet system, it is hard to imagine that there is a hard and clean division between civilian and military productivity (although we do know that salaries and incentives are considerably higher in the military sector, and, as a result, productivity is probably better), and so we may presume that the same, or similar, factors are at work throughout the entire system. This low productivity is of course closely linked to the poor performance of the Soviet workers and to the mindlessness imposed by centralized planning in all sectors of productive activity. But the spectacular drop in productivity when a specific system moves from West to East suggests that there are additional factors at work, of which one is surely the failure of the Soviet system overall to guarantee a steady flow of supplies to the factories. As one particularly insightful analysis concludes, "Until an economic reform sufficiently radical to obviate supply uncertainty supervenes, Soviet industry cannot afford high productivity."[8]

I am sceptical of attempts to quantify Soviet economic performance whether made by independent scholars or by government agencies. My scepticism is based on the fact that it is difficult to measure the value of anything in the Soviet Union because prices often fluctuate according to class. As explained by the brilliant Soviet emigré Michael Voslensky in a book just out in English,[9] at best only the economic data that refer to ordinary citizens can be taken at face value because the elite—the *Nomenklatura*—pay less for the same goods, often pay in foreign currency, and have hidden subsidies to their income, their housing, their transportation, their medical care, and their food and restaurant bills. In other words, prices vary with social status, and, consequently, it is impossible to determine real costs, on the one hand, and real value, on the other hand. Establishing what a given item would cost (and, thus, what it would be worth) in a Western society (the method adopted in some recent CIA studies) begs the central question. One may sympathize with the methodological difficulties, but this does not save us from the obligation of attempting to understand what actually goes on. Nor is the situation improved by concentrating on gross production figures, for these frequently reflect the requirements that the various productive units meet published (Gosplan) goals rather than reporting real output. Finally, given the fundamental structural irrationalities of the system, a certain proportion of Soviet production is "conspicuous production," that does not contribute to useful activity but meets the political requirements of the system.

Given such considerations, it would appear to be virtually impossible to use economic data to try to analyze Soviet productivity. If this can be done at all, it can only be attempted through a detailed study and analysis of discrete sectors of the system, comparing the performance of a given factory in the Soviet Union with its Western counterpart, taking into account all of the specific variables. But gathering such information is exceedingly difficult and has, to my knowledge, rarely if ever been done successfully. Indeed, it is a crime to reveal economic information to foreigners, even information about such mundane activities as working hours, wages, and prices; these are considered state secrets.[10]

All is not lost however. Although we may not have satisfactory data on the detailed costs of Soviet manufacture, we do know a great deal about the functioning of Soviet industry. This information comes from a wide variety of sources, ranging from Western entrepreneurs who have worked in the Soviet Union and its satellite countries; from Soviet engineers, managers, and technicians who have emigrated to the West; and from Western experts who have managed to maintain good contacts in the Soviet Empire, especially in the more "Western" parts, such as Hungary, Poland, and Czechoslovakia.

In one of the most celebrated cases of technology transfer from West to East, the Italian automobile company, Fiat, built a model plant in the Soviet Union in the mid-sixties, creating a new city named Togliatti, named after the late general secretary of the Italian Communist party. The Togliatti project was carried out under nearly ideal conditions: the Italian government extended long-term credits at favorable rates, the most modern equipment was shipped to the Soviets and installed by the best Italian specialists, and thousands of Russian engineers, supervisors, managers, and workers were trained by their Italian counterparts, some in Italy, others in the Soviet Union. When the project was completed in the late sixties, it was widely proclaimed the most advanced automobile plant in the world, earning itself the sobriquet, "factory of the eighties" more than a decade before its time.

Togliatti might well have been ten years ahead of anything else if it had been built in the West, but in the Soviet Union it never functioned up to its capabilities. More important, it remained precisely as the Italians built it. The Soviets were unable to modernize the plant, improve production methods, update designs, or refine techniques in any substantial way. When, ten years after the construction of Togliatti, Italians pointed out that the Soviets should start to manufacture newer model cars, a new assembly line was built only when a minister intervened directly. It had been impossible for any plans for modernization to come "up the line" from those involved in automobile manufacture. Even when the decision was finally made, the technology had to be brought in from the outside; the new assembly line was imported in toto from Italy.

The technology was transferred, then, but the developmental know-how and the management skills and attitudes were not, and it is dubious whether the latter sort of transfer can be achieved. Although the Soviets have effectively acquired Western technology (whether by purchase or theft), including the most modern plant designs complete with managerial structure and worker-training programs, they have not been able to use technology as a component of a steadily evolving system. Instead, each acquisition represents a separate unit, unrelated to the overall process.

To be sure, the Soviets certainly have an overall plan, but each acquisition stands by itself and does not provide a developmental impulse to the whole system. One of the central features of Western industrial societies is the ongoing effort to improve efficiency and modernize equipment and procedures; thus, we in the West conduct ongoing research and development aimed at improving the current model and planning future ones. Nothing of the sort seems to take place in the civilian sector of the Soviet Union, as demonstrated by the case of Togliatti. No change in the automobiles was made for more than a decade; when it was decided to produce a new kind of car, the Soviets simply bought another assembly line from the Italians. Moreover, when Togliatti was built the Soviet copied not only the technology, but the organization of the workers within the factory as well.

All this shows that the Soviet Union lacks not only the ability to keep up with modern technological development by itself, but—more seriously, in my opinion—it has failed to develop the creative managerial and productive skills that are required of any industrial society. The consequence of this lack of independent managerial creativity is that the Soviets will remain doubly dependent on the West for its future "development": they will need to acquire both Western technology and the know-how that accompanies it. This is the reason for the increasing stress on buying so-called "turnkey" factories from the West: Western companies simply replicate their own factories in the Soviet Union, train the workers and managers, and walk away, leaving the Soviets to turn the key and start production. This kind of technology transfer is particularly valuable to the Soviets, for it gives them both equipment and know-how. As will be seen, the Soviet secret intelligence service has embarked on a massive espionage program to steal Western technology, but the KGB at its best cannot steal know-how; this has to be learned. In the West, the method of production is constantly refined to meet new market or staffing demands, but in the Soviet copy, the productive process remains the same unless local conditions *in the originating country* dictate a change, which may then be imported to the U.S.S.R.

There is an additional glitch in the Soviet Union's program of legally acquiring modern technology from the West, for the Kremlin cannot coordinate the purchases of the various foreign trade associations (FTAs) in a rational way. Each FTA is assigned a set of goals and is given a budget in foreign currency. The foreign currency can be spent only for the stipulated goals and *only within the FTA to which the funds have been assigned.* By law, foreign currency cannot circulate within the Soviet Union, and this restriction applies to transactions between the FTAs as well as to transactions between individuals or other entities. Consequently, no transfer of funds between FTAs is possible (of course every FTA is expected to exhaust its annual budget by the end of the fiscal period). If, as often happens, it is discovered that funds have been poorly allocated during the course of a given five-year plan, the system is nonetheless compelled to carry out the plan's instructions.

This institutionalized rigidity leads to absurd purchasing policies. If, for example, a given sector (say, agriculture) requires a new overall technique (say, a combination of new farming equipment and new fertilizers), efforts to institute the new method will be limited by the allocations of the Central Planning Committee. In a case I recently encountered, a European group offered for sale a package of farm equipment and fertilizers designed to meet the needs of the current and projected five-year plans. The Europeans had to deal with several different FTAs (it being impossible to deal with the farm sectors as such), and the package, thus, had to be divided into several parts to meet the Soviets' bureaucratic requirements. In the end, almost all the machinery and some of the fertilizer were purchased, but in combinations that made little sense for the agricultural units. Some had too much machinery, others too much fertilizer, and so forth. Yet no other solution was possible. Moreover, it is evident that, in such cases, the Soviet agricultural units were at the mercy of the Europeans' ability to restructure their proposals in more or less rational ways.

It follows from all this that the Soviet Union is far more dependent on foreign trade and illegally obtained Western technology and know-how than is generally assumed. If the Soviets found themselves commercially isolated from the West, they would lose not only the ability to acquire the most modern technology, but would also lose the expertise, the management skills, and the know-how necessary for any reasonable modernization. In confirmation of this hypothesis, Soviet agriculture, the area most effectively isolated from Western know-how, is now a chronic failure; the machinery is there, but the expertise is lacking. The Kremlin is accordingly compelled to make up for its own failures by importing ever more costly quantities of grain, fertilizers, and technology from the West. On the eve of the First World War, Russia was the world's greatest grain exporter; after nearly seventy years of communism, it has become the world's greatest grain *importer*.[11]

The Soviets are well aware of the depth of their problems, and they have taken steps to make sure that they will have access to Western scientific and technological advances, whatever the policies of Western countries. It is no surprise that the Soviet Union has devoted vast resources to the conduct of technological espionage.

Technological espionage is a relatively new phenomenon, the result of the confrontation between the world's two great political-economic systems. Although the Soviets set about this task shortly after the revolution, technological espionage in the European satellite countries was created at Soviet request shortly after 1952, on the graduation of the first generation of engineers educated under the various Communist regimes. In that year, Lavrenty Beria—at that time the chairman of the Soviet State Security organization (later known as the KGB)—asked for the establishment of a technological section within the Rumanian foreign intelligence service (the CIE), explaining that

> a new form of intelligence collection, developed during the dramatic confrontation following the October Revolution of 1917, has become an important Soviet state policy. . . . Since World War II, technological intelligence has proven to have a significant, positive influence on our national defense, as well as on our economy. . . . A well-organized, aggressive, common technological intelligence system could . . . provide substantial support for our Marxist-Leninist-Stalinist revolutionary struggle.[12]

The creation of the Rumanian technological espionage organization was supervised by Sergei Petrovich, a Soviet general of the secret intelligence service. Petrovich told the Rumanians that the U.S.S.R. made a real commitment to technological espionage only after the outbreak of World War II and that the activities of the Rosenbergs in the United States "was no less important than the whole victory over Germany. They not only hastened the end of the imperialist nuclear monopoly but also, by dying without confessing, founded modern anti-American, anti-imperi-

alist propaganda and the antinuclear peace movements. . . .
They inaugurated a new era in which technology has become a
vital support for politics."

Special technological groups were set up in all Warsaw Pact
intelligence services, copied from the Soviet model. The KGB
controlled all these activities, for every scrap of scientific and
technological information was destined for Moscow. In the early
1950s, the Soviets created a huge organization called "Evalua-
tion, Verification, and Indigenization" that employed more than
a thousand engineers, translators, and draftsmen. This organization today continues to draw up requirements for the KGB and
the secret services of the other Warsaw Pact countries, receives
all technological and military-technical information, and sepa-
rates useful and accurate information from fiction and misinfor-
mation. Finally, this unit translates the intelligence received and
transforms it into "Soviet projects." Only then is the technological intelligence—whether from a Soviet agency or another East
European intelligence service—sent to a civilian ministry, the
Ministry of Defense, or a KGB-sponsored technological center.

THE BUCHAREST SCENE

Over the years, the Rumanian Interior Ministry built up its own
industry in Bucharest. In every hotel designed for tourists, telephones could be tapped by simply turning a switch; micro-
phones, carefully hidden in every room, could easily be acti-
vated; and closed-circuit television provided round-the-clock
surveillance of restaurant rooms, corridors, and bathrooms. Television cameras—installed outside the Athenee Palace, Intercontinental, and the Lido and Nord hotels—together with infrared
equipment were used to cover foreigners' movements outdoors.
Surveillance officers working under cover as managers or waiters
in the leading restaurants could easily put transmitters on the
tables, concealed in ice buckets or ceramic ashtrays. A small
army of prostitutes, 80 percent of whom were agents handled by

the counterespionage directorate, worked the bars, hotel lobbies, restaurants, theaters, opera, concert halls, circus areas, movie theaters, streets, and parks. Foreigners studying at Rumanian universities, most of them black Africans, were recruited by the security service and sent out to solicit illegal money exchanges or homosexual relations.

In the autumn of 1961, several prestigious companies from West Germany, Great Britain, France, and Italy were in Bucharest with bids for sheet iron and wire-rolling mills, which Romania planned to add to the old metallurgical plants of Hunedoara and Resita. This was among the first major Rumanian openings toward the West since the Communist party had come to power, and the Rumanian foreign intelligence service together with its counterespionage and countersabotage organizations were kept busy. They photographed every single piece of paper carried in by the foreigners and surveilled every delegation member in order to arrest subversive Rumanians and recruit foreigners. The most prominent personage who appeared at that time was a West German by the name of Herbert Kamper. The chief representative of a German consortium, he had the best organized team and he eventually opened a permanent office in Bucharest. Although he was observed having several affairs with married women, he was not blackmailed. Instead, an educated, intelligent, and attractive young Rumanian woman, Rodica Oanta, who was working for a foreign airline in Bucharest, became his mistress. She was of course an agent.

In early 1963, Kamper himself became an agent. In exchange for a better life with Rodica in Rumania—and favored treatment for his business ventures—he furnished valuable technological documents about rolling mills and other metallurgical equipment. On one of his trips to Germany, Kamper returned with data for a new advanced rolling mill for ultrahard alloys needed for a new generation of military and space rockets. Kamper explained that this was a brand new American project and that American engineers were still working out its final de-

tails. He said that the data had been offered for sale to a West
German company—which had already received several thousand
plans and thousands of pages of technical specifications—and
that through a friend of his in that firm, he could obtain the
whole project for a mere $64,000. Obviously, Rumania could
not build and manage such a project, but Kamper suggested that
the information might be worth more than its weight in gold to
the Russians. The Rumanian leader, Gheorghiu-Dej agreed, and
two days after Gheorghiu-Dej's next trip to Moscow, four Soviet KGB generals arrived on a military airplane and were put
in a safe house where they set up their order of priorities for
designs and technical specifications; then they waited for the
delivery of the documents. It took more than six months and
dozens of trips to Germany for Kamper to deliver the whole
project.

Another story offers perhaps the most flagrant example. In
the mid-seventies, Colonel Christian Scornea, then one of the
most experienced Rumanian intelligence officers for West German and Austrian operations, spotted a potential source of information on chemical weapons: a professor of engineering
named Dr. Horst von Hajek. Hajek was born in Germany and
had been a ranking Nazi officer in the chemical troops during
the war. To shield his past, he moved to Portugal after the war.
There he started his own business as a military consultant and
armaments engineer and dealt with various African and Asian
countries. Later, he built an armaments factory in Cascais (near
Lisbon) that produced napalm bombs and artillery shells, which
von Hajek illegally exported. Years later, he returned to West
Germany where he became a technical advisor to NATO. The
Rumanian investigation revealed that von Hajek had plenty of
money but that he had family difficulties; thus, he was vulnerable to an approach using women. Invited to Bucharest, he was
introduced to Adriana Oros, a beautiul young girl who corre-
sponded to von Hajek's fantasies about having a meaningful
romance. She was then but 21, worked as an agent in a good

restaurant, where she was a waitress, and had some experience in operations against West German tourists.

A passionate love affair developed, all recorded on film and audiotape by the Rumanian service. Von Hajek was deeply in love, spent about $40,000 on a house in Brasov for Adriana and her mother, and began to spend at least one week there every month. In 1977, he was recruited, and an official contract was signed showing von Hajek as a consultant for the Rumanian Ministry of Chemical Industry. He made major contributions to the modernization of the Rumanian chemical forces. Based on his information, a supernapalm factory was built in Bucharest under cover of a detergent plant. Napalm bombs were built based on designs smuggled from Portugal to Rumania vio Africa. Napalm rain and other substances were experimented with by the chemical forces, and a secret exposition and practical demonstrations were organized by President and Mrs. Ceausescu.

Von Hajek was well known as an agent at the highest levels of the Rumanian regime when a letter arrived for Mrs. Ceausescu from von Hajek's wife in West Germany. Mrs. von Hajek stated that her husband had been trapped into a love affair in Rumania and was being used by the intelligence service. She emphasized that she had firm evidence of his illegal activities but that she would not inform the German government if Mrs. Ceausescu would order the Rumanian service to cut all ties to von Hajek and cancel his permanent entry visa. The president's wife asked her people to handle the matter in a discreet way. She said, "He looks to be an excellent fellow. I think it would be a good idea to move his girlfriend out of Rumania and set up secret communications with him abroad. . . . For us, it is important to keep him as a close friend."

The ways in which the Warsaw Pact countries acquire Western technological secrets are basically the same in each Communist country. The material that follows deals with Rumania, but similar examples could be drawn from throughout the Soviet bloc.

Cultural and Scientific Accords   Although they do not afford access to highly classified information, agreements and exchanges with Western scientists and engineers are significant sources of technological information. In 1978, more than 90 percent of the Rumanian engineers, medical doctors, economists, and teachers sent abroad under bilateral accords were intelligence agents; some were even intelligence officers. When the CIE was reorganized in 1972, Ceausescu ordered that every citizen sent abroad, whether in a diplomatic capacity or as part of a bilateral agreement, should either be an intelligence officer or a collaborator with the CIE.

An old case may illustrate the dimensions that such technological espionage can assume. Shortly before 1960, Alexandru Moghioros, who was the minister of agriculture, became fascinated with American hybrid corn because of its resistance to the vicissitudes of climate and its exceptional productivity. Moghioros was a former farmer himself; after five consecutive years of drought he realized that hybridization was the only hope for Rumanian agriculture. Unfortunately for his goal, at that time Ceausescu was obsessed with the development of the nation's industries and, thus, not a penny was available for the importation of the necessary genetic materials.

Moghioros turned to the intelligence service for help and volunteered the assistance of several distinguished agricultural engineers, including his own technical director, Nicolae Covor, who later became a colonel in the intelligence service and operated under deep cover. Medals and glory were promised for those individuals who brought back hybrid corn to Rumania. The intelligence service took the project and over the next five years several dozen agricultural engineers were sent to the United States, every one an intelligence officer or agent. They went to federal or state research institutes as well as to private organizations and farms. In five years, they collected thousand of pounds of the genetic materials essential to developing hybrid corn in Rumania. A special diplomatic-pouch system was developed that permitted the materials to be transported to Bucharest without any significant biological deterioration. The Rumanians recruited several valuable American specialists, including one scientist working at the Agriculture Department's Research Center in Beltsville, Maryland. This man alone supplied the entire American hybrid collection containing some 14,000 assortments and species, thus providing the basic standard for all subsequent research in Rumania. Based on this operation and seven more years of intensive selective reproduction, Rumania became an important producer of genetic material and one of the largest producers of hybrid corn in Europe.

American brands disappeared and were replaced by "Rumanian hybrids." This theft of U.S. agricultural technology not only cost American farmers and seed producers the possibility of exporting seed corn to Rumania, but also their proprietary rights to a significant part of Europe that switched to Rumanian hybrid seeds. In 1978, the total savings to Rumania were estimated at roughly $300 billion. Colonel Covor was given an academic degree, and the Fundulea National Institute of Agriculture, which had performed secret research on the stolen genetic materials, received the highest awards of the state. In 1962, Khrushchev visited Rumania; when he heard of the new "Rumanian" hybrids, he asked for a complete genetic collection. This became the basis for the so-called "Soviet hybrids."

Commercial Trade   Trade with the West is the most important source of technological intelligence. In 1978, approximately 70 percent of the Rumanian foreign trade personnel abroad consisted of intelligence officers; the rest, save for a few unimportant exceptions, were agents. In the Ministry of Foreign Trade, for example, the first deputy, five other deputy ministers, and eleven directors were deep cover intelligence officers, and thirty-eight out of the forty-one heads of state foreign trade enterprises were intelligence officers or agents. Every single contact with Western firms was analyzed for intelligence purposes.

Every new foreign specialist encountered in the course of commercial trade negotiations was reported, and every transaction was first screened for its technological intelligence potential. In fact, over 90 percent of all the technological operations run by Rumanian intelligence have their roots in foreign trade.

One of the most spectacular examples of such operations was the acquisition of information concerning the West German Leopard II tank. The Rumanian military intelligence service acquired a Leopard II engine through a source working for the German firm Kirschfeld, A.G. in Düsseldorf, but the manufacture of this engine was too complicated for the Rumanians. Thus, their defense specialists sought help from the tank's developer and producer, the German firm MTU. One of the senior officers at MTU was judged a good candidate for recruitment as an agent, and he was given the code name, Leonard.

Leonard was quite willing to help the Rumanians and explained that the Leopard I and Leopard II tanks were developed for NATO; therefore, without formal approval from the West German government, it was quite difficult for any part of the tanks to be exported. However, MTU had just designed a new diesel engine that was entirely based on the Leopard II design, with two basic differences: it was heavier, being made of cast iron instead of aluminum, and the lubrication system was different. This engine was the property of MTU, and MTU was prepared to sell to Rumania a license and a production line. Moreover, Leonard was willing to sign a confidential agreement under which a Swiss firm specially set up for a one-time contract would design and deliver every necessary component to transform the MTU engine into a tank engine. Moreover, every employee of the Swiss firm was to be a retired MTU employee with on-the-job experience with the Leopard II engine. In effect, the only difference between the Leopard engine and the one the Rumanians got was the stamp on the blueprints.

The Leopard II operation showed that retired foreign specialists are an excellent source of technological intelligence. In

1977, the CIE began compiling an inventory of retired specialists in Western countries and eventually discovered that most of these specialists did not have to sign any secrecy agreement on retirement, even if they had worked on classified projects.

Cooperative and Joint Ventures After some experience, the CIE used every new cooperative venture to infiltrate small armies of intelligence officers, agents, and photographers. Franco-Rumanian cooperation in producing a compact car, known as the Dacia, brought more than one hundred French technicians to Rumania. They arrived with quantities of technical documents covering more than the equipment legally purchased "in case" they were needed. In a confidential letter to the CIE, the Rumanian Minister of Machine-Building Industry, Ion Avram, expressed his profound gratitude for the clandestine photography of all the French documents, emphasizing that in this way it had been possible to eliminate the importation from France of more than thirteen thousand improvements in the basic car that had not been included in the cooperative contract. This saved Rumania several million dollars.

After a joint venture was arranged in the late 1970s, more than one hundred fifty Rumanian engineers and technicians were sent to France to study the new Citroën compact. Some of them, intelligence officers or agents, arrived with new minicameras and photographic contact paper. When the films and other sensitive materials sent back to Rumania were studied, they were found to contain many secrets, which Citroën had carefully tried to keep out of the new joint venture, as well as important technical data on other Citroën products.

Another joint venture with a West German firm producing turbotransmissions brought to the city of Craiova a considerable number of German specialists. They brought "secure" safes that contained technical documents. The local Rumanian authorities obligingly delivered these safes free of charge, promising careful protection. The Rumanian intelligence service and the local security authorities spent one month secretly photographing the contents of the safes, yielding, among other things, part of a new design for a tank turbotransmission. These papers belonged to a technician who had worked on military turbotransmissions for many years, and he was drawn into a love affair with a young woman who was a Rumanian agent. Once recruited by this woman, he was paid to take monthly trips by car to West Germany, ostensibly to visit his family. His case officer, Vasile Vago, waited for him at the Yugoslav-German border every time, taking from him the rest of the information on the Leopard tank turbotransmission.

Contacts with Consulting Firms   Consultants provide good access to valuable, even if not highly classified, information because such firms employ or engage the services of people who work with classified information. For more than ten years a London consulting firm, owned by a British citizen who became a Rumanian agent, furnished thousands of reports from the United States that had been restricted from Rumania. In another case, in 1958, an engineer living in Frankfurt and working for the American Battelle Institute, was recruited by the CIE. Over a twenty-year period he furnished information based on classified information to which he had previously had access; this information helped introduce into Rumania more than fifty new technological processes.

In the early 1970s, an American citizen who was the chairman of a California company was recruited by the CIE, and he reported that the chief engineer of a Ford glass factory was prepared to sell secretly for $200,000 a complete Pittsburgh plate glass technological process. Rumania, a traditional glass producer and exporter, was quite interested in acquiring this information. A meeting was set up to buy the information, but before it was over, the participants were arrested by FBI agents. The engineer was fired from his job and had to face an investigation.

Yet, two years later an American citizen who was the head of a consulting firm proposed a contract to design a Pittsburgh glass factory in Rumania. It was the same engineer! He was immediately recruited by his former case officer and was hired, this time as a consulting engineer with a legal-looking contract. A relatively large Rumanian team of engineers and draftsmen moved into a safe house near Bucharest, and under the engineer's supervision, a project for a new factory was designed. This installation was in experimental operation by 1977 within an older plant, the Scaeni Glass Factory. The American engineer received several hundred thousand (tax free) dollars and began other "consulting" work for the Rumanian glass industry. By 1978, Rumania had become an important exporter of Pittsburgh glass and was ready to produce a new type of glass called "float," without having bought any licenses or paid any royalties to the American companies that did the research and development.

Third-Country or One-Time Firms When direct importation of technology was forbidden, either by standing legislation or extraordinary embargo, the Soviet Union and her satellites resorted to the use of firms created specially for the illegal diversion of such technology, which in almost all cases had military applications:

In 1975, a fictitious one-time company was established by a recruited Japanese entrepreneur in Tokyo to ship to Rumania high-grade microelectronic equipment that had been imported into Japan from the United States, West Germany, Great Britain, and Italy.

Highly advanced, high-pressure hydraulic presses for sensitive uses were imported from Sweden and South Africa by using a one-time firm registered in Helsinki by another intelligence agent, in this case a West German citizen.

An import-export company was created in Vienna by a Rumanian intelligence officer for the illegal transfer of sensitive Western optical equipment through Austria.

A British export firm set up by an agent in London was used to purchase radar and other military equipment and special computers, which were transshipped to Rumania through various third countries.

Emigrés Ever since the Bolshevik seizure of power, emigrés have been used for foreign intelligence purposes. In the Rumanian case, once emigration restrictions were loosened after 1972 in an effort to achieve better relations with the West, more than ten thousand departing citizens were recruited for intelligence purposes. To be sure almost all of them failed to use their secret correspondence codes, but some of them, either in need of money or to protect relatives left behind, cooperated with the CIE.

As of 1978, more than 60 percent of the intelligence agents among Rumanian emigrés were being used to obtain technological information, compared with 25 percent used to penetrate and subvert emigré organizations, and a mere 15 percent in political and military intelligence.

Illegal Intelligence The most secret intelligence activities are those in which agents and officers operate without any sort of Rumanian identities. A number of CIE officers were given new German, Greek, Turkish, Israeli, and even French and Italian identities together with false birth certificates, university diplomas, and other documents that were able to withstand scrutiny. Usually they left Rumania illegally so that once abroad they could avoid being connected with their homeland in any way. During the early years of illegal operations—all of which were conducted under direct KGB control—an illegal officer was required to have been a Party activist (preferably a Communist party member) before the time that the Communist party was legal in Rumania. This rigorous requirement was dropped for the second generation of illegals; after 1965 Rumania sent many doctors, scientists, engineers, and scholars abroad.

The large German-speaking ethnic minority in Rumania made it relatively easy to infiltrate a number of illegal officers into Germany, Austria, Switzerland, and some other European countries. In Austria, illegal officers penetrated most of the state-owned industries: Voest, famous for its Linz-Donauwitz technology; Alpine, with its nuclear power section as well as the Alpine foundry; the headquarters of Elin-Union, another renowned metallurgical corporation; the chemical company Stickstoffwerke, including its new melamine section; and the prestigious engineering firm of Wagner-Biro. There were illegal officers in private companies as well, such as the electrical firm Siemens-Austria and Norma microprocessors.

In West Germany, illegal officers with good professional training and forged credentials worked their way up into important positions in companies like Siemens in Erlangen and its nuclear section in Karlsruhe, the electrical company AEG in Düsseldorf, the chemical company Hoechst in Frankfurt, and the steel giant Thyssen. Smaller companies, including Telemechanik and the Nitrohirsch container company, along with the universities in Karlsruhe and Giessen were used primarily as springboards for better positions in Canada and the United States.

The operations of illegal Rumanian agents, though relatively limited, were of high quality, consisting mainly of highly classified, original projects, copies of which were identical to the originals kept in companies' most secure vaults. To mention just a few examples from the late seventies:

A complete project for Linz-Donauwitz technology, which was immediately introduced into Rumanian metallurgical factories, saving production time and many millions of dollars.

Various projects for nuclear power reactors and their security systems.

The complete construction project for a heavy water installation for a nuclear power plant.

The project for an artillery shell installation designed in West Germany for Egypt.

THE UNITED STATES AND EUROPE

All Warsaw Pact countries have had considerable difficulty in penetrating American corporations in the United States. Among the explanations for this situation are the limited extent of bi-lateral trade relations, the aggressive work of the FBI and the CIA as well as military intelligence, and the general anti-Com-munist attitude of the American public. Rumanian intelligence has had little success in obtaining technology directly from the United States, but it has had far greater success in getting such technology indirectly from European subsidiaries operating un-der American license. The same holds for the other Warsaw Pact services.

One of the most important targets of Rumanian espionage was the silicone technologies, which were strictly embargoed for the Communist countries. Repeated efforts in the United States got nowhere, but in the 1970s, an American subsidiary in France, which had previously sold Rumania two production lines for German semiconductors, kept its doors open. A single French citizen furnished file after file of data, until the whole technol-ogy, supplied under license from the United States, was passed to the Rumanians. Soon thereafter a secret installations in an electronics factory located on the highway between Bucharest and the Otopeni International Airport began the industrial pro-duction of silicone semiconductors.

The technology for growing silicone crystals, which is under strict control in the United States, was provided to Rumania by an Italian electronics company in Milan under a special arrangement that included part of the equipment needed for this process.

Similar methods were used to obtain information on integrated circuitry. Unable to get the information directly from Texas Instruments in the United States, cooperation was undertaken with a prestigious British firm that produced microelectronics equipment under a Texas Instrument license. This yielded thousands and thousands of photocopies of technologies embargoed by the United States.

THE VALUE OF TECHNOLOGICAL ESPIONAGE

In 1978, the CIE reviewed a decade of technological espionage. Its conclusions were impressive indeed: over 35 percent of the inventory and development of Rumanian industry was due, at least in part, to intelligence operations. The chemical industry had been the major beneficiary, with whole factories built in Borzesti (polystyrene), Iasi (polyurethane and synthetic leather), Brasov (melamine and photosensitive materials), Transylvania (color films and photographic papers), Codlea (coloring agents), Victoria (plastic explosives), Bucharest (radial tires), and elsewhere.

The medical-pharmaceutical industry was next in line, followed by metallurgy (with an impressive number of new technologies for high-alloy steel, metallic carbides, and nonmetallic alloys as well as for modernized steel mills and rolling mills together with a new aluminum industry). Silicone semiconductors and integrated circuits were the most important contributions for the electronics industry. New digital machine tools, diesel engines, and Bosch injection pumps were all the results of intelligence operations. The nuclear energy industry reported that it had received enough information to build an industrial heavy water installation, 30 percent of the components of its nuclear reactors, and 40 percent of their security systems. These are just a few examples, for it was estimated that for the decade under review, between $600 and $800 million had been saved by replacing legal but expensive imports with illegal and inexpensive products secured through covert intelligence activities.

These cases show the enormous effect of Communist intelligence services, which are able in many instances to compensate for the basic inferiority of the Soviet Union's technological establishment by stealing secrets from the West. General Zakharov, the chief of the Soviet foreign intelligence service, once explained the matter to one of his Rumanian colleagues in these terms:

> When it comes to agents, agents who cannot be replaced by satellites, we need your help and the help of our other sister socialist countries. Taken together, you and they have trade with the West that is greater in volume and in diversity than we have. Together you have more representatives abroad than we do. You have many more recent emigrés and a broader basis for building up illegal officers. . . . We badly need agents, more agents . . . together, and only together, we can change the present relatively even balance of military power into a decisive socialist superiority. And only together can we make our technological intelligence into one of the most productive and prosperous businesses in history.[13]

THE PROBLEM OF THE WORKING CLASS

The Bolshevik Revolution was supposed to give power to the working class, instead it led to a new, more systematic form of repression. The condition of the Soviet worker can be briefly described, using the words of Fyodor Turovsky:[14]

> Those who are obliged to work have no vested interest in their work. Their pay is not enough to feed them and their families, and this explains the absenteeism, drunkenness and laziness of those who regard their work not a matter of "honor, glory and heroism," as Stalin taught, but something which they are intimidated into undertaking. That is why

Soviet industry produces so many rejects, the quality of production is so low and the losses through lack of productivity so great, with equipment and lorries standing idle for days. Moreover, the worker in the Soviet Union preys upon the means of production, upon raw materials and the finished product, breaks things by accident and on purpose, and causes wastage all the time; things have come to such a pass that theft at work, not only small, but large-scale theft, has become the norm throughout the country.

An entire police force has been created to track down stolen property, even though the practice is well-nigh universal, and, given the necessity of generating additional income, a long string of Potemkin industries—which exist only on paper to justify payment to people who in fact do no work at all for the industries in question—has come into being. Like other forms of corruption, it is impossible for the Kremlin to shut down such activities for fear of wrecking the entire system.

Turovsky calculates that as of the late seventies, a family of three would need a monthly income of 450 rubles a month to meet requirements for the bare necessities of life: a modest food budget, a few clothes, a modest rent, a telephone, and an occasional film or concert. Yet, the average wage for the country as a whole was 150 rubles a month, and most workers did not earn that much. Thus, even with two parents working full time, a monthly deficit of between 150 and 200 rubles a month was normal; where did the additional income come from?

Turovsky lists various activities: "Stealing time" from one job so as to be able to work extra hours at a second job. "Some," he writes, "do not appear at all, others leave their factory during the working day, or sit idle at work so as to save their strength for working somewhere else in the evenings." As Turovsky points out, this method was invented by the government itself when it gave phantasmagorical positions to full-time "amateur" athletes. Others copy the model. Falsifying the books; that is, workers are paid for labor that has not in fact been performed. In this case, the failure belongs to the system, not to the workers. Because the distribution is so bad, it is impossible for work to go on at a normal rate—"sometimes machinery stands idle because some essential spare part is missing . . . sometimes there is no cement on the site . . . if the crane driver does not turn up for work." But if the workers are paid only for work performed, they would leave for some other work site, thus producing the failure of the project and the ruination of the managers. So, they are paid anyway. But this produces a new problem, because the Central Bank pays only for work completed, and it is clear that much of this work is *not* completed. This problem is solved by an elaborate subterfuge, which was publicly explained in the pages of *Literaturnaya gazeta:*

> What saves our skins . . . are the one-off buildings, the ones that are not built according to a stereotype plan.
>
> Organizations which need a non-stereotype building to be built on time will comb the whole of Moscow until they find a contractor willing to take on their building over and above the buildings which he is obliged to construct in order to fulfill his plan, and which he will have to answer for with his head. And this is the saving of us: we accept the job on condition that we will have the right to readjust the estimated costs. The client looks the other way and nods in silence, since he is well aware of the true reason for our insisting on this condition: for we will include bills for work which will never be carried out, and is not even needed, except for the fact that by "doing" this work we will receive money that we need to pay the workers standing idle on the building being put up to ordinary stereotype plan.[15]

Imaginative solutions to the structural problems of the Soviet Union, such as the ones described here, obviously only solve the problems at the cost of creating even greater difficulties, and the Soviet workers have made their displeasure known. Although not nearly so dramatic as the labor unrest in Poland, there is, nonetheless, a surprising amount of proletarian protest within the Soviet Union. There are some ten to fifteen free labor unions, with the pitifully small number of some two hundred members, and these are obviously in constant jeopardy. Yet, they do exist, and strikes do take place, sometimes on a national scale. According to one of the few scholarly articles on this important subject, it is impossible to document fully the extent of such national manifestations, yet "it is not unreasonable to suggest that awareness of one strike was a factor in the precipitation of another," and some of the strikes have produced concrete results.[16]

But it is, of course, the Polish case that has exposed the problem of the working class in the Soviet Empire in its full gravity. To quote one of the most brilliant students of the Soviet Union, Frane Barbieri:

> From 1956 on, no working class in the world has fought so hard for its rights as has the Polish. And no people has so followed the movements and demands of its workers as have the Poles. They have routinely been declared in violation of the law, in conflict with socialism, in the name of a system that calls itself socialist. In general, the problems of the socialist countries have sometimes been caused by the imposition of national interests on social ones; sometimes by the imposition of social interests on national ones. In Poland the sacrifice is complete: the Poles are victims of both national and social interests.[17]

The Polish case cannot possibly be unique; the workers in other countries of the Soviet Empire have undoubtedly created their own "Solidarities," and are closely watching events in Poland to judge their own next moves.

THE PROBLEM OF NATIONALITY

Hand in hand with the problem of the working class goes the simmering issue of the nationalities, which has perplexed Soviet leaders since Stalin's essay on the subject in the 1920s. Current demographic trends in the Soviet Union point toward a relentless growth of non-Russian nationalities, and by the turn of the century the Russians are projected to drop under 50 percent of the total population, although they will remain the largest single national group. But the problem facing the Kremlin is not one of mere numbers, it is rather the situation that derives from the shift in population distribution, above all the economic implications of the employment problems and the nature of regional development. The Soviet Empire is losing its Russian workers at the expense of non-Russian groups; that means that the Empire is losing skilled workers, and the situation is rendered more damaging still by the fact that the non-Russians are reluctant to migrate to the areas where labor is needed. In Central Asia, where population growth is substantial, the labor requirements are insufficient to absorb the greater numbers. Throughout the Soviet Union, the countryside is overpopulated: the Ukraine has 0.7 persons per cultivated hectare, Uzbekistan has 2.1 persons, Tadzhikistan 2.4, Georgia, 3.3 persons. Moreover, the obvious solution—developing the areas where the population is growing most rapidly—has political costs because such a policy would both give strength to the non-Russians and tempt the Chinese across the border. Moreover, if Central Asia *is* developed, who will do the work in the now-developed regions?

In keeping with the overall model of Soviet life, decisions are taken at the top and then implemented down the line, but as in the economic sphere, the control of the Kremlin comes at a high cost, and the Russians do not fully trust the other nationalities. If reports are accurate, non-Russians had to be replaced with native Russians in Afghanistan because the Kremlin feared large-scale defections. There was probably another reason: the linguistic integration of the non-Russian nationalities has not gone well. Hardly any of the Muslim minorities speak Russian as a primary language; even as a secondary tongue, it is spoken by less than one-fifth of the Kirghiz, Tadzhik, Azeri, and Uzbek peoples—and the trend is downward rather than upward. In general, assimilation can be achieved with the tinier minorities, but the largest ones are becoming ethnically, linguistically, and even religiously more distinct. Nonetheless, they have little autonomy, even when a certain degree of independence would probably serve the long-term interests of the state. Instead, the sessions of the local soviets always take place after those of the Supreme Soviet, consequently, the local organizations merely repeat everything that has been said in Moscow; they do not serve as sources of information for the leadership in Moscow.[18]

The most careful Western student of the minority problem has written that "of all the problems facing Moscow, the most urgent and the most stubborn is the one raised by the national minorities. And like the Empire that it succeeded, the Soviet State seems incapable of extricating itself from the nationality impasse."[19]

THE STRUCTURAL CRISIS II:
ACCOMMODATION TO A FILLED SYSTEM

By now the failure of the Soviet economic system is so manifest that even their own official spokespersons acknowledge it; the question facing the Kremlin—and, alas, the West as well—is whether the situation can be remedied without an explosion that might involve the world at large, not merely the Soviets and their subjects. For the most dangerous of nations is one that is militarily potent but that faces internal breakdown. A proper appreciation of the Soviet crisis is consequently a matter of grave international concern.

In analyzing the structural crisis, we must beware of applying Western standards to Soviet society; the Kremlin, of course, is not subject to the pressures from below that determine the actions of our governments, and the Soviet people have an impressive tolerance for misery and repression. Solzhenitsyn, as one would expect, puts the matter in its baldest form:

> The Soviet economy has for its primary goal not development, nor the growth of overall production, nor better pro-

ductivity or even profit: it is only the functioning of a powerful military machine and abundance for the ruling class.
The Party bureaucracy is incapable of effectively organizing
production or trade; it only knows how to confiscate that
which is produced. The system excludes all individual responsibility. Incapable of managing the economy, the authorities substitute a generalized violence. Economic life is
shackled, compressed by various administrative edicts that
are aimed at preventing the social forces from acting freely.[20]

Solzhenitsyn correctly identifies the two primary internal
goals of the Kremlin: military power and the enrichment of the
ruling elite. Both have been successfully achieved, and they are
closely related to each other. The impressive military machine
speaks for itself; indeed, it has now apparently given the Kremlin a degree of confidence that it never had before. Although the
war in Afghanistan may constitute a real problem for the Soviet
Union—here again, our information is spotty and often contradictory; people with excellent credentials and apparently good
sources disagree on whether the fighting is going well for the
Soviets—the initial invasion was impressive. Such military prow-
ess strengthens the rulers, for it suggests in a highly visible way
that the Communist forecast of ultimate triumph is correct. "As
Brezhnev used to say, foreign policy is our most important domestic problem."[21]

The external success of the Soviet Union is critical for the
elite in another way, for it justifies their privileged existence. In
Moscow, as in few capitals in recent history, the entire system
revolves around the small number of men at the top of the repressive apparatus. It is they, and only they, who benefit from
the wealth produced by the system, just as they and only they
determine how resources shall be allocated, who shall govern,
and how the Soviet Union shall conduct its foreign policy.

The elite, known as the *Nomenklatura,* is totally removed
from the population at large. The members of the *Nomenklatura*
not only receive more than ten times the income of the workers,
but also enjoy special shops (where the same articles cost less

than they do in the ordinary stores), live in special apartments in Moscow, have luxurious *dachas* in the countryside, and get superior medical treatment—a meaningful perquisite in a country where life expectancy is actually dropping—and all manner of special privileges. Indeed, in Voslensky's words,

> A family of the *Nomenklatura* can pass its entire life in the U.S.S.R., from birth to death, can work, rest, eat, go shopping, get sick, and enjoy itself, without ever encountering the Soviet people, which the *Nomenklatura* claims to serve. The isolation of the *Nomenklatura* from the mass of the population is the same as that of foreigners in the Soviet Union. The difference resides in the fact that foreigners are not permitted to have contacts with the population, while the *Nomenklatura* doesn't want to have any.[22]

The privileges of the elite are such that the *Nomenklatura* constitutes a state within a state. And like all such powerful and privileged castes, it has become corrupt. According to one of the most thoughtful of the recent Soviet emigrés, Konstantin Simis, corruption has become the defining characteristic of Soviet society. Top officials earn salaries that are disproportionately high, and their privileges are virtually limitless, ranging from cars to telephones (all bugged) to apartments in Moscow and to *dachas* in the countryside, paid vacations, the latest in Western leisure-time gadgets, the finest food at bargain prices, and the most up-to-date clothing. But because Soviet society is based purely on power—leaving no room for fairness or orderly and stable careers—the position of the members of the *Nomenklatura* is eternally precarious, and they are consequently driven to obtain the maximum gain in the minimum time. The most characteristic method of ensuring rapid advancement and enduring power is the bribe, a method that also serves to lubricate a system that otherwise cannot function satisfactorily. As Simis puts it in a recent article:

> The typical pattern of corruption in trade, emerging from the data of hundreds of trials and in part from material pub-

lished in the Soviet press, gives clear evidence that without
deception, bribery, and falsification of documents Soviet
trade simply cannot function.[23]

The same kind of statement can be made for all areas of
"productive" activity. Because the five-year plan makes demands
on managers and functionaries that cannot possibly be fulfilled
legally, they are compelled to resort to illegal actions to meet
their quotas and thereby save their careers. Some of these actions border on the hilarious. I once spoke to a West European
engineer who had been hired by the Soviets to work on the
Trans-Siberian Railroad. He needed to find two I-beams with
which to repair a bridge and was told that it was impossible to
find just two beams—to get them, it was necessary to order an
entire carload of them. This was done, the railroad car arrived
somewhere in the outer reaches of the steppes, and the bridge
was repaired. The problem then arose: what to do with the re-
maining dozens of beams? There were two solutions. The legal
solution was to abandon the beams, and let them rust. The illegal
solution was to try to find some useful purpose to which they
could be put.

We are used to thinking of corruption as a negative force
in society, but it is evident that in the Soviet Union corruption
plays a positive role. Given the nature of the society, there is no
legal way to make the system work (it can be destroyed and replaced with a more reasonable system, but the rulers will not
accept that solution), and illegal acts are, therefore, required to
achieve reasonable success. Furthermore, the ubiquity of corruption acts as a cement for the ruling class, from the center to the
periphery.

As has been seen, corruption also pervades the working
class, both because workers are inevitably caught up in the illegal activities of their managers—thus becoming accomplices
to the corrupt activities—and because the salaries paid to the
workers are insufficient for subsistence. Like every other ele-

ment in the Soviet system, the rules being irrational, rational behavior is inevitably illegal. Thus, a second economic system has come into existence, one that functions more effectively than the official system (at a minimum, more effectively than the civilian sector; we don't know enough about military production to be able to judge the official system in toto). Well enough; but there is a political price to be paid for the parallel systems. Because almost everyone participates, willy-nilly, in the illegal activities, everyone is vulnerable to anticorruption campaigns. There is not a single Soviet official of any importance who cannot truthfully be condemned for illegal actions, save those few bureaucrats who have gone by the book (and, consequently, contributed mightily to the ruination of the country). One should accordingly see the periodic anticorruption campaigns—like the one launched by Andropov immediately upon his accession to power—in a double light: both as an attempt to remedy some of the more egregious sins committed by officials, great and small, and as a purely political operation (because if the campaign were serious, virtually everyone of any importance would have to go to the *gulags*).

Corruption at the center—Moscow—derives from the easy availability of wealth; corruption at the periphery is driven by scarcity. The salaries of local officials are low, but their power is proportionally as great as that of the Kremlin *Nomenklatura*, so, they are able to extort payment from those beneath them. The officials at the center are loath to expose the corruption of the periphery, both because anticorruption campaigns tacitly threaten everyone and because the elimination of corrupt practices in the more distant regions of the empire would require the center to increase the legal payments to local officials. Thus sanctioned at all levels, corruption predictably expands even further, reaching all levels and regions of the Empire.

If the central planning system does not work, there must be institutions to remedy its defects, and these over time have come to constitute a fairly complete underground economy. Thus, there is a systemwide criminal network, linked primarily to local and regional authorities:

> Although not conceived as such by its creators, this Soviet variety of organized crime naturally is derived from and has become an organic part of the dictatorship of the *apparat* of the . . . Communist Party. . . . Organized crime in the Soviet Union bears the stamp of the Soviet political system, the Soviet economy, and, in general, everything that may be lumped together as the Soviet regime.

> [T]he ruling district elite acts in the name of the party as racketeers and extortionists of tribute, and . . . it is the criminal world per se who must pay through the nose to the district *apparat*.[24]

Thus, corruption may fairly be said to be a defining characteristic of the Soviet system, required by the fundamental irrationality of the centrally planned economy, and present in all sectors of the state.

THE STRUCTURAL CRISIS III: PEOPLES AND CONTINUITY

The problems of the Soviet Union would tax the most dynamic and imaginative of leaders; the actual ruling class in the Kremlin is aged, conformist, and provincial. The geriatric Politburo replaced Brezhnev with an ailing and aged Andropov, and Andropov with the ailing and aged Chernenko, and although it is said by some Kremlinologists that the Kremlin leaders have now decided to bring in a new generation, as yet no such transformation has occurred. As a matter of fact, by the summer of 1984, the most often-told joke in the Soviet Union was reportedly this one:

Q: Where was Andropov finally buried?
A: Between Brezhnev and Chernenko.

In any event, mere youth will not resolve the problems of a political system that rewards caution, that still has not provided for orderly transition from one leader to the next, and that punishes innovation and individualism. The resistance to change of the Soviet leadership is one of the few rational elements of the system, for the internal balance of the Soviet Empire is so fragile and the potential rage of the populace so intense that any sign that the Kremlin's control is weakening may serve as the beginning of the end.

Every time a new dictator has emerged in the Kremlin, Western observers have predicted a shift in policy. The predictions have almost always been wrong (Khrushchev constituting the one notable exception to this otherwise iron rule of Soviet oligarchy), and will most likely continue to be wrong for the foreseeable future. Every now and then a Khrushchev or an Andropov come along and act as if they were about to undertake sweeping changes. Khrushchev was serious about it, and this was the basic cause of his removal. Following the fall of Khrushchev came the long era of Brezhnevian inactivity, which led to Andropov. Andropov surely recognized the necessity for internal change, but from the standpoint of the Kremlin, the risks entailed in structural change must far outweigh the potential benefits, especially as there is no pressing reason for immediate action (aside from the Polish crisis, which the Politburo may feel can be tolerated indefinitely).

Any meaningful change, from a simple streamlining of the bureaucracy to more substantive, even revolutionary moves (like decentralizing certain sectors of production or creating free market zones) would challenge the privileges and the power of the *Nomenklatura*. A meaningful change would constitute an act of political suicide by the ruling class of the Soviet Empire, an act not often taken voluntarily by any ruling class. As Walter Laqueur puts it:

> Some argue that the system *must* change to remain competitive and productive, to keep pace with the rest of the world,

or for whatever other reason . . . we know from history
that political elites can cling to power for decades, perhaps
even for centuries, even if they have long since fulfilled their
historical role (assuming they ever had one), even if they
have lost faith in their doctrine and mission, even if they no
longer have the active support of their followers.[25]

Furthermore, dictatorships are far more common than democracies, and there is no evidence that there is a natural tendency toward democracy among all nations of the earth. Fascism,
to take a recent example, was a successful political movement
that was only removed from power when it was defeated in battle by forces external to the system; internal resistance was never
sufficient to challenge its hegemony seriously. Why should we
presume that communism will be more vulnerable?

In truth, we lack a model for the failure of totalitarianism
from within. The Nazi and Fascist totalitarian regimes of the
first half of the century did not fail as such; they were defeated
from without, not removed from within. Yet these regimes were
of such short duration compared to that of the Soviet Union
that internal pressures did not have the time to build to sufficient force. Alternatively, it may be that the seventy-year survival of the Soviet Union has brought it to a point at which it is
better able to suppress internal dissent, no matter what the pressure. The modern totalitarian state with all the method of control available to it in the post-Orwellian period is simply too
new to be able to make confident predictions about whether or
not it can sustain itself indefinitely unless defeated from without. But careful study of the nature of Soviet communism suggests that it may indeed be subject to internal disintegration of
a sort that we cannot now anticipate. After all, the regime's
legitimacy rests on a vision of history, both of its own development and of the expansion of its domain. If its development is
revealed to have been a failure and its expansion is reversed,
may there not be serious repercussions undercutting its very
existence? Or, at a minimum, may this not drive the leaders of

the system to take more risky acts to demonstrate that the prophecies of the founders were true after all? Again, we do not know, and the most likely forecast is that things will continue more or less as they have to date. As Walter Laqueur has nicely put it:

> The unique character of the Soviet regime, a frozen revolution which can neither advance nor find its Thermidor, makes prediction dangerous. It would be foolish altogether to rule out radical change in the Soviet Union in the foreseeable future. All one can say is that at present it seems unlikely, and that, if it should occur, it would be triggered by circumstances and by forces which cannot possibly be anticipated today.[26]

A similar view is expressed by one of the principal characters in Alexander Zinoviev's novel, *The Radiant Future*. "Communism," he wrote, "is a completely natural and normal social structure. There is less artificiality in it than in the societies of Western civilization."[27] Yet, at the same time, the struggle against communism is an integral part of the system itself and must be carried on: ". . . if you are not content, if you don't like it, fight against it. How? However you are able. For the best forms of struggle can only be found from experience of the struggle. And for the moment, there is too little such experience for useful conclusions to be drawn." Zinoviev agrees that we do not know how such a system can be defeated, but there is ample evidence of its internal crisis to make the search for successful resistance a meaningful one.

I believe that Chernenko is well aware of the internal failure of communism and that he shares with Andropov the conviction that foreign policy is the most important domestic program for the Soviet Empire. Although it may be impossible to predict the future of the Soviet system and although any drastic change in the system is certainly unlikely in the near future, these considerations were manifestly not sufficient to calm the anxieties of a Soviet dictator who had carefully studied—and fought—the various manifestations of discontent for a decade and a half as the head of the KGB. If, as I believe the evidence suggests, Chernenko is gravely concerned about the structural failure of the system and recognizes the deep dependence of the Soviet Union on Western technology and Western know-how, he may seek quick, decisive gains to reassure himself and the Russians that the communist prophecy will indeed be fulfilled, notwithstanding the current travails of the Soviet people. With quick domestic reform impossible, Andropov's search for success must of necessity be conducted internationally. In this manner, an Empire not otherwise vulnerable exposes itself to a potentially mortal challenge. By raising the stakes of the game, the Kremlin may bring its own stability into question.

THE STRUCTURAL CRISIS IV:
THE FOREIGN CHESSBOARD

The international objectives of a revolutionary regime are always the same: export of the revolution by all means considered legitimate and defeat of "counterrevolutionary forces" wherever possible. At issue are the tactics, and these in turn depend on varying circumstances, relative strengths and weaknesses, and calculations of possible gains and losses. The Russians are chess players and are used patiently to deploy their forces in various positions around the board, probing their opponents' defenses, and preparing for various possible reactions.

The notion of the world as chessboard fits neatly with both the Russians' national pastime and their vision of the steady advance of communism. Yet, such a vision of policy leaves little room for sudden, unexpected developments nor for strokes of imaginative courage. To remain with game-playing analogues, one can gain some insight into Russian national character by watching Soviet soccer teams, all of which play according to carefully prepared schemas and are quite lacking in the creativity that has distinguished the truly great teams like those from Brazil, Italy, and, earlier, Hungary. There is a predictability to the Soviet teams that makes effective defense rather easier than it is against the Brazilians or the Italians, who excel in improvising new ways to score goals. So it is in foreign policy, and it should surprise no one who takes Marxism seriously. For just as the Soviets believe they have found the one true guide to theory and practice and a political method that guarantees them success, so they search for the "correct method" in other fields as well, including sports, and they stick with that method once it has been sanctioned as "correct."

The vaunted "conservatism" of Soviet foreign policy, much of which is the predictable caution of a nation confronted by an opponent who has traditionally been much stronger than the U.S.S.R., also stems, in part, from confidence in the eventual accuracy of communist prophecy. Because the triumph of the Soviet bloc is guaranteed by historical laws, incidents along the way need not be taken seriously. Yet, confidence of this sort can be shaken by the repeated—and now evidently chronic—internal failure of the system, and confidence can turn to despair and confusion in the face of evidence that history has changed course. Judging by recent Soviet policy moves, we may be at the beginning of such a process.

Yuri Andropov's moves in 1983 to block the deployment of American Cruise and Pershing missiles in Western Europe looked very much like efforts to demonstrate that the Soviet Union could dictate terms to the Europeans. How else is one to explain the tone of Soviet statements, the constant threats of dire consequences if the Europeans held to their commitment to deploy the missiles if reductions could not be negotiated with the Soviets, the strident tones with which Andropov intervened in the German elections and in the affairs of the Williamsburg Summit? Crucial here is not so much the effort to block or delay the deployments—that was normal pursuit of advantage in the international game—but the selection of bullying as the most appropriate technique. The choice is puzzling—past experience having demonstrated that the West responds better to sweet talk than to blunt threat—unless it is explained on the basis of a real sense of urgency in the Kremlin. Andropov had not only to achieve results, but he had to do so in a way that could not be misunderstood: the West had to be seen to bend to Soviet desires.

Any single event can be explained in many ways, but a pattern of behavior requires a coherent assessment, and the pattern of behavior of the Andropov period and the first several months of Chernenko's rule suggest a Soviet drive to achieve quick and unequivocal foreign successes clearly identifiable as such both on the world's stage and at home, and preferably at the expense of the United States. Nothing is left to the imagination and no subtlety is employed: the Soviet Union simply stated its demands and awaited the obedient response.

It is both amusing and instructive to recall that when he succeeded Brezhnev, many Western commentators almost plaintively described Andropov as a sophisticated, almost Westernized politician, the master of subtlety and charm rather than the throwback to the Stalinist stereotypes of the pre-Khrushchev era that he really was. The destruction of the Korean passenger airliner—and even more to the point, the Soviet handling of the event—was managed in such a way as to say to the rest of the world, "whatever your own standards, let there be no doubt that we simply destroy anyone who ventures over our territory." This was of a piece with the other Andropov initiatives, brutally threatening those who did not behave as he wished. And the very consistency between the airline destruction and the tough talk to the Americans and Europeans led many to reconsider their view of Soviet intentions regarding the arms race. Since Chernenko's accession to power, things have continued along in much the same way, with an intensification of anti-American rhetoric from Moscow along with a parallel drive to achieve quick results at our expense both in Europe and in other areas. The most interesting case in point is that of Afghanistan, where the Soviets staged a major offensive in the Panshir Valley in the spring of 1984. Widely heralded in the Soviet media, this was clearly designed to break the back of the most vigorous Afghan resistance group, which had been a thorn in the Soviet side for more than three years.

Accompanied by fighter-bombers and armored flamethrowers, Soviet troops moved into the Panshir, but unlike the original invasion of the country—which was a strategic triumph—the attack against the guerrillas in the Panshir Valley was poorly designed and poorly executed. First, there was no element of surprise; the guerrillas were prepared for the attack, had already moved out of the main valley, and had taken refuge in caves in the smaller ravines that made passage difficult for the armored Soviet columns. Even the bombing attacks were poorly executed, and in the end directed against Potemkin villages because the main population grouping had been evacuated in anticipation of the attack.

The spring offensive, then, bore marks of political urgency and military improvisation; a marked contrast with the events of four years earlier, which had demonstrated political and military confidence and professionalism. The Soviets appeared to be frustrated by the slow tempo of fighting, irritated that the guerrillas had seemingly grown stronger over the past few years, and in a rush to achieve a clear-cut success. They, consequently, got what they deserved in the Panshir Valley: large numbers of casualties and a significant loss of face.

Such events are usually dictated by political requirements rather than by strategic assessments, and the sense of urgency that one detects underlying the attack against the Panshir Valley—with the attendant use of massive firepower, heavy bombing, and the spectacular-looking, but inappropriate, flamethrowers—is of a piece with the deepening Soviet concern about the flow of events both at home and abroad.

There are different ways to describe the attitude of the Soviets toward the current international situation, but they all add up to the same result: a sense of urgency. Some of the more common Kremlinological ruminations include:

The closing window of vulnerability view suggests that the Soviets developed a certain edge in strategic power during the seventies and early eighties and are now seeking to translate this military advantage into political gain and enhanced geopolitical security before the advantage is lost. Although there was no need to rush things so long as the overall strategic trends favored the Soviets, once the Reagan administration committed the United States to a program of rearmament, time became crucial. There are differing views of when (or even whether) the United States will draw even with the Soviet Union at current spending levels—one problem is that we do not have a good picture of Soviet military programs until their results appear in parades in Red Square in Moscow—but there is considerable agreement among a wide spectrum of defense analysts that whatever advantage the Soviets acquired is going to start diminishing shortly.

The decline in East-West relations view suggests that the Soviets had come to believe détente was a more or less permanent feature of international affairs and that détente constituted universal recognition that the U.S.S.R. had achieved superpower status. The Reagan administration's early rejection (rhetorically, at least) of the principles of détente, in particular the President's harsh words for the nature of the Soviet regime, were said to drive the Russians toward an intransigent position and provoke them to challenge the United States in a more direct manner than previously.

The ascension of the generals in the Kremlin view suggests that Andropov was chosen by a combination of old-line politicos (Gromyko in the first rank) and the military elite (Ustinov, Ogarkov) and that the same alliance installed Chernenko. According to some Kremlinologists, the real repository of political power in Moscow has shifted from the Politburo to the military committee and that the Soviet Union is, accordingly, headed toward some kind of "Bonapartism." This makes possible such shows of force as the Korean airline episode and encourages the use of military power in the search for geopolitical advantage because the generals (whether in the armed forces or in the KGB) are confident of Soviet military strength and are eager to demonstrate Soviet might to the rest of the world.

These may all be true (or false or partially true) without changing the overall picture. Most likely there are elements of truth in all these perspectives, especially the fear on the part of the Kremlin—and the military officials therein—that the United States is resolved to achieve and maintain an acceptable military balance. To be sure, the Soviets can take solace in their past experience with American spending surges, from the Marshall Plan to the post-Sputnik years, because they know that American enthusiasm for such programs inevitably wanes, the isolationist trends inevitably return, and the challenge to Soviet expansionism ebbs. But the current American surge comes at a time when the U.S.S.R. faces unprecedented internal difficulties, and—ominously—there are signs that the international trends are beginning to shift against the Communist tide.

The first great shock of the Reagan years came in late 1983 with the invasion of Grenada and the removal from power of the New Jewel Movement of Maurice Bishop. Though the Soviets had been careful to operate in Grenada through proxies (primarily the Cubans, although East Germany, Czechoslovakia, and even Bulgaria served in this role in specific areas), they had made a major, direct commitment in the Caribbean. Grenada was not so important in itself as for what it could represent for the Empire: the first Soviet outpost in the English-speaking world of the Western Hemisphere; a staging and training base for clandestine operations in the Caribbean and northern Latin

America (particularly against Venezuela); a highly useful relay
point aimed at the United States. And the Soviets made their
commitment to the Grenadians quite explicit when Marshall
Ogarkov told the ranking officer of the Grenadian army, Major
Einstein Louison, that the revolution in Grenada was irrevers-
ible, thus extending the Brezhnev doctrine to the Caribbean
region.

But for the first time, the Brezhnev doctrine failed; a Soviet
advance was reversed. As if to signal a sea change, the bloody
Bouterse regime in Suriname, which had seemed bent on joining
the Empire, expelled its Cuban advisers. And to make matters
even worse, the defeat came at a time when a similar setback
was looming in Angola, where the forces of Jonas Savimbi's
UNITA* guerrillas had established control over much of the
country, even though more than thirty thousand Cuban soldiers
were on hand to shore up the Soviet-supported regime of the
MPLA.† By early 1984, the U.S.S.R. was compelled to announce
increased military support for the embattled Angolan regime,
with the eventual outcome very much in doubt (rumor had it
that François Mitterrand had decided to restore the clandestine
French support for Savimbi late in the previous year). Were the
Angolan regime to fall, the entire Soviet strategy in the Third
World would inevitably be called into question.

These geopolitical setbacks occurred against the background
of other Soviet actions that suggested the Kremlin had been
looking for new methods to achieve its fixed objectives. In particular, the Soviet-supported international terrorist network was
an indication that the traditional method of Communist expansion—subversion of established governments and groups fighting against dictatorships through the use of local Communist
parties and front groups—was not succeeding. The terror network was (among other things) a way of intensifying the pressure on the West to make space for the extreme Left. But ter-

* Union for the Total Liberation of Angola.
† Popular Movement for the Liberation of Angola.

rorism was expensive, and even though the terrorists could resort to bank robberies and kidnappings to fill their coffers, this was apparently not good enough, for in three major theaters (Turkey, Cuba, and Italy), the terrorists were working hand-in-glove with organized criminal bands to run both drugs and arms. In the case of Cuba, the government itself became so deeply involved in the trafficking that a federal grand jury in Florida indicted four members of the Central Committee of the Cuban Communist party for involvement in drug-running. This was probably a reflection of the inability of the Kremlin to meet its heavy obligations; Cuba was taking $3 billion a year in aid (without which its own failed economy would not survive) and needed the extra revenues from the drug and arms businesses.

By forming a working alliance with organized crime, the Kremlin was taking an uncharacteristic risk (another sign of urgency) and paid for it with the breaking of the Italian Red Brigades (unravelled by Italian police investigations of the drug network) and the successful infiltration of at least some of their Latin American operations (notably the Colombian terrorist group M-19) by local governments and American agents. To be sure, a formidable terrorist threat remained with the vast PLO-supported network, the Armenian groups, and the Cuban network (undoubtedly extended into the continental United States during the seventies and early eighties), but the trends were not encouraging.

Combined with the indecisive Soviet actions in Poland, Lebanon, and Afghanistan, these developments called into question the direction of world events. Would such setbacks weaken the Soviet regime itself or simply add to the sense of urgency in the Kremlin? Or would American confusion about our own strategic objective eventually save the Soviets from their numerous errors? To these, yet another question needed to be added: Given an aging ruling class, would Soviet policymaking be paralyzed following the death—or incapacitation—of each successive dictator? Virtually immobile for the last few years of the Brezhnev era, the Soviet Union became even more unpredictable when An-dropov fell ill and disappeared from public view, and yet the Soviets chose as Andropov's successor another septuagenarian—Konstantin Chernenko—whose health seemed at least as bad as that of Andropov. It seemed, at least, to some observers that power had been distributed among a variety of persons—that there was no longer a single commander. Had the failure to solve the succession problem become chronic?

Whatever the answers to such questions, the other nations of the world were fully justified in looking with apprehension toward the two superpowers whose strategies were supposed to be the polar stars of the international firmament. Moving in eccentric orbits, the superpowers could not guarantee an orderly universe, and the growing chaos seemed destined to intensify.

DILEMMAS

I have argued that the increased risk of war in the world has resulted from a lack of control by the superpowers—a consequence of their incoherence and unpredictability. The increasingly aggressive and sometimes desperate actions of the Kremlin stem from a structural crisis that has no obvious solution, at least in the immediate future; American social, political, and economic structures are solid enough, but there seems to be little chance that the national elite can design and conduct an effective foreign policy. Soviet policy is conducted seriously, but is made against the background of internal crisis; American policy is conducted against the background of relative calm, but is not serious. Lacking clear direction, the risk of direct conflict is increased as the superpowers' unpredictability leads other countries to take greater risks on their own. This is the course on which we are now embarked. It remains to consider possible ways to lessen our danger.

THE SOVIET FUTURE

The Soviet Empire is driven by its revolutionary ideology and its vision of the future to expand; the internal crisis intensifies its drive to expansion. Ideally, one could hope for a combination of internal reform and a "mellowing," less aggressive leadership that would in time transform the Soviet Union into a country like others, one with which the West could eventually reach a stable accommodation. Many Kremlinologists foresee such a future; in fact the imminent if not actual arrival of Soviet "normalcy" has ben quite widely predicted with each recent succession in the Kremlin.[1] Given enough time, this may well come about, but it is small consolation today when we face the most dangerous of all adversaries: an opponent with great military power and a deep domestic crisis combined with a structural failure to provide for an orderly succession from one dictator to the next.

The situation may be growing even more dangerous because of the arrival in power of a new generation of Soviet leaders. Here, as usual, our information is poor; one can only speculate on the significance of this slow transition at the apex of power in the Kremlin, but it is certainly reasonable to assume that younger leaders will be more adventuresome than their predecessors. Quite aside from the natural differences between young and old, the terrible losses taken by the Soviets during the Second World War are said to have produced a profound aversion to warfare among the Brezhnev/Andropov/Chernenko generation, and the newcomers have no such experience. But more important, the older leaders participated in the creation of the modern Soviet Empire; whatever their failures to provide for the comfort and happiness of the people, the Kremlin's power and influence have grown considerably in the past generation. The newcomers may want to put their own stamp on things and, therefore, may be more easily tempted to take risks. Finally, they are more likely than their seniors to recognize the internal problems, for they have more recently arrived at the top.

A great deal has been said about the conservatism of the Soviets, but those who point to Soviet moderation often ignore the fact that the balance of power has only recently swung away from the West. When the strategic balance was clearly on the Western side, conservatism was the best Soviet alternative to a resounding defeat (as was demonstrated during the Cuban Missile Crisis). Only in the past five or ten years could the Soviets reasonably contemplate more aggressive military actions or use their military power to intimidate nations outside the Soviet sphere of influence. It is no accident, as the Soviets would put it, that in this period we have witnessed the first use of the Red Army outside the boundaries of the Warsaw Pact (Afghanistan) and an impressive military airlift in the Horn of Africa to demonstrate the possibilities of rapid intervention (Ethiopia). Both operations were carried out with great efficiency and indicated great self-confidence, neither of which characterized Soviet behavior in the past. And as Edward N. Luttwak has noted, this suggests a more aggressive use of military power in the future:

> We are therefore confronted by clear evidence of an utterly novel boldness on the part of Soviet military leaders, and of an equally new confidence on the part of the Kremlin leaders in the professional competence of their military colleagues . . . Now that boldness and an elegant economy of means characterize Soviet military operations, it is natural that a more confident and far less prudent external policy should also be in evidence.[2]

If this impressive growth in military power had taken place against a background of similar improvement in the structure of the empire, we could anticipate a continuation of Soviet prudence in international affairs, for the leaders in the Kremlin would then have every reason to look forward to the future with considerable confidence. But this is not the case, and indeed not only are the Soviet leaders concerned about internal matters, but also by a series of international setbacks, thus increasing their anxieties and heightening the probability that they will be tempted foolishly to use their great military might in a sudden effort to reverse quickly the external trends.

It is tempting to suggest that the West should help the Soviets "solve" their structural problems, thereby reducing the impetus to foreign adventurism. Although détente was never described in precisely such terms, it was implicit in some of the things Kissinger and Nixon said about it. The theory is that close ties in commerce and technology transfer would in the end increase Western leverage over the Soviet system. The generally unstated element in the theory is the notion that the Soviets would become "Westernized" by such contacts, thereby learning that a wealthier, more consumerist society is better than the poorer empire they currently rule over. In time, the Soviets would become more like us, and thanks to our goods and services they would become less militaristic and aggressive. In short, if the West promotes détente, it eventually produces reform within the Soviet system.

The theory is attractive and even elegant, but it is unlikely to work. In the first place, the Soviet people, let alone the *Nomenklatura,* do not need détente to realize that life is better on the Western side of the Yalta line; they know it already. As a matter of fact, they know it so well that a massive espionage network has been organized to make sure that they are able to steal what they cannot buy in Western science and technology. But the legal or illegal acquisition of the most advanced computer systems or even the latest in American hybrid corn seeds will not greatly affect the Kremlin's outlook on the world because the Western technology will be put to the service of the Soviet system and its current objectives.

Thus, instead of promoting change within the Soviet system, placing our technology in the Kremlin's hands only strengthens the rulers and, thus, makes change less likely. Many Westerners like to think that technology transfer is something that can be used as a diplomatic "carrot," something with which we can reward the Soviets and other countries for behavior of which we approve; in reality, each time a new advance in science or technology goes eastward, we have simply strengthened our adversaries—we have not encouraged them to change their behavior. Why should they change if we continue to give them what they want—and often extend them the credits with which to pay for it?

If we were seriously interested in using technology and trade to alter Soviet behavior, we would have to do so in concert with all the other advanced nations of the West. For, as Ion Mihai Pacepa has revealed and dozens of recent examples have confirmed, most of the American technology that reaches the Soviet bloc does not come directly from the United States; it is acquired through American subsidiaries or licensees overseas, mostly in Western Europe. But, as was seen when the Reagan administration tried to block the Soviet acquisition of equipment for the Yamal Pipeline in 1982, if the United States tries to stop this flow, there is great outrage from the Europeans, who feel *they* are entitled to make this decision, even though the equipment in question is manufactured under American license.

Consequently, the use of the technology "weapon"—like the use of the grain "weapon"—depends not only on American will, but also on our ability to forge a united Western front, and this is very difficult, indeed, especially after the extended period of détente during which several American administrations endorsed the notion of extending the commercial relations between East and West.

But even if we were in a position to generate a coherent Western policy on the subject of East-West trade, it would be difficult to use it to produce internal reform within the Soviet system. Reforming the Soviet system means striking at the status and wealth of the *Nomenklatura* generally and the military establishment more particularly. There is no reason to think that a system that rests on the systematic repression of the people and the systematic enrichment of a small elite will voluntarily tinker with itself, especially when there are substantial risks to be derived from such an experiment. Quite aside from the potential damage to particular members of the elite, the in-

troduction of change in a system that has been imposed at such
a cost and defended with such tenacity is fraught with danger,
for how can reform be contained within manageable parameters? Once begun, where would it stop? Russian history con-
tains several cases of leaders—both czars and dictators—who
attempted to liberalize the society; without exception the reformers became reactionary (or, as in the case of Khrushchev,
were removed) after the liberalization either failed or got out of
hand.

Khrushchev's failure suggests that we should be pessimistic
about chances for successful reform. If there are going to be
serious changes in the Soviet system, they will most likely be
wholesale and violent rather than gradual and peaceful. The system can be abandoned, abolished, or destroyed, but reform is
the least likely method of change. Thus, a policy of "linkage,"
whereby Western trade concessions would be tied to changes in
Soviet policy, may be used to isolate the Soviet Union or to try
to weaken or even to destroy it, but one should have few illusions about the prospects for "reform" of the Soviet system.

This is not to say that we should not have a policy of "linkage"; quite the opposite. I believe it is strategically foolish and
morally wrong to abandon control over the information and
technology that provides us with our most reliable margin of
safety. Moreover, I believe that a policy of linkage, resolutely
applied for several years, would have a considerable effect on
the Soviets. If they were unable to obtain our technology and
know-how without moderating their international activities, the
Soviets would have to choose between spending far more money
to keep up in the technological competition—and, therefore,
either reducing their military expenditures or increasing the
misery of their people—or coming to terms with the West to
maintain access to our technology.

However, although there may well be a breakdown of the
system, we are not in a position to predict it; thus, for policy

purposes, we must act as if the Soviet system will continue more or less as it is with its internal problems intensifying for the foreseeable future. Because we cannot evaluate the intensity of the Soviet structural crisis accurately enough to judge whether it has reached a critical moment, we will probably be unable to gauge when or whether Western assistance could "save" the system from its moment of truth. Our policies will have to be designed on the basis of a long- or medium-term analysis rather than an accurate short-term assessment.

At the moment, the medium- and long-term pictures from the Kremlin are not cheery; before looking at our policy options, it should be stressed again that both the internal crisis and the flow of international events help drive the Soviet Union toward foreign adventures that might produce quick victories for the Soviets. It is not merely pessimism about the future of the Soviet system, but also a pattern of setbacks around the world that call into question the accuracy of Lenin's prediction that communism will eventually prevail. If events show that the tide of history is running against the Soviets at the same time that what they themselves might term the internal contradictions of Soviet society are becoming clearer for all to see, then the Soviets might well lash out in desperation.

There is unlikely to be any substantial improvement in the internal situation, and it is hardly to our interest to attempt to influence international events in a direction more agreeable to the Kremlin. We can, accordingly, expect that the Soviets will push harder and harder for "victories," and crack down on anyone at home who tries either to challenge or to reform the system. In short, we cannot improve our chances for a safer world by hoping for, or encouraging, change within the Soviet system; nor can we hope that initiatives for making the world more peaceful and more equitable will come from Moscow. If we are going to make the world safer, the initiative will have to come from the West, and primarily from the United States.

WHAT SHOULD WE DO? CAN WE DO IT?

There are many ways to deal with the Soviet threat, all aimed at convincing the Soviet Union that violent action directed against the West is counterproductive. We can try to remain strong and resolute, attempting to contain Soviet expansion and wait for better times. We can try to "buy time," coming to various forms of accommodation with the Soviets, granting them greater influence, and hoping that they will eventually either mellow or collapse. Or, we can appease them, giving them what they demand to avoid a conflict that some fear more than the consequences of Soviet victory on a global scale. These are "defensive" strategies, essentially abandoning the hope that we can have a decisive influence on Soviet behavior (except insofar as, by granting them commercial and territorial concessions, we hope to moderate their appetites at least temporarily). They are based on a recognition of the enormity of Soviet military power and are designed to either guide that power in directions less dangerous to us or to "draw lines" on the dimensions of Soviet expansion or to yield in an orderly fashion. There are both pessimistic and optimistic advocates of such theories: the pessimists believe that the Soviets are destined to dominate much of the world in any event; the optimists believe that if we can get through the current phase, the Soviets will eventually cease to threaten us.

Some of the advocates of these defensive policies argue that the Russians aren't a real threat to the West at all and, consequently, that we need not threaten them. In their extreme form, these theories take the form that it is always the West that provokes the Soviets and that every act of Soviet aggression is somehow prompted or caused by an antecedent act by the West, generally the United States. All such policy recommendations in essence abandon the objective of defeating the Soviets. Some advocates of defensive policy grant the possibility that the Soviet Union may somehow collapse, but they do not believe that we should attempt to bring this about. By making the Soviet Union inviolable, such persons ascribe superpower status to the U.S.S.R., even in areas where it is clearly a secondary power, such as culture and economics.

Alternatively, there are more aggressive lines of action available. We might try to exploit the structural problems of the U.S.S.R. by withholding those elements that the Kremlin needs most desperately: grain, certain hi-tech products, and so forth. After we had established that a Western embargo could be maintained, we might then offer to trade these products for the sort of international behavior we desire. In addition, because the Soviet system rests on the systematic repression of its peoples, we might take a more active role in encouraging the repressed peoples to challenge Soviet hegemony. For example, the West seems to have done relatively little to help the Afghanis fight against the Red army; we could increase support to them, as to the various peoples fighting against Soviet proxies in Africa and Central America.

Such policies have been limited more by tradition and lack of imagination than by serious objections to them. The Soviet Empire is fragile, and the Kremlin's sensitivity to any suggestion that their legitimacy and authority are less than total betrays the Soviet leaders' own doubts about the solidity of their system. They are quite frightened, indeed, by the possibility that their subjects might have free access to international communications or even receive radio and television broadcasts from the free world. Their fear of ideas contrary to their own is so intense that when Jimmy Carter announced his human rights policy, the KGB conducted an intensive internal investigation, convinced that the Americans had arranged some kind of uprising. This kind of insecurity is confirmed by the billions of dollars' worth of effort the Kremlin devotes each year to jamming Western radio broadcasts aimed at the Soviet Empire as well as the additional billions spent on their own propaganda, both at home and abroad. Many Westerners are impressed with the Soviets' disinformation effort, as well they should be, but they forget the underlying insecurity about their own system that drives the Soviets systematically to distort reality for their own citizens as well as ours. With such insecurity in the Kremlin, we should be confident of our ability to strike effective blows against them.

My own preference is for a relatively aggressive policy in support of the democratic revolution throughout the world because I believe that this is both in keeping with our own traditions and most likely to strike at the evils and weaknesses in the Soviet system. We need to support those democratic forces that challenge dictators, whether of the right or the left. If the United States were to put itself solidly behind the forces of the democratic revolution, we would have far greater success in combating communism. We often forget that the Communists have sometimes worked to create dictatorships of the extreme right because with such regimes in power, the Communists believe that their own chances are greatly enhanced. But they cannot tolerate successful democratic revolutions, and Soviet foreign policy constantly shows this. The most recent example of this long-standing principle of Soviet foreign policy is Central America, where the Cubans created a unified guerrilla movement in El Salvador only *after* the democratic revolution in 1979 that removed the old oligarchs and led to the first presidency of José Napoleon Duarte. In Honduras, the guerrilla movement became a serious threat only after the country was firmly committed to the path of free elections and civilian governments.

Communist rhetoric has always vilified moderate democrats and democratic socialists, whether in Europe or in the Third World, because they cannot tolerate peaceful, successful transformations of societies under the moderating influence of the principles of law. The Soviet Union and its proxies insist that only a sudden, violent transformation of the world is possible and that all other kinds of change are bogus. It is up to us to demonstrate that they are wrong; indeed, this is the heart of the ideological conflict between us. If we wage this war of ideas enthusiastically and energetically, I believe the Soviets will eventually regret their challenge.

But no policy will succeed without constancy and resolve, and the most admirable worldview will be insufficient if the conduct of policy is incoherent. The question before the nation today is whether we can find the individuals capable of leading us, and put them in a position to do it. As things currently stand, it seems impossible to achieve this with our own people. Many of the reasons for this sad state of affairs—above all, a view of the world that makes it quite difficult for our own elite to define and pursue our vital interests—have already been discussed. To these must be added two more structural elements: the triumph of bureaucratic interest and blind legal formulae over individual initiative and personal accountability, and the failure to maintain bipartisanship in foreign policy.

Our system rewards caution and the acquisition of bureaucratic turf. There are no penalties for policy failures and only the rarest rewards for courage and imagination. In other words, there is no accountability within our bureaucracy. In our efforts to strike a reasonable balance between a society of people and a society of laws, we have chosen the second alternative, thereby confirming the Iron Law of Oligarchy, as currently defined and enforced by the lawyers that so afflict us. In the American government today, the privileges and security of the collective are enforced even when the public interest is thereby damaged. It is virtually impossible to fire anyone for incompetence, and this quite predictably undermines discipline and breaks the chain of command. Not so long ago, a junior officer in one of the bureaus of the Department of State wrote an analysis of an important policy question and, quite on his own, had his work printed and distributed. When the director of the bureau investigated the case, he found that the officer in question had, until a couple of years earlier, been in charge of filing for a different office. Being poorly educated, this officer had misfiled a considerable quantity of information, for which his supervisor attempted to fire him.

The good officer filed a protest, claimed to have been subjected to discrimination, won his case, and was promoted to the position of analyst from which he issued his report. After all this, no one dared challenge his right to do so, even though the report had not been requested, the officer had no qualifications for his position, and his analysis was at odds with the position of the bureau from which it was finally issued.

With such a system, it is no surprise that the wheels of government grind so slowly and that talented individuals are reluctant to make sacrifices to serve in it. We have to restore accountability, but this is easier said than done. No professional (that is, no member of the military services or officer of the foreign service) can be fired unless he or she has committed a crime (things are different with political appointees, who can be terminated quite quickly, as in the case of a scandal); with the various legal and bureaucratic remedies available, an individual can even resist transfer for nearly a year. Without the power to fire subordinates or, at least, to move them quickly out of the way when they perform badly, no manager can effectively enforce discipline; yet, the professionals fear—with considerable justification—that if their bosses were free to hire and fire, these decisions would often be made on purely political criteria. Moreover, the professionals can legitimately argue that often their (politically selected) superiors are far less qualified in the field of foreign affairs.

The national interest requires that policymakers be qualified and that they have effective power to design and conduct policy. Without the proper qualifications, they will be unable to articulate and advance our vital interests and will, in any case, be considered illegitimate by the professionals; without power over the system, they will be unable to enforce discipline and produce timely decisions. The two ingredients go hand-in-hand: given the right people, it will be possible to entrust them with the kind of power that they need. But they must be placed in key positions in both the executive and the legislative branches of government, for without bipartisanship foreign policy cannot be conducted effectively.

The lack of bipartisanship in foreign policy not only makes it more difficult for us to design and conduct policy, it also offers our adversaries the opportunity to win in Washington what they cannot gain in their own direct efforts in the international arena. Indeed, every president in recent memory has complained about the constant "interference" in foreign policy from the Congress. While no one challenges the legitimacy of Congressional oversight of foreign policy, the main problems derive from the attempt of some members of Congress to exercise an almost daily control over the conduct of international affairs by the executive. This is clearly a recipe for a very bad policy, for it is hard enough to design and manage policy with the very large bureaucracy that is charged with such responsibilities; it is impossible when one adds more than five hundred legislators and thousands of staff assistants.

The most desirable relationship between the president and Congress would be one in which the general discussion of foreign policy problems was conducted at the outset of an administration, the outlines of policy were agreed on, and then Congress stepped back and permitted the president to conduct that policy. Barring some major crisis, Congress should give the executive branch maximum flexibility in the conduct of foreign policy, and the White House should strain to keep members of Congress fully briefed; after all, the diplomatic requirement for full consultation of allies should apply domestically as well as within the international alliance structure.

Of course, that is easier said in the abstract than done in the real world. The central issue still remains: When, and with what frequency, can Congress legitimately play a major foreign policy role? It is clearly intolerable, for example, for Congress to attempt to "fine tune" policy, as in the case of Central America in 1983–84. With repeated requirements that the president "certify" the performance of the government of El Salvador, Con-

gress in effect held a fiscal sword of Damocles over the head of
the Salvadorans and gave to both political extremes in that be-
leaguered country the chance to terminate American aid. Presumably, all that was necessary for an end to American assistance to El Salvador was a major eruption of something that
could be identified as the activity of "right-wing death squads."
Thus extremists of the right, or other people successfully posing
as right-wing killers, could jeopardize the survival of El Salvador
by murdering a sufficient number of innocent civilians or moderate politicians. This clearly ran counter to both the interests of
the United States and to the interests of the people of El Salvador, for the United States was attempting to provide security
for El Salvador—victimized by a guerrilla movement that was
sponsored by neighboring Nicaragua (and there was no disagreement about the facts of the case, even by those who opposed
American policy in Central America)—and for America herself.
If the pro-Soviet Communist regimes of Cuba and Nicaragua
were permitted to expand into El Salvador and to move north
toward Mexico and the Texas border, the United States could
find a guerrilla movement on her doorsteps, and at a minimum
would have to cope with an unprecedented movement of refugees from south to north. The Congress might be justified in
demanding an improvement in the human-rights performance of
the Salvadoran Government and elements of her armed forces,
but such improvements are usually slow in coming, and with
such vital security interests at stake the least one can say is that
it was highly imprudent for the Congress to demand such frequent reviews of the internal Salvadoran situation.

Just as excessive politicization of arms control makes it
more difficult for any administration to conduct successful negotiations with the Soviet Union, so the excessively frequent involvement of Congress in Central American policy made it more
difficult for the administration to exert steady pressure on El
Salvador. Internal reform is always easier to achieve when it is
clear that the country in question is not being asked to commit

political suicide, and Congressional behavior not only encouraged panic in El Salvador, it also encouraged the Nicaraguans, the Cubans, and the Salvadoran guerrillas to play for time and to meddle in the internal debate in the United States. In short, our adversaries in Central America were offered the chance of winning in Washington what they could not possibly gain in the Salvadoran war. This was reminiscent of the situation in Lebanon, where the Syrians and their Druse and Shi'ite allies were led to believe that if they only killed enough American diplomats and marines, Congress would eventually compel the withdrawal of American (and thus the Italian, British, and French) military forces from the country.

There was another similar shortcoming in the discussions of both Lebanon and Central America: in each case there was an unwillingness to identify the central adversary of American interests. Just as it took a very long time to realize that Syria was fundamentally opposed to Western interests in Lebanon, neither the Kissinger Commission nor the participants in the broader public debate were able to deal with the problem of Cuba in Central America. This is quite understandable, since Cuba is both unpleasant and difficult for American policymakers to deal with. Yet just as we could not achieve our objectives in Lebanon unless we dealt with Syria (and behind her, the Soviet Union), so we shall not be able to achieve our objectives in Central (and Latin) America unless we deal with Cuba (and behind her, the Soviet Union). Castro may be amenable to some sort of arrangement with us, especially since recent events have not been favorable to him. His forces are apparently leaving Ethiopia, they have been defeated in Angola and Grenada, and the Cuban- and Sandinista-backed guerrillas in El Salvador are not winning that war either. As the Soviet Union finds the cost of Cuba ($4 billion per year) increasingly hard to bear, there may be some chance for a settlement that would put an end to Cuban adventurism in Central America, in exchange for American assistance for Castro. On the other hand, he may insist on his revolutionary destiny and, as he has so many times in the past (most recently, so far as I know, in a conversation with Ambassador at Large Vernon Walters in 1982), reject efforts to normalize our relations and his behavior. If that is the case, then the United States, one hopes in tandem with other democratic states in the region, will have to design a strategy to either contain Cuban actions or challenge Castro's regime itself.

In the bipartisan Kissinger report, both the security threat and the underlying misery that gives the Cubans, the Sandinistas, and the guerrillas such willing allies are addressed properly as integral parts of a single problem. In the partisan political debates in Congress—and those between the administration and its critics—these two elements are often dealt with independently of each other, and by the late spring of 1984 Congress was often acting as if one could separate the Salvadoran problem from that of Nicaragua. With the presidential campaign in full swing, it seemed highly unlikely that bipartisan support for the bipartisan recommendations of the Kissinger Commission could be mustered to both assist El Salvador and continue pressure on Nicaragua—and the all-important matter of Cuba was not discussed at all. This was not simply the result of the differences between those engaged in the political debate and those with the luxury of more detached ratiocination, for a highly politicized group—the members of the Kissinger Commission—had reached a significant consensus on the most highly charged foreign policy issue before the country. Instead, it was yet another symptom of the broader problem: the lack of informed and resolute persons who are prepared to fight for the national interest. Without such a policy elite we shall not have good policy. Is it possible to develop such a group?

I have argued that the United States does not produce a satisfactory foreign policy elite, both because of our current political practices and because of our national traditions. There are exceptions, to be sure. But it is difficult to find them, to convince them to come to Washington, to have them make the necessary considerable sacrifices now required for government service, and to remain in government long enough to make a difference. We should consider the possibility of creating a policy-making elite from the broadest possible base, drawing on the talent that now exists throughout the Western world and enlisting it to help us design our policies and simultaneously educate a new generation of Americans in the intricacies of the world as it now exists. In short, we should attempt to recruit some of our foreign policy officials from other Western countries and not limit our talent search to the United States alone.

Many of the best American foreign policies have come from abroad, for the basic pattern in our history is that we react slowly to challenges, arrive relatively late in the day in major crises, and then often overcompensate in our response. Men and women who have watched this pattern from allied capitals understand better than we the enormous consequences of our actions and inactions on the rest of the world, and their counsel has often been of great value to American presidents and secretaries of state. Roosevelt's policy of assistance to Great Britain prior to our entry into World War II was shaped by Churchill, and the Marshall Plan was as much a West European product as it was an American one; the same can be said of détente. Much of our current policy in the Pacific region is the result of years of education from the likes of Lee Kuan Yew of Singapore and a new generation of Japanese leaders, and so it goes. But the input of foreign leaders is intermittent and inevitably skewed by the domestic political considerations of the foreigners. If they were able to come to Washington as private Western citizens (not advocates for a narrow national interest) to work for the president on a more or less permanent basis, they would be freed of their own political constraints and would be able to look at the world from a broad, Western perspective, informed by their own experiences and by their geopolitical visions.

Every president has recognized the necessity of having available the politically disinterested advice of wise men and women whose experience and judgment makes them uniquely qualified to serve the country. Such persons often serve, for example, on the President's Foreign Intelligence Advisory Board (PFIAB), a largely unknown group of great talent (it is currently headed by Ambassador Anne Armstrong and Leo Cherne) that helps the president evaluate the performance of the intelligence community and design ways to improve it. PFIAB works well because it is helpful to both the White House and the intelligence community. In those cases where the community has functioned poorly, PFIAB is in an ideal position to examine quietly the causes of failure and work to correct them without exposing the persons involved to harsh public criticism and the unhelpful politicized recriminations that characterize so many postmortems. From the president's point of view, PFIAB is a reliable source of information and a dispassionate source of advice, two precious commodities.

There is another secret to PFIAB's success that speaks to one of our major problems: its activities do not make news. As a result, its members are generally reacting to real problems rather than to those that have been defined by the latest news broadcast or the latest front-page story.

A similar institution could be created for foreign policy and overall strategy, including (although not limited to) distinguished figures from other allied countries. At present, there are several such individuals "available" for work of this type, all former prime ministers or foreign ministers: Helmut Schmidt of Germany, Francesco Cossiga of Italy, and Adolfo Suarez of Spain, to name just three. What a splendid contribution they could make to our strategic thinking if they served on a presidential advisory board with men like Henry Kissinger, James Schlesinger, Dean Rusk, and Harold Brown.

In addition to serving the president directly, such men and women would, by their regular presence in Washington and their ongoing contribution to our foreign policy discussions, broaden and deepen the quality of our debate. For the first time, they could participate in such discussions as direct contributors to the creation of Western policy and not merely as advocates of their national causes. It is entirely appropriate for them to participate directly in our foreign policy decisions; they have already done so from the outside, and they know, perhaps better than most of us, that American foreign policy must represent the interests of the West as a whole. Their participation as "insiders" is both proper and useful.

But it is not sufficient to draw on foreign talent simply in an advisory capacity; such individuals should be placed in positions of authority where their examples and their instructions can be brought to bear on our own professionals and political appointees. This is not the place to consider the specific positions and the individuals who should fill them. But if, for the sake of argument, the president and his top advisers came to believe that the finest strategist in the Western world came from a foreign country, but was willing to become an American to serve the Western cause, then why not invite him to serve as national security adviser to the president where he can both advise the president and bring his own unique discipline to bear on the entire system?

The notion of importing strategists from abroad is neither new nor all that unusual. When Richelieu approached the end of his life and searched for a suitable successor, he turned to Italy and brought Cardinal Mazarino to Paris to manage French foreign policy for much of the "splendid century." Suitably recycled as "Mazarin," this brilliant Italian made a notable contribution to the creation of a stable European system, to the enduring advantage of the French national interest. At that time, France served as the model and guide for many other countries, and the men who designed French policy did so with this broader vision in mind. American policy should be designed and conducted with a similarly broad vision, and those who have lived and worked in other Western countries can help us realize that vision.

This process has functioned well in the past, albeit on a somewhat slower timetable than the one I have in mind and on a random rather than a planned basis. The likes of Henry Kissinger and Zbigniew Brzezinski have come from abroad to make a significant contribution to our foreign policy, and the country is the richer for their presence.

There are political advantages to this method as well as the obvious strategic ones: by bringing some of our policymakers from a political context other than our own, we spare them the scars and wounds that our own political leadership brings to government. A Cossiga or a Suarez, for example, would represent a politically neutral component in our policy debate and would be spared a good deal of the politicized criticism that now inevitably weakens the members of our own elite. The presence of such persons would not only give us an elite of more varied experience and deeper understanding than the current group but would help to drive home the point that American foreign policy must be designed and conducted above the domestic political battlefield, for there are broader and more enduring interests at stake than those defined by the day-to-day American political conflict.

But even the introduction of the world's finest minds to Washington will not save us without bringing accountability into the foreign policy process. This means that failure should incur some cost and success should be rewarded, a concept that would seem to be the essence of fairness. Yet, after years of permitting our bureaucrats to function in an environment where there was a premium on *not* taking risks and where accommodation rather than the desire to shape the world was the dominant leitmotif of the foreign service, anyone who tries to reinstitute accountability will be accused of trying to politicize the foreign policy process. Here again, by bringing in men and women who have no vested interests in the Washington political game, there is a fair chance that we can get through the transition without fatal stresses and strains. If this can be achieved, we will be well on the way to assembling a policymaking bureaucracy that will effectively fight for our interests.

POLICY AND LEADERSHIP

With good advisers and a bureaucracy motivated by a desire to excel rather than by a fear of standing out from the crowd, we can expect good recommendations to reach the desks of the president and his cabinet secretaries. But will our leaders be able to use them to best advantage? And will they be able to overcome their political blinders and make policy "on the merits" rather than on the basis of domestic political considerations? Once again, the answer is probably no unless some changes are made.

Our political system will inevitably generate candidates who are out of touch with the basic foreign policy issues so long as the presidential campaign lasts several years. The best way I can think of to help presidental candidates stay up to date on the state of the world is to reduce the length of time they are forced to study issues from a purely political standpoint. Would it be possible to forbid the creation of presidential campaign organizations until there is just one year left until election day? I don't know the answer, but at least some of the political experts I have asked about this believe there is some chance. If it can be done, it would be helpful, for it would permit political leaders to study foreign policy questions without the necessity of making pronouncements all the time. In this way, it would be possible to educate some of our leaders before the campaign so that the eventual winner would not be years out of date on November 5.

All of this requires that the media will permit the political process to become more rational and the foreign policy process to achieve a certain independence from the daily political tumult. Without the cooperation of the media, no one of good character will accept appointment (or run for election) to high office, for he or she will be unwilling to have every detail of his or her life subjected to minute analysis. The media will have to strike an acceptable balance between the public's curiosity about the lives of leading Americans and the minimum of privacy required to make public life tolerable.

But granting a certain integrity to the private lives of our leaders is insufficient, for the media must also stop treating foreign policy as one more element in the domestic political debate. Our journalists and broadcasters must recognize that there are such things as national interests and that their definition and defense are vitally necessary, regardless of which party or leader is in command at the moment. Without this recognition we are doomed to the continued politicization of foreign policy, and this is a prescription for folly, unpredictability, and disaster. It is hard enough to come up with good foreign policy under the best of circumstances, but it is impossible when the media are competing with foreign intelligence services for American secrets and when the leak of sensitive information has become a basic weapon in the debate over foreign policy.

Can our journalists, editors, broadcasters, and producers be convinced that it is not a good idea for them to make public a dramatic scoop if it jeopardizes national security? Who is to convince them of this? Certainly, they are unlikely to listen sympathetically to government officials, and the judges and lawyers have tended to take the side of the media in the ongoing struggle between the keepers of the secrets and those who wish to make them public. Finally, anyone who believes that the media will be able to police itself, whether in the area of respecting national security or in that of respecting the privacy of other citizens, is likely to be disappointed. Doctors and lawyers have not been able to regulate themselves, why should we expect superior performance from the press? In the end, media responsibility will have to be defined and the media monitored, just like other professions. Those who desire a moderate solution to the ongoing conflict between media and state need to move quickly before the absolutists on both sides of the First Amendment insist on extreme solutions.

The other main requirement for the media is one that I have already discussed: rigorous libel laws with automatic penalties for those who commit libel. There is some legitimacy to the claim by First Amendment advocates that a few big libel decisions might have a "chilling effect" on free speech, but at least, for the moment, this risk is decidedly less than that of the chilling effect of journalists on elected and appointed officials as well as on distinguished private citizens.

THE FUTURE

The Soviets need to find a way to cure the structural defects of their political and economic system; the Americans must somehow create a foreign policy elite capable of leading the free world. Neither seems likely to solve its basic problems, and the unpredictability and incoherence of the superpowers are, therefore, likely to continue. I believe that we in the United States have a real chance to take the initiative in international affairs if only we will give foreign policy the importance and the integrity it deserves, insisting that our various institutions—especially the media—respect that decision. If that can be accomplished, it may then be possible to manage the explosive crisis of the Soviet Empire and, thus, navigate the treacherous waters that lie ahead of us. If we do not take these matters seriously, if we continue to permit the tactical to prevail over the strategic, the domestic over the international, and the transient over the enduring national interest, then we shall have earned the crisis into which we shall surely enter, without understanding how or why it happened, or how we might escape its terrible consequences.

NOTES

CHAPTER 1. THE GRAVE NEW WORLD

1. In the mid-thirties, for example, Stalin believed that the situation was ripe for a Communist uprising in Italy and Germany; the result of his call for open revolution against Nazism and Fascism was a devastating setback to the Communist parties in those countries. This episode is well known, but perhaps the most interesting description and analysis is in Giorgio Bocca's excellent biography, *Palmiro Togliatti* (Rome and Bari: Laterza & Figli, 1973), pp. 195–248.

2. This little-known plan of the Americans is documented by material I recently obtained through the Freedom of Information Act. It will appear in my forthcoming book on West European Communism and American foreign policy (New Brunswick, N.J.: Transaction Books, 1985).

3. This, in turn, has brought about the end of one of the most important myths of the postwar period: that the West could lend money to any country in the Soviet Empire with full confidence that the Soviet Union would eventually make good. This so-called umbrella theory has now collapsed; as a result, the Empire is having trouble raising money in the West.

4. Walter Lippmann, "The Dangerous Amateurs," *New York Herald Tribune*, February 5, 1952. Quoted in Clinton Rossiter and James Lare, eds., *The Essential Lippmann* (New York: Random House, 1963), p. 368.

5. It may come as a surprise to many Americans to learn that in dis-

cussions between Western statesmen at the highest level, Soviet support for (*not* creation of, or total control over) the Western peace movements has long been taken for granted. One European foreign minister told Secretary of State Alexander M. Haig, Jr., for example, that in his long years of political activity he had never seen so much Soviet money in his country as during the antimissile campaign of 1981–82. European intelligence services were able to document this Soviet activity in considerable detail; the Dutch service's study was leaked to the press and published in the Netherlands and in Germany. And in Denmark, the Foreign Ministry took the extraordinary step of expelling a Soviet agent, annoucing the name of the person in the Danish peace movement who had been working with the Soviets, and inviting him to sue the Government for libel if he desired.

The documentation on KGB involvement in the peace movement is quite vast. (Again, lest there be any misunderstanding, I am talking about Soviet efforts to manipulate the movement, not Soviet *creation* of the peace movement or total Soviet *control over* the movement.) To take the Scandinavian cases first, here are some excerpts from an unclassified State Department cable in December of 1981 that was sent to all European posts:

> The Norwegian case involved a Norwegian peace activist, Bjarne Eikefjord, who was quoted in an article in a Norwegian newspaper as having "Top Secret" documents indicating U.S. Government plans to target parts of Norway for nuclear attack. Eikefjord had brought copies of these papers to the U.S. Embassy for verification, but had gone to the newspaper with his "evidence" before waiting for a reply from the embassy in Oslo. What Eikefjord had in fact appears to be a version of Soviet forgeries circulated for years, based on Army documents stolen in the early 1960s by Army Sgt. Lee Johnson, who was later convicted of espionage. The embassy in Oslo has written a letter to the editor of the newspaper explaining the true nature of the "Top Secret" plans.

> *Denmark.* Danish Foreign Minister Kjeld Olesen confirmed in a November 6 press conference newspaper reports detailing the circumstances surrounding the October 1981 expulsion from Denmark of a KGB operative working under the guise of Soviet Embassy second secretary in Copenhagen.

> According to newspaper reports, the Soviet, Vladimir Merkulov, acted as KGB case officer for Arne Herlov Petersen, a Danish author, member of the Danish-North Korean Friendship Associa-

tion, and KGB agent-of-influence associated since the early 1970s with the Soviet intelligence service.

On at least one occasion, Merkulov is known to have provided Petersen with a letter, forged by the KGB but appearing to have originated in the United States, purporting to detail the substance of alleged U.S.-Chinese discussions aimed at preventing North Korean negotiations (presumably with the PRC). Petersen was instructed by Merkulov to pass the letter on to the North Korean Embassy in Copenhagen, the purpose being to arouse North Korean suspicions of Chinese intentions and ultimately move North Korea closer to the USSR. . . .

Petersen's value to Merkulov as an agent-of-influence was also evident by virtue of his contacts among Danish artistic and journalistic circles, according to media reports. Petersen apparently arranged at Merkulov's instruction for some 150 Danish artists to sign an "appeal" calling for a Nordic nuclear weapons-free zone. With money supplied by Merkulov, Petersen then had the appeal placed as an advertisement in a number of local newspapers. In addition, Petersen was believed to have made a number of recruitment attempts among his journalist colleagues on behalf of the KGB. Petersen's activity in this sphere was intended to increase the number of journalistic assets in the clandestine intelligence net which Merkulov was coordinating in Denmark. In all, it was estimated that Petersen had received approximately 10,000 Danish Kroner in exchange for his assistance to Merkulov and the KGB. He was arrested by Danish authorities on November 4.

According to the Danish press, Merkulov's activity was not confined to running and coordinating the operations of agents such as Petersen.

Merkulov and other members of the Soviet Embassy in Copenhagen reportedly maintained contact with the Copenhagen-based Committee for Cooperation for Peace and Security, an umbrella organization of approximately 50 smaller peace-related associations and groups with well-established ties to the Soviet-dominated World Peace Council. (The World Peace Council is a well-known Communist Front and a primary conduit for Moscow's financial and other support to segments of the European peace movement.)

In Germany, to take one example among many, there was the remark of Defense Minister Hans Apel, reported by John Wallach and Bernard Kaplan of the Hearst Newspapers from Bonn on November 1, 1981 (I quote from the *San Francisco Chronicle* of that date):

Bonn. "I heard your remarks, general, about the communist in-

filtration of these protests and I agree with you," West German
Defense Minister Hans Apel snapped, interrupting his command-
ing officer, Maj. Gen. Peter Tandecki.

"There's no doubt about it. The money comes from them, the in-
frastructure. The bus arrives on time. The soup arrives on time.
All those things which can only be organized by a military or
para-military organization."

. . . German authorities believe a sizable portion of the money
needed to stage what was, in effect, a gigantic public spectacle
was channeled through East Germany. Most of it came from the
Evangelical Church there.

Funds from east of the Elbe also helped to finance last June's
dress rehearsal for the Bonn rally, a church congress in Ham-
burg attended by 100,000 "peace partisans."

The Dutch story, perhaps the most interesting, played out over
many months, and would take too much space to describe in complete
detail here. But the general outlines of the case were well described
in the Dutch newspaper *De Telegraaf* on June 3, 1982. The headline
read: "West German Security Service: Money from Moscow for 'Stop
the Neutron Bomb.' " Datelined The Hague, the article went on:

"Stop the Neutron Bomb" was partly supported financially by
Moscow. Former Minister Drs. Van Thijn denied this a half year
ago in the Second Chamber. The West German security service
made these accusations in a confidential report which was leaked
last month in the General Republic, a report entitled, "Left Ex-
tremist Influence on the Peace Demonstration of 10 October
1981 in Bonn." The Second Chamber member Drs. Aad Wagenaar
(RPF) will put a question this week about the report to the new
Minister of Internal Affairs, Mr. M. Rood. Drs. Wagenaar stated
yesterday that he had learned from reliable sources that the information which had been leaked in Germany is based on two
reports of the Dutch internal security service (BVD). According
to the Parliament member, "former Minister of Internal Affairs
Drs. Van Thijn was playing bluff poker when, last year in September in the Second Chamber, he declared that there was only
talk of a 'slander campaign' against the Dutch peace movement,"
said Drs. Wagenaar. On that occasion, the minister of internal
affairs called the "so-called American evidence" for the contacts
between the East bloc and the Dutch peace movement "neither
rock solid nor butter soft."

"This West German report goes against the assertions of ex-
Minister Van Thijn," claimed the RPF Second Chamber member.

In the report of the West German BVD, which was compiled in

November 1981, it was said, there is no doubt that the Netherlands committee "Stop the Neutron Bomb" is led in an orthodox
Communist manner, with financial assistance from the Soviet
Union and with the aid of Russian functionaries from the international section of the Central Committee of the Communist
Party. "Stop the Neutron Bomb" organized in the Netherlands
actions against atomic arms in general and against the neutron
bomb in particular. Orthodox Communists are also present in a
number of cells of the IKV (Inter Church Peace Council) according to the German security report.

For those who wish to read more on this subject, there was a two-
part series in a Rotterdam monthly, *Ons Leger*, by J. A. E. Vermatt,
published in October and November of 1981, and a six-part series in
De Telegraaf of Amsterdam, written by J. G. Heitink, published July
22, 23, 25, 29 and August 1, 1981.

6. The best recent study of the Cuban role in international terrorism
is Edouard Sablier's *Ie Fil Rouge: Histoire Secrète du Terrorisme international* (Paris: Plon, 1983), especially Chapter X, "Un Fidèle Sous-
traitant."

CHAPTER 2. THE CHARACTERISTICS
OF AMERICAN POLICY

1. The quotation from Schlesinger is taken from an unpublished address he made under the auspices of the Georgetown University Center for Strategic and International Studies in 1982. I am grateful to
him for the text of that address.

2. S. Robert Lichter and Stanley Rothman, "Media and Business
Elites," in *Public Opinion* (Washington, D.C.: October/November,
1981). This article, quite rightly in my opinion, has become a water-
shed in the analysis and understanding of the American mass media.

3. I'm indebted to Professor Bernard Lewis of Princeton University
for this striking quotation.

4. Jimmy Carter, *Keeping Faith: Memoirs of a President* (New York:
Bantam, 1982), p. 19.

5. Ibid., p. 143.

6. Not only did the United States fail to help Spain in this matter,
but the Government of France—which had a unique opportunity to
close down ETA—also declined to participate in a serious antiterrorist
campaign. The government of Giscard d'Estaing refused request after

request from Madrid, even though it was public knowledge that ETA terrorists lived undisturbed (albeit not surveilled) in the Basque regions of France. Any time that the French chose to do so, they could have co-operated with the Spaniards to shut down the bulk of ETA's operations by the simple expedient of denying them the safe haven and tranquil atmosphere in which they operated in France. This was not done, on the pretext that the traditional French policy of giving asylum to "political exiles" prevented them from moving against the Basques. This excuse might have had some credibility while Franco was in power in Spain but not in the new democratic era. The real reason was more pragmatic and, as usual in such matters, had to do with internal concerns: Giscard was afraid that if he helped with the Basques there might be terrorist trouble in France.

For once, there was a certain justice to the course of events. The French Government persisted in its unhelpful stance under Mitterrand, and indeed carried the illogic of its position one step further: not only did the French fail to help the fight against Spanish terrorists, they also largely dismantled the excellent internal security structure that had been in place for some years, thus enabling terrorists to begin operating in France itself. Waves of bombings (mostly directed against Jews and carried out by radical Arab groups) swept Paris, producing a public outcry and a belated attempt on the part of the government to reinstitute some sort of antiterrorist organization. Even then, there was no help for the Spaniards and there would be none until the elections of late October 1982 signaled that the Socialists would take power in Madrid. Then, with a solid political excuse to reverse years of error, the French began to cooperate with Spanish security organizations.

7. I was told this story by a former leading American official who spoke privately with Lopez Portillo shortly after the meeting with Carter. William Safire later published an almost identical account in his column in the *New York Times*.

8. The much-maligned State Department "White Paper" on Nicaragua and Salvador that was issued in the first months of the Reagan administration was based almost entirely on information gathered during the Carter period.

9. This quotation, from an article by Cottam in the spring 1979 issue of *Foreign Policy* magazine, is cited in Michael Ledeen and William Lewis, *Debacle: The American Failure in Iran* (New York: Knopf, 1981), p. 210.

10. Ibid., for a more complete exposition of these themes, especially pp. 127 ff. and pp. 208 ff.

11. Ibid., p. 212.

12. This is developed in detail in my forthcoming book on West European communism and American foreign policy (New Brunswick, N.J.: Transaction Books, 1985).

13. There is another notable difference, which has already been cited: dictatorships of the authoritarian Right, as Ambassador Kirkpatrick has pointed out, do often evolve into fully participatory democracies, whereas those of the totalitarian Left and Right seldom, if ever, do.

14. Rossiter and Lare, *Essential Lippmann*, p. 82.

CHAPTER 3. THE FAILURE OF THE AMERICAN ELITE

1. This is painfully clear regarding the discussion of nuclear weapons, where the three crucial questions—deterrence, proliferation, and the overall strategic balance of power—are frequently overlooked in the passion of the rhetorical fray. Instead—and this is typical of the general problem—we hear a great deal about freezes, unilateral gestures, and other fashionable claims to innovation in an area that has long been frustratingly unresponsive to attempts at total resolution. As in other areas of foreign policy, attempts to withdraw from the game or fundamentally alter its ancient rules result in automatic defeat.

2. Charles Krauthammer, "Deep Down, We're All Alike, Right? Wrong," in *Time* magazine, August 15, 1983.

3. Ibid.

4. Walter Lippmann, "Everybody's Business and Nobody's" in the *New York Herald Tribune*, April 10, 1941, quoted in Rossiter and Lare, *Essential Lippmann*, pp. 98–100.

5. Brzezinski's memoirs make this evident: he knew that he was going to have to fight with Vance over basic issues, so the first months were devoted to efforts to box out the State Department. Haig makes the same point in his memoirs, for this was the explanation for the early infighting between Haig and other cabinet members in the Reagan administration. It revolved around Haig's early memo that would have given him control over the foreign policy process. And, to take the analysis back one more administration, Kissinger fought the same battles with Rogers and others.

6. This information came from both official and unofficial sources. Although it is obviously impossible to describe the sources in detail, it is worthwhile noting that some of the sources were present at quite small meetings in which Castro spoke with real urgency about his convictions. The sources stressed that Castro was deeply concerned precisely because he was equally convinced of the Soviet determination to crush Solidarity and the American decision to make Cuba pay the price for the Soviet action.

7. See Ledeen and Lewis, *Debacle*, pp. 171–175.

8. Ironically, the much-maligned shah was actually the most progressive leader in the area, and his regime was more respectful of those human rights values we in the United States cherish than those of any of his immediate neighbors, his predecessors in Iran, or his successor.

9. See Secretary of State Haig's account of the numerous occasions on which he tried to prevent the Israeli action in Alexander M. Haig, Jr., *Caveat* (New York: Macmillan, 1984). Haig was not alone in these efforts; other members of the cabinet and senior State Department officials were similarly energetic with their Israeli interlocutors.

10. The series covered several different "area studies" programs in leading American universities. The analysis of Latin American studies was written by Professor Ernst Halperin (*Washington Quarterly*, vol. 1, no. 3, 1982).

11. The range of estimates I saw while in the State Department in 1981–82 ranged from 5 to 15 percent, and this matches the estimates I heard from various foreign observers, including several quite favorable to the guerrillas. Even some of their European supporters—who had come to El Salvador expecting to denounce the elections—were amazed at the widespread rejection of the guerrillas by the population at large.

12. For a discussion of American intelligence on Iran, see Ledeen and Lewis, *Debacle*, pp. 123–135.

13. Walter Lippmann, "The New Imperative," quoted in Rossiter and Lare, *Essential Lippmann*, pp. 202–203.

CHAPTER 4. BARRISTERS, JUDGES, BROADCASTERS, AND JOURNALISTS

1. For a detailed description and analysis of the American media treatment of the war in Lebanon, see, above all, Joshua Muravchik,

"Misreporting Lebanon," in *Policy Review* (Winter 1983). Several people who read this chapter were unfamiliar with the episode of the baby, so here is what Muravchik wrote about it:

> Near the end of the siege of West Beirut, Secretary of State Shultz said: "The symbol of this war is a baby with its arms shot off." Israel and its supporters came to agree. The baby in question had appeared swathed in bandages in a UPI wirephoto captioned:
>
> > Nurse feeds a seven-month-old baby who lost both arms and was severely burned late yesterday afternoon when an Israeli jet accidentally hit a Christian residential area in East Beirut during a raid on Palestinian positions to the west. The baby was being cared for in a hospital hallway, which is considered an area safer from shelling than the room normally assigned. [*Washington Post*, August 2, 1982]
>
> Israel protested that a PLO shell, not an Israeli bomb, had caused the child's injuries. A few weeks later Israel produced photos and affidavits proving, even to UPI's satisfaction, that the child had not lost his arms and that his injuries were not very severe. The story seemed to symbolize the exaggeration that Israelis felt permeated news reports about the casualties resulting from its attack on the PLO in Lebanon.

2. Lichter and Rothman, "Media and Business Elites."

3. Ibid.

4. Walter Lippmann, *The Public Philosophy* (New York: Little, Brown, 1955), Chapter 9, quoted in Rossiter and Lare, *Essential Lippmann*, pp. 193–196.

5. Carl Bernstein and Bob Woodward, *All the President's Men* (New York: Simon & Schuster, 1974), pp. 35–36.

6. Ibid., p. 192.

7. See the front-page story in the *New York Times*, May 25, 1981.

8. In keeping with the constant effort in the *Post* to discount all suggestion that the KGB was involved in the attempt to kill the Pope, Sari Gilbert's lead paragraph in the *Washington Post* on January 6, 1983, read:

> Rome, Jan. 5.   The impact of an Italian Cabinet minister's accusations that a Soviet Bloc state was involved in the attempt to assassinate Pope John Paul II has been significantly tempered here by the conviction that his charges were at least partly related to domestic Italian politics.

Having made such a claim, Gilbert then used an anonymous source to "document" her assertion that "many Italian and foreign observers tend to view [Defense Minister] Lagorio's statements with the traditional grain of salt. . . . They have described his comments . . . as 'hasty' and 'irresponsible.' " Not one of these "observers" is identified.

9. See Marvine Howe's story, headlined "Turks Say Suspect in Papal Attack Is Tied to Rightist Web of Intrigue," in the *New York Times*, May 18, 1981.

10. Georgie Anne Geyer, "Lessons from the Turks on Handling Terrorists," in the *Washington Star*, May 15, 1981.

11. Joseph Kraft, "The Dark Side of Islam," in the *Washington Post*, May 19, 1981.

12. Joseph C. Harsch, "Thoughts on Terrorism," in the *Christian Science Monitor*, June 2, 1981.

13. George Armstrong, in an article headlined "Agca in Rome: Too many pieces for open-and-shut case," in the *Christian Science Monitor*, May 18, 1981.

14. David B. Ottoway, "Interrogation of Agca Turns Up Several Baffling Mysteries," in the *Washington Post*, May 21, 1981.

15. Henry Kamm, "Israelis and Germans Doubt Bulgarian Link in Attack on Pope," in the *New York Times*, December 18, 1982.

16. Henry Kamm, "Bulgarians Regret a Tarnished Image," in the *New York Times*, January 27, 1983.

17. Bernard Gwertzman, "U.S. Intrigued but Uncertain on a Bulgarian Tie to Pope," in the *New York Times*, December 29, 1982.

18. *Newsweek*, January 3, 1983.

19. *Time*, January 3, 1983.

20. I do not have the full text of Georgie Anne Geyer's article, only my notes; but she has confirmed the accuracy of the quotation.

21. Flora Lewis' op-ed piece appeared in the *New York Times*, April 3, 1983.

22. Robert Toth's article appeared in the *Los Angeles Times*, January 31, 1983.

23. The Hersh series appeared in the *New York Times*, August 7, 8, and 13, 1979.

24. Jenkins said the following on his radio interview within days of

the massacre: "There is no doubt in my mind that Israel aided and abetted the whole operation. . . . These men passed through Israeli lines . . . they were fed by the Israeli Army, were given water between their shooting sprees . . . the final proof to me was I walked and found what was a mass grave in a corner of the camp. When you stand just on top of that and you raise your head and you look up at a seven-story building about three hundred yards away which is the Israeli Army's main observation post, a place where they set up before their own advance into the city, set up giant telescopes for spotting snipers. As I stood there Saturday morning and looked up there were six Israelis looking straight down at me. They stood and watched throughout this whole horrible tragedy as people were brought here, shot, dumped in this grave and packed up. . . . I saw not one person who seemed to have died in a position of fighting or resisting. This was basically an undefended civilian camp. . . . There were no hard-core PLO cadre there." I have transcribed this from National Public Radio, "All Things Considered" #820920, "Massacre Eyewitness."

Yet it was well known long before the massacre that Shatila was one of the PLO's main terrorist training centers. As Sablier notes in his book on international terrorism, "Among the 8,000 fighters evacuated from West Beirut in August 1982, approximately 1,000 were not Palestinians; they had kept themselves in the PFLP [Popular Front for the Liberation of Palestine, one of the most extreme PLO groups] camp at Shatila, known under the name of "the Europeans' camp." See Sablier, *Le Fil Rouge*, p. 126.

And in the most recent study of the PLO, based on firsthand research in Lebanon during 1982, Jillian Becker writes:

> There were three main training camps for foreign terrorists: Chatila, Burj al-Barajneh and Damour. Basque terrorists were trained in Chatila with Germans and Italians. . . .

As far as Israelis watching the massacre from the surveillance post described by Jenkins, there is no confirmation of his claim in the exhaustive investigation conducted by the Kahan Commission, which found Israelis to be indirectly responsible for the massacre. The Kahan Commission found that Israelis had received only "reports," not that there was ongoing Israeli observation of the killing. See Jillian Becker, *The PLO: The Rise and Fall of the Palestine Liberation Organization* (London: Weidenfeld and Nicolson, 1984), pp. 191, 192, 211–213.

25. Richard Neely, *How Courts Govern America* (New Haven: Yale, 1981), p. 128.

26. Ibid.

27. William Reese Smith, Jr., "How Many Lawyers Are Enough?" in *American Bar Association Journal*, March 1981, p. 244.

28. James B. Stewart, *The Partners: Inside America's Most Powerful Law Firms* (New York: Simon & Schuster, 1983), p. 45.

29. Ibid., p. 47.

30. Riesman is quoted in "Why Everybody is Suing Everybody," in *U.S. News & World Report*, December 4, 1978.

CHAPTER 5.   THE SOVIET EMPIRE

1. Forty years after being overrun by the Red Army, Poland remains a Catholic country, not a Communist one; the rest of Eastern Europe, with the possible exceptions of Bulgaria and Albania, would almost certainly reject communism if free to do so.

2. Edward N. Luttwak, *The Grand Strategy of the Soviet Union* (New York: St. Martin's, 1983).

3. "Pour une politique à l'égard de l'Union Sovietique," in *Commentaire*, Automne 1982.

4. I do not have the date of Safire's column in the *Times*, but it appeared in late 1983 or early 1984. His central thesis was that the fact that the report was leaked to several major Western journalists indicated that the Andropov faction was using it to criticize Brezhnev's (and therefore Chernenko's) policies in the past.

5. Leo Wieland, "Letter From Moscow: Comrade Andropov's Basic Problem," in *Encounter*, November 1983. Wieland gives a more sophisticated (and in my view, more realistic) appraisal of the significance of the report, and stresses the limits on our knowledge and understanding:

> In contrast to the early burst of economic activity, the later Brezhnev years were characterised by a clear stagnation uninterrupted by any sign of new event-making decisions. The first period of the Andropov era has, behind the sound and fury of foreign-policy activity, indicated some signs of a general approach. Soviet economic experts have obviously been encouraged to look a little beyond the food on the Russian table, and to peer a little into the experiences (and even "experiments") of other—Socialist—economies. Above all, this involved the fairly efficient industrial combinations in the East German DDR and the working

agrarian arrangements in Kadar's Hungary. Even Chinese ways
of doing things, including the so-called "Brigade contract" which
seems to offer both the individual and the collectivity more and
better results, are suddenly being studied attentively. In the Cau-
casus, in Central Asia, and in the "little models" of the Baltic
states, there are the very modest beginnings of a tentative approach to something more like a bigger "market economy" involving state farms and collectives.

This is hardly enough to be called a reform programme. What is
still missing is a whole host of decisions involving the most basic problems: the autonomy of factories; a realistic method of
cost accounting; flexible relations between wages and productivity; the sensible calculation of prices; quality control of all goods
actually produced. Here the good old "Soviet model" will surely
prevail—until Andropov clearly indicates that he holds it to be
capable of reform. It could be that, like Brezhnev, he will content himself with the minimal achievement of fulfilling minimal
needs with a modest minimum. . . .

6. The most famous of these studies is Hélène Carrére d'Encausse,
Decline of an Empire (New York: Newsweek Books, 1979). See also
the relevant sections in Archie Brown and Michael Kaser eds., *Soviet
Policy for the 1980s* (Bloomington: Indiana University Press, 1982),
a very useful book.

7. Luttwak, *Grand Strategy*, p. 115.

8. David A. Dyker, "Planning and the Worker," in Leonard Shapiro
and Joseph Godson, eds., *The Soviet Worker* (London: Macmillan,
1981), p. 65.

9. The book was originally written in German. I have used the Italian translation: Michael S. Voslensky, *Nomenklatura: La Classe Domi-
nante in Unione Sovietica* (Milan: Longanesi, 1980).

10. See Murray Seeger, "Eyewitness to Failure," in Shapiro and Godson, eds., *Soviet Worker*, pp. 79–80.

11. Given the political realities of East-West trade, the Kremlin has
made a rational decision: it would be far more costly to try to make
Soviet agriculture work well than it is to buy wheat, corn, and soy-
beans from the West. So long as the West is willing to supply (and
unable or unwilling to stop the flow of) information, technology, and
know-how to the East, the Soviets will simply continue to cash in on
an international division of labor. Their problem derives from the
possibility that the West may one day effectively limit the transfer

of high technology and foodstuffs to the East, as well as from the
growing realization–underlined by the constant discussions of grain
sales and technology transfer—that the Soviet system is a failure by
most standards.

12. This section is based on conversations with, and written material from, Ion Mihai Pacepa, who defected to the West in 1978 and
was the former deputy director of the Rumanian Secret Intelligence
Service and adviser to President Ceausescu. I believe that I am the
first private citizen to talk with Mr. Pacepa about these matters since
his defection. Beria's statement was provided, in writing, by Pacepa.
A shorter version of this material was published in *L'Express* (Paris),
July 3, 1984.

13. The quotation was provided, in writing, by Ion Mihai Pacepa.

14. Fyodor Turovsky, "Society Without a Present," in Shapiro and
Godson, eds., *Soviet Worker*, pp. 158 ff.

15. The article is quoted by Turovsky, ibid., p. 164.

16. Betsy Gidwitz, "Labor Unrest in the Soviet Union," in *Problems
of Communism*, November–December 1982.

17. Frane Barbieri, "Polonia: Esiste una Soluzione?" *Affari Esteri*,
Winter 1983, pp. 20–24.

18. All these points are exhaustively documented in Carrére d'Encausse's *Decline of an Emipre*.

19. Ibid., p. 274.

20. Alexander Solzhenitsyn, "La Russie à l'heure Andropov," *L'Express*, December 17, 1982.

21. Walter Laqueur, "What We Know about the Soviet Union,"
Commentary, February 1983.

22. Voslensky, *Nomenklatura*, pp. 276–277.

23. Konstantin Simis, "Andropov's Anticorruption Campaign," *Washington Quarterly*, Summer 1983.

24. Konstantin Simis, *USSR: The Corrupt Society* (New York: Simon & Schuster, 1982), pp. 94–95.

25. Laqueur, "What We Know."

26. Ibid.

27. Alexander Zinoviev, *The Radiant Future* (New York: Random
House, 1980), p. 286.

CHAPTER 6.   DILEMMAS

1. Many of the predictions at the time of Brezhnev's death verged on the hilarious. See Edward Jay Epstein, "The Andropov File," *New Republic,* February 7, 1983.

2. Luttwak, *Grand Strategy,* p. 60.

INDEX

Acheson, Dean, 10
Adventurism, international, American-Soviet strategic confusion and, 4–5
Afghanistan
  Soviet invasion of, foreign policy confusion over, 37–38
  spring 1984 offensive in, 192–93
Agca, Mehmet Ali, attempted assassination of Pope by, reporting on, 115–30. *See also* Pope John Paul II, attempted assassination of, reporting on
Agriculture, Soviet, failure of, 160
Allies
  American-Soviet strategic confusion and, 4
  effects of American failure in Lebanon on, 91–92
  as investigative journalism targets, 130–31
American-Soviet strategic confusion, consequences of, 4
Andropov, Yuri
  deception by, 11–12
  foreign policy of, 191–92
  misreading of, 192
  Soviet future and, 189–90
  Western European policy of, 17–18
Angola, Soviet setback in, 196
al-Assad, Hafez, misreading of, American policy and, 81
Anticommunism, disfavor of, among New Left, 51–53
Armstrong, George, on attempted assassination of Pope, 117–18
Authoritarian regimes and totalitarian regimes, distinction between, 26–27
Automobiles, Rumanian espionage on, 169

Barbieri, Frane, on Polish working class, 179
Beirut. *See also* Lebanon
  attacks on Americans in, 85–86
  siege of, 79–84
Beria, Lavrenty, on technological espionage, 161
Bernstein, Carl, on Watergate investigation, 112–13
Bill, James, on Ayatollah, 48–49
Bradlee, Ben, on *Post* error on Watergate coverage, 113
Brzezinski, Zbigniew, on Iranian crisis, 70
Bucharest scene of technological espionage, 162–74
  commercial trade in, 167–69
  contacts with consulting firms in, 170–71
  cooperative and joint ventures in, 169–70
  cultural accords in, 166–67
  emigrés in, 172
  illegal intelligence in, 172–74
  scientific accords in, 166–67
  third-country or one-time firms in, 171–72
Bulgaria in attempted assassination of Pope, 116, 118, 119–20, 122–23, 126–28, 130
Bureaucracy, American, accountability of, need for, 209–10

Carlos, Juan, in Spain's transition to democracy, 40–42
Carter, Jimmy
  on Afghanistan invasion, 37–38
  on communism, 27
  economic situation under, 30
  foreign policy approach of, 38–39
  on Nicaragua, 42–43, 44–45